Education
Theory and
Practice

Caribbean Perspectives

Second Edition
Edited by

Tony Bastick
University of the West Indies
Former Director of the Education Research Centre

Editorial Consultants
Austin Ezenne
John Hayter
Hazel M. Salmon
Kola Soyibo
June Degia

Department of Educational Studies, University of the West Indies
Kingston, Jamaica

2003

Copyright © 2000, 2003 by The Department of Educational Studies,
University of the West Indies,
Kingston, Jamaica.
All rights reserved.

Education theory and practice: Caribbean perspectives /
Tony Bastick, editor; 2nd ed.
p. cm.
Includes bibliographical references.
ISBN: 976-632-038-1
1. Education - Caribbean, English-speaking. T. Bastick, Tony
LA475 . E37 2003   371.2

Cover and section illustrations from 'Year of the Child' by Claude Rahir assisted by two students, Doreen Kong and Robert Ramsay. The original wall mural, depicting the work of UWI Faculties, is at the Assembly Hall, UWI, Mona, Jamaica. Copyright © University of the West Indies.

Cover design and text layout, T. Bastick.

Printed in the USA

INTRODUCTION

CONGRATULATIONS.

It is a pleasure to see the publication of this collection of articles on Caribbean Education. Research in Education in the region has been going on for generations, but the dissemination of this work has not kept pace, yet it is precisely this information and the ideas generated that will help to shape a better quality of education more appropriate to our context and problems. It is particularly pleasing to see the breadth of areas covered, since it reminds us of the holistic nature of education and stimulates our thinking in and synthesizing of the multiple facets.

The School of Education can be proud of this latest strengthening of scholarship, product of the combined efforts of so many staff members. We look forward to further works of this kind arising from the encouragement it gives to practitioners and thinkers in the field of Education. We applaud the new insights and knowledge these articles bring to the theories and practice of education in the Caribbean context.

Joseph Pereira
Deputy Principal, Mona, UWI
Former Dean
Faculty of Arts and Education
University of the West Indies
Jamaica

Contributing Researchers

Oliver Mills
Sonia Jones
John Hayter
Tony Bastick
Kola Soyibo
Austin Ezenne
Beverley Bryan
W. Madge Hall
Dian McCallum
Joycelyn Barton
Susan Anderson
Olga James Reid
Hazel M. Salmon
Rosemarie Johnson
Valerie J. Hardware
Beatrice Boufoy-Bastick
Marguerite Narinesingh

CONTENTS

Introduction by Joseph Pereira, Deputy Principal, Mona. Former Dean, Faculty of Arts and Education, University of the West Indies, Jamaica   iii

SECTION 1

PROFESSIONAL DEVELOPMENT   1

Chapter 1
Is There Still Room for the Model Teacher?
Sonia Jones   3

Chapter 2
Using an In-Service Programme to Develop as a Teacher:
Working on Expectations
John Hayter   9

Chapter 3
Teaching History in Secondary Schools: Organising for Instruction
Dian McCallum   19

Chapter 4
Practical Stress Management for Education Students
Rosemarie Johnson   27

Chapter 5
The Teacher and Instructional Development in the Classroom
Austin Ezenne   33

SECTION 2

LANGUAGE EDUCATION   41

Chapter 6
Promoting Language Awareness through Language Study
Beverley Bryan   43

Chapter 7
Two Contrasting Foreign-Language Teaching Orientations
Hazel M. Salmon   49

Chapter 8
Foreign Language Teaching Strategies and Students' Performance in Spanish
Joycelyn Barton and Hazel M. Salmon   61

Chapter 9
Revisiting Methodological Approaches to Foreign Language Teaching: From Communicative to Actional Language Teaching
Béatrice Boufoy-Bastick   77

SECTION 3

SCIENCE EDUCATION   95

Chapter 10
Planning Lessons for Science Teaching
  Kola Soyibo   97

Chapter 11
Questioning Techniques in Science Teaching
  Kola Soyibo   111

SECTION 4

EDUCATIONAL ADMINISTRATION   121

Chapter 12
Management of Student Discipline and Behaviour in School
  Austin Ezenne and Oliver Mills   123

Chapter 13
Teachers and Stress Management in Schools
  Austin Ezenne and Olga James Reid   131

Chapter 14
The Role of Educational Foundations in Teacher Education
  Oliver Mills and Austin Ezenne   137

Chapter 15
Models of Leadership Behaviour for Educational Organisations
  Austin Ezenne   143

SECTION 5

ASSESSMENT AND EVALUATION   151

Chapter 16
Assessing the Predictive Validity of the ATLP-75 Selection Test for Caribbean Nurses
  Valerie J. Hardware and Tony Bastick   153

Chapter 17
Is Validity more Reliable than Reliability is Valid?
  Tony Bastick   167

SECTION 6

PHILOSOPHY OF EDUCATION   173

Chapter 18
Education and Choice: The Family or the State?
  Oliver Mills   175

Chapter 19
Spirituality and Education: Epistemology as Ethic
  Oliver Mills   187

SECTION 7

PSYCHOLOGY OF EDUCATION   199

Chapter 20
Facilitating gifted learners in Jamaican primary schools:
Challenges and explorations
  W. Madge Hall and Marguerite Narinesingh   201

Chapter 21
Subjectivist Psychology and its Applications to Teaching
  Tony Bastick   209

Chapter 22
Learning Styles as a Foundation of Instructional Activities
  Susan Anderson   219

Afterword
The Honourable Burchell Whiteman, Minister of Education and Culture, Jamaica.

x

Section 1

Professional Development

Chapter 1
Is There Still Room for the Model Teacher?
    Sonia Jones 3

Chapter 2
Using an In-Service Programme to Develop as a Teacher: Working on Expectations
    John Hayter 9

Chapter 3
Teaching History in Secondary Schools: Organising for Instruction
    Dian McCallum 19

Chapter 4
Practical Stress Management for Education Students
    Rosemarie Johnson 27

Chapter 5
The Teacher and Instructional Development in the Classroom
    Austin Ezenne 33

Caribbean Perspectives

CHAPTER

Is There Still Room for the Model Teacher?

SONIA O. JONES

ABSTRACT

There is yet to be a major thrust to discredit the critical importance of education to national development. There is no denying that education contributes much to the economic development of a country. Consequently, a system of education that is manned by persons who believe in excellence and are committed to quality education is the type of system that will drive economic growth and development. Enabling this growth and development requires the kind of human resources who will remain a model of professionalism despite the number of challenges faced by schools in terms of security, proper remuneration, adequate supply of instructional materials, to mention a few. Are the challenges so insurmountable or so overwhelming that every teacher is professionally challenged? Or is there still room for the model teacher?

Perhaps in these last few years of the 20th century it is somewhat out of step to talk of the model teacher. The Oxford Reference Dictionary (1991) gives a number of definitions for the word model. In the context in which the word is used here the definition which is most apt is "a person or thing regarded as excellent of its kind and proposed for imitation" (p. 537). The challenges which face the teaching profession are numerous and varied. The increasing threat to schools from violence without and within, the call for better working conditions and increased funding for education in the form of higher salaries and an adequate supply of materials and equipment create an environment less than conducive to effective teaching and learning. The model teacher has to be able to create harmony out of disharmony, order out of disorder and make students the centre of the teaching-learning process. It is therefore the humanising of the environment in which teaching and learning take place that is the model teacher's central role. A classroom that feels comfortable as you enter and emanates warmth is a classroom that inspires student involvement and stimulates them to be active contributors to their own development.

Harmin (1994) takes the position that all of us at one time or the other have had the experience of inspiring *some* of our students. She expresses the view that if we should visit the inspirational classroom we would find high levels of five qualities:

1. **Dignity:** Students look confident and are ready to learn. They are proud of themselves and their abilities
2. **Energy:** Students are fully involved. The classroom hums with activity
3. **Self management**: Students are self managing and are self-motivating and take responsibility for themselves

4. **Community:** Social relationships are well established with peers and persons of authority
5. **Awareness:** Students are alert to what is happening in the classroom. Creativity, awe, diligence and concentration are in evidence.

These qualities would be in evidence in the classroom of the model teacher no matter how difficult the situation in which such a teacher works. Yet as complaints are made to the media and professional organizations by teachers highlighting their discontent with the status of the teaching profession and behaviours exhibited as are articulated in the following case, the question must be asked "Is there still room for the model teacher?"

CASE

TEACHING AS THE SIDELINE

Concerns about teaching and the teaching profession are many and varied. The greatest concern, however, must be the emergence of teaching as a second or third job for many teachers. Robert Benjamin started teaching at Louise Armstrong High School in 1989. Not much of a talker he went about his daily task with alacrity, wasting little time to exchange gossip or pleasantries with his colleagues. Despite the efforts of a number of his co-workers to get him to be more involved in social gatherings Robert maintained a polite but safe distance from these 'sanity maintainers' as the gatherings were dubbed. After two years of trying, he was accepted as a Party Pooper but a nice guy nevertheless. In November 1992, his colleagues conspired behind his back to trap him in the staffroom for a full hour to find out, among other things, how he was able to afford a new car and assume a mortgage on a two bedroom townhouse on the salary teachers were paid. Robert worked on the morning shift and did most of his marking and preparation for the next day before leaving school each day.

On November 25, 1992 at 1.00 pm he settled down in the corner of the staffroom and started marking the previous day's homework when he found himself surrounded by eight of his colleagues. Appearing not the least bit perturbed Robert asked his colleagues to what did he owe the pleasure of their company. Richard Long, the staff member closest to him told him that they wanted to ask him a few questions. Robert put his pen down, folded his arms and responded that they had five minutes, as that was all the time he could spare since he needed to get away by 2.00 pm. Carrie Moore, a member of Robert's Department protested that five minutes would not be enough to answer all their questions. Robert interrupted her, pointing out that they were wasting precious time and time was money. Taking his cue from Robert's response, Richard blurted out the first question, "We wanted to know how you are able to drive a Toyota Camry on your salary and afford the mortgage on a two bedroom townhouse in such a high priced neighbourhood?" Robert's mouth dropped open. Before he could recover his composure, Amelia Kennedy injected quite hastily, "I am sorry if you believe that we have been prying in your affairs, for one thing you drive your car to work and the agent you are purchasing your house from happens to be my sister-in-law. Not that she was discussing your business, she wanted to get in touch with you urgently when she remembered that we taught at the same school."

Robert took his time to respond, and kept looking from one to another of his colleagues as if he were trying to memorise the features of each of them. When he spoke it was as if his voice was coming from far away. He told them inter alia that his salaries were responsible for his assumed superior economic base. At first the word "salaries" escaped the notice of his colleagues until one by one they realised the implication of Robert's response. Several questions followed. This was what was learned by Robert Benjamin's eight colleagues on the afternoon of November 25, 1992:

1. When he took the job at Louise Armstrong High School he already had two part-time jobs.
2. Throughout his teaching career Robert always had two jobs. He took his present job because he could work on the morning shift, leaving the afternoon free to do his second job.
3. Teaching although Robert's first love was not providing enough either financially or psychologically for him to devote all his time to it.
4. The demands on the teacher to be baby-sitters, counsellors, instructional experts, community worker, to mention a few of the roles teachers perform are too much. What is worse the salary is not commensurate and many of these roles have little to do with teaching.
5. Robert's part-time job at Electrical Works was really his main job since that was where he earned the most money.
6. Any teacher who can live on the salary he or she is paid is more a magician than a teacher!

Robert's last retort evoked loud laughter from his colleagues. One by one they confessed that they suspected all along that the money he made from teaching was not enough to keep him in the lifestyle that he was obviously enjoying. Miranda Toch, the Guidance Counsellor reminded him that the Principal was expecting every teacher to be involved in the new School Community Outreach Project to be launched in January. The project required teachers on the morning shift to do their community outreach work in the afternoons and those on the afternoon shift to do theirs in the mornings. Robert thanked her for the reminder but stated that he would have to use his Sundays to do the work and if that were not acceptable he would resign since nothing was going to get in the way of his other job. He concluded by saying that the school's involvement in community projects was going to cause more teachers to leave the profession.

Reluctant to leave well enough alone, Lola Hutch asked Robert what time he did his lesson plan. "My what", Robert replied, "how much am I being paid for that?" "Come now", Lola continued, "you want to tell us that you have not been writing lesson plans all this time?" "No, no, no", Robert replied, "I write one at the beginning of each term". "And you have got away with that all the years you have been working here?", Lola asked. "That cannot be true." Two of her colleagues exchanged meaningful glances but said nothing. Just then Richard asked Robert to forgive them for seeking to find out so much about his private life and for taking up a full 55 minutes of his time. The reference to the time catapulted Robert into action, he quickly gathered his belongings and fled from the staffroom.

As if prearranged, everybody spoke at once, "Why not, if we cannot earn a decent salary at our main job, make it the sideline." Miranda Toch had the last word, however, "What of the students?" she asked.

Questions

1. What is/are the main issue(s) in the case? Can the/these issue(s) be resolved? If yes, how? If no, why not?
2. From your experience, how pervasive is the sentiment expressed by Robert's colleagues "Why not ...... sideline". What is your position on the matter?
3. Why do you think Robert believed that the school's involvement in community projects would cause more teachers to leave the profession?
4. Why do you think Miranda asked the question, "What of the students?"

These questions should be answered and examined in the context of what is the status of the teaching profession at the present time. Whether members of the teaching profession like it or not there is still a very very large segment of the world's population that still regard the practitioners of the profession as exemplary and believe that they should demonstrate a level of professionalism that should set them apart from the rest of the population.

Newspapers as well as the electronic media have carried reports of increased corruption in many areas of the public and private sectors. Sometimes the feeling of being trapped in a totally immoral society immobilises the mind albeit momentarily. Yet at all times there is the promise of new minds open and ready for the kind of guidance that will transform them into young adults capable of setting right a world bent on its own self destruction.

The teacher has been given this promise to gentle into caring, human beings. Can teachers afford to renege on this promise? If teachers can, then the answer to Miranda Toch's question is a sad indictment on the teaching profession. So again the question is asked "Is there still room for the model teacher?"

It has become painfully clear that the traditional model of the teacher that focused on conduct, that is, moral conduct and his/her role in the community, has undergone some changes. The professional improvement of teachers is one of the main ingredients of an effective education system. It is vital that teachers understand that professional growth and development is a continuous process. That is, they must keep professionally informed, actively participate in professional groups and attend professional meetings. After all, one of the indicators of the teacher's professionalism is his/her competence. As the environment in which teaching and learning take place becomes more hostile, and less rewarding to the teacher in terms of monetary compensation, and praise for a job well done the place for the model teacher is under threat. Can any society afford to lose this place?

The society should make every effort to facilitate excellence in education. There are teachers who are working in very volatile areas yet they are among some of the most dedicated in the profession. This should not be the standard against which comments like "If teachers can work in economically disadvantaged communities and excel why then is there so much dissatisfaction among teachers in much better neighbourhoods" is judged. A teacher no matter how committed, how dedicated, will become disenchanted, disillusioned and dissatisfied with a society that gives lip service to providing quality education for the citizens. Parents and other community members faced with the demands of employers for students to enter the job market with qualifications that can fit them for entry level jobs join in the call for better and more education for their children. Many of them have children who have left school functionally illiterate increasing the pool of the "unemployable". There is little for parents to be happy about or to support if education fails to live up to their expectations. Many parents often ask the question, "Where would teachers be without our children?" A question which is sometimes very awkward for teachers to answer. Ayers (1995) contends that teaching demands thoughtfulness. It is this thoughtfulness that all teachers must continuously bring to the teaching-learning situation.

Self-Evaluation

As teachers manage their careers in a constantly changing environment, self evaluation is a very good way of monitoring their effectiveness on the job. As an approach to this monitoring it would be useful if teachers evaluate themselves to see the extent to which they are maintaining a high level of professionalism on and off the job. Such an instrument could examine three main areas as depicted in Figure 1.

Fig. 1 Level of Professionalism (Self Evaluation Profile)

Where Am I?	Where Do I Want To Be?	How Can I Get To Where I Should Be If I Am Not There Yet?
1.		
2.		
3.		
4.		

The answers to all three questions must not be superficial. A critical look at all areas of the job must be done and the understanding that professional development is integrally intertwined with personal development must be acknowledged if this model is to provide the kind of guide that will lead to effective teaching and learning. A society may fail its teachers but teachers should not fail the society by providing poor quality professional service that will retard students' progress and keep the teaching profession in the ambiguous state of what some refer to as the "semi-profession". Ball and Goodson (1985) remind us that:

> Occupational status is one of the most widely studied aspects of the social stratification system... studies of occupational status show that teachers rank far below most professions (physicians, pharmacists, lawyers and so on) and in the lower third of white collar occupations. (p. 80).

The people who can raise the status of the profession to what it should be are teachers who have made the commitment to be in every respect true professionals.

BIBLIOGRAPHY

Ayers, W. (Ed.). (1995). To Become a Teacher: Making a Difference in Children's Lives. New York: Teachers College, Columbia University

Ball S., & Goodson I. (1985). Teachers Lives and Careers. London, Falmer Press

Harmin, M. (1994). Inspiring Active Learning: A Handbook for Teachers. Alexandria: Virginia Association for Supervision and Curriculum Development.

CHAPTER 2

Using an In-Service Programme to Develop as a Teacher: Working on Expectations

JOHN HAYTER

Abstract

Students start major in-service programmes such as those at the University of the West Indies with varied intentions and expectations. Often these seem to be carried subconsciously without clear recognition or productive resolution by the students or the tutors. This article invites students to examine the kind of teacher they are in relation to three types - *intuitive, conditioned* and *reflective* and to think about causes and their own movement with respect to these types over the period of their professional lives. Some common 'blocking' expectations are examined and students are encouraged to develop a realistic agenda for their use of the programme for their own professional development and thereby to develop strategies which can enable longer term continuing professional development.

Prologue

Althea, Bertram, Carole, Dian and Errol meet for the first time waiting for the registration process to unfold. All teachers, and from different schools, they are enrolling for the same programme and use the time to share hopes and expectations of the upcoming course.

Bertram: *These queues are terrible, man. Why can't they be better organised. I hope it isn't all going to be like this. I could be resting or kicking a ball.*

Dian: *This place is so much bigger than my TTC – I'm not sure that I shall ever find my way around. Still the social life seems good, it was a great party last night and I hear the weekend starts on Thursday afternoon here. All the family are back in Trelawny and I'm a student again -for two years! Still there are all those course credits to collect – did they say*

66, used to be 60, is this educational inflation? I already have a chart on my wall — credits earned by Dian; gold star for each 3 credit course passed — this will be a real measure of progress. Do you know, I will be the first with a BEd in the family?

Carole: Not really sure why I'm here. I'm already head of department in a comprehensive high school and teach mainly CXC classes. The principal pushed me into coming but I'm already trained and have a good reputation as a teacher. The students are queuing up for my extra classes and the income from this makes all the difference to my lifestyle. This could be two years wasted out of my life, but hopefully I can cruise. Still the thought of that extra pay coming with the BEd will keep me going.

Errol: Have you seen the course handbook? It takes some understanding but there are some interesting possibilities. 'An Introduction to Information Technology' — I have been waiting to be computer literate and I know the Principal is keen to get IT started at my school. Also Assessment courses — I didn't realise how significant this matter was when I was at College. There has to be a better way of assessing than using just exams — though I notice some of the Out-of-School courses seem to depend heavily on examinations. These tings always freeze me, man. There is a lot in my subject field both the subject itself and also on its teaching. Should be some experts in this place; perhaps I will be one after two years here! Plenty of late nights on assignments too, I would guess.

Althea: It feels like a dream come true, I didn't think I would ever get a place here. They wanted to interview me but that turned out to be really interesting, because I was able to talk about my work in the classroom and share some of the problems I am facing and things that I want to know more about. I'm really looking forward to the teaching courses but am worried about the Out of School subject work. It's going to be tough but I shall work at it. Am still looking for some satisfactory accommodation, does anyone know of a room?

Carole: I think there's a spare room in my place, why don't you come round after we get through this business.

Bertram: Well I'm here for the content — the more the better I say. The education stuff was covered at College — not that it did much for me. Guess what, they are sending us back into school for more practice. I shall try to get back to my school — I can't fail there! Hey the queue just moved — is this progress?

Errol: No worry man, we've got two years and the company seems just fine to me. Did you hear the one about the three women teachers …….?

Beginnings are special

Five students, all on the threshold of a new programme of study. They all hope for the same award at the end but have different backgrounds, different abilities and most significantly different expectations of what the programme will do for them. Some are keen about titles of courses, others have already shut down on parts of the programme, some are seeing it in a more holistic way - a two year experience to be endured, to have fun or to achieve personal and professional growth. We get only glimpses of what they might understand by professional development – more pay, more knowledge, a new label acquired through meeting the demands of a remotely determined academic system.

Nothing very unusual about this scenario even if the new UWI registration system does not give them time for such a protracted conversation. Where do the students' expectations come from? Largely, one imagines, from earlier experience, from personal motivations and from the image projected by publicity material and by former students on the programme. Beginnings are special, as are senses of direction; it seems important to examine purposes and possibilities before becoming engulfed by the particular demands of a programme.

This chapter endeavours to examine what professional development can mean in general terms, while recognising that it will be a unique journey for each individual. The article will be written to give emphasis to some *noticings* (Mason, 1992) of a relative newcomer to Jamaica – this is risky since it will display ignorance, but could also be valuable because new experiences bring a clarity of noticing which familiarity dulls. In a similar way, starting a new course can generate powerful *noticings* for students; these need to be captured, worked on and used in the early days of the course

Professional development can be narrowly or broadly defined. Here I want to see it as different, though not necessarily unrelated, to career development. One aspect of a profession is that its members have a substantial degree of self-determination in their working lives; clearly this is both an opportunity and a responsibility. Much is left up to them and their consequent action will determine whether the job is well done or not. Hoyle (1974) suggested two models – the *restricted* professional and the *extended* professional. Notice that each type is assumed to be doing a thorough, responsible job but the extended professional has built in potential for development – moving on in knowledge, thinking, skills and areas of activity.

Becoming a Teacher

Jamaica must have as many routes into teaching as any country – a mix of people educated to the level of CXC, A level, diploma and degree, trained and untrained, experienced in Jamaica, the Caribbean and even from more Foreign than that. What a rich set of resources, yet what differing perspectives on what it means to become and to develop as a teacher. Sadly, so much of the potential is unrealised as teachers beaver away at work in their separate classrooms, seldom if ever talking about what makes them the teachers they are. In part, this is a matter of time, but more significantly, it is about recognising who we are as teachers, knowing how we became the professionals that we are and seeing the potential of reflecting on our own work and sharing understandings with others.

One way to categorise teachers is: the *intuitive*, the *conditioned* and the *reflective*. A pen portrait of each type might help to capture the nature of each:

THE *INTUITIVE* TEACHER

The *intuitive* teacher responds to the teaching situation using their intuition – it may just be the way they react to a class of children, it may reflect their own experience as a student, but in general it happens without considered thought. Such a teacher would find it difficult to give reasons for what they do. They may be supremely confident or worryingly anxious; they may be quite successful as judged by the motivation of the students and sometimes by the learning that is being achieved. However they may be in a class where little learning is taking place and they may not be aware of it or know what to do about that situation.

THE *CONDITIONED* TEACHER

The *conditioned* teacher works by a set of rules for teaching good lessons, for assessing student work and for managing their classroom. Such an approach may have its roots in the expectations of the institution in which they work, but seems more likely to arise as an outcome of their training. (Such an outcome may or may not have been the intention of their trainers.) This kind of teacher may draw confidence in the tight structure which they use, though they may be frustrated and blaming at the limited learning that is sometimes evident in their classroom. The teacher can quote chapter and verse as to why they teach as they do or they may refer to what their training required, as justification. Students in their classes are likely to gain a view of a tightly structured world in which things are done in a certain way because someone says so.

THE *REFLECTIVE* TEACHER

The *reflective* teacher brings knowledge of their subject, the students, the teaching context and their own skills as teachers to bear on what they do. They adopt an approach to teaching in which feedback from their work with individuals and the class is used to progress. For some this approach appears to come naturally, for others it has emerged from grappling with mixed experiences in the classroom. For yet others, their approach started when as confident professionals on a course, they came to recognise in a new way that the classroom and the learning needs of students are complex and difficult to handle; there are no simple solutions. Gattegno (Mason, 1987) claimed that only awareness is educable. An aware teacher is now in a position to work on issues and move forwards. Asked why they work in the way they do, they are likely to take you into a description of their practice, perhaps illustrated by an anecdote of their work with a particular class. It will be an incomplete picture and the reasoning behind it may be difficult to grasp, for it is a very personal account not immediately transferable to others. Their students are likely to be aware of the untidiness of the world being present in their classroom – more questions than answers, no simple solutions even in Mathematics where they had previously thought that questions had a single answer – right or wrong. Speculating about, sharing with, thinking through, are the order of the day. There is an implicit belief that this might be a more effective education for life as it is beyond the classroom.

Three models of teaching and probably no pure and perfect example of any of them can be found. But even with this partial understanding of the models we can perhaps think of teachers who seem characterised by the different types.

Looking at ourselves as teachers (Slow down this section needs time!)

Think about your own work as a teacher in the classroom. How do you rate yourself with respect to these three models?

One way to tackle this is to represent yourself on a diagram like that below. Put a single cross in the triangle to show how distant or close you are to each of the models described. If possible, find time to share and explain your response with another student.

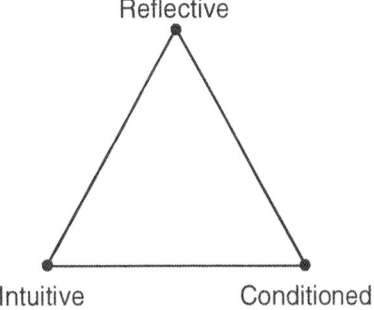

As you consider your position on the diagram, reflect on whether it has changed during your professional career.

Think about the nature of the change and the causes. Was it self-motivated, did it arise from experiences in the classroom, from books read, from people encountered in the school or outside? Did the changes occur a long time ago or more recently; was it conscious or unconscious change?

Are you presently 'at rest' or 'still moving' with respect to your position on the diagram?

Share your story with a colleague and hear theirs. Note similarities and differences – be comfortable with both. What emerges from this reflection together on your work as teachers?

Revisit the characters encountered at the start of this article. Think about them in relation to their initial ideas about the course and their capacity for change.

The models and professional development

For the purposes of this discussion, we might define *professional development* in terms of movement on the diagram reflecting change in our professional philosophy and practice in response to growing understanding. The reflective model is seen as a more mature response to the complexities of the classroom but is not seen as necessarily guaranteeing effective teaching and learning – some people reflect endlessly while all manner of chaos surrounds them! Philosophy has to be turned into personal practice and will then need further change through a reflective cycle. As a result, further professional development can occur.

If professional development is conceived in this way, the importance of having some idea where we are at present is clear. Such knowledge opens up the possibility of significant change. This type of change occurs at a 'depth' within us, as we become more aware. It may not have much to do with any content learned or notes conscientiously written or examination questions satisfactorily answered. Such change seems to come almost naturally for some, starts as a flash of insight for others, emerges slowly like a day dawning for yet others. Sadly, it seems quite beyond the experience of some, who leave the course with their certification, but are much where they started, except for a load more knowledge and the necessary credits.

Working on Expectations

At the start of a programme, students inevitably have expectations - conscious or unconscious. These can be motivating and provide a sense of direction. But, if unexamined, they can also be stumbling blocks which prevent the most being made of the opportunities which a programme can provide.

Experience of working with students suggests that it is worth addressing the issue of expectations at the start of a programme – challenging, rejecting, confirming and adding to these may enhance the possibilities of significant development.

First let us consider some student expectations which may 'block':

"N credits is the major goal"	Yes but the quality of the experience is the key determinant of ultimate professional value.
"Strategies on my last course/programme will work again"	They may, or they may simply hinder if not reviewed; as a professional you should be clearer what you need and be aware of ways to get it.
"All programmes represent rules without reasons; I do what they ask."	At the tertiary level (and elsewhere) students should seek clarification and reasons for what is provided. Sense-making has to be largely in the hands of the student - but tutors and institutions have a responsibility to assist.
"Tertiary trainers should be perfect models of teachers"	They have a variety of skills and experience to share but none is perfect – some have glaring inadequacies alongside major talents; value the latter, learn from both – students at school have to cope with your deficiencies! Think about the implications of education in the hands of the imperfect. Talk to tutors about what makes difficulties for you; the skills of negotiating understanding and ways to progress will always stand you in good stead in your professional life.
"Play safe, I can't live with insecurity."	Learning has to involve risk if change is to occur; risks can be small (e.g. questioning what a lecturer has said or expressing your own tentative ideas in an assignment) or larger (e.g. exploring a major shift of methodology in your classroom teaching).

"The lecture is the vital bit – except when I don't get up in time"	Not really so, but your use of that experience may be; also preparation for it may largely determine its value. Your contribution from experience, knowledge or thought can be vital. The corresponding contribution of others may have most to offer you in a session.
"It's only grades that matter"	Grades, like urinating, are a necessity in life. The value of any assignment comes mainly from the thinking and activity that goes into it. There is additional value where you can interact with the lecturer (face to face or in written form) about your work and where you can share the ideas and /or the product with your colleagues. Hopefully the assignment will get back to you for your future reference.
"Treat each part of the course as it comes – one hurdle at a time, concentrate on immediate needs."	Real problems here! This may be a worthy survival strategy and get you through each course but may not do much for your professional development. The whole programme needs to be much more than the sum of the constituent parts. The challenge is for you to continually relate and evaluate a number of aspects – your current study on a course, your work on other courses, your professional experience and base (i.e. the school from which you come and are likely to return), yourself as a conscious, reflective learner. (This is obviously not going on all the time but should be in active mode frequently! Deal with inconsistencies, challenge relevance, acknowledge change etc.)
"Accumulating knowledge (especially 'content') is what Its all about."	Accumulation as such can be a self satisfying but an ultimately non-productive activity. Something needs to happen with that knowledge in its interaction with the learner for it to become professionally valuable. Accumulating bricks doesn't make a house.
"I enjoy meeting new ideas, my problem is turning them into action"	The awareness is there – this is a major step; now work to make the links. Observe yourself at work in the process of trying out new ideas, share the exploration with a peer and/or a tutor. Reflect on the experience as new and old ways accommodate to each other. Keep going until the new becomes the familiar, and all the more comfortable and effective.

Ways to achieve Professional Development

Awareness of need and of related issues such as those raised above, make for a good start. It can enable a more realistic and worthwhile agenda to be established. The skills of reflective practice can only emerge over time. If professional development of the type discussed here has become a personal aim and expectation then work at it, discuss it, pursue it – understanding more about its nature, turning ideas into personal and professional skills. Keeping a journal can provide the opportunity to reflect in a private but more ordered way, as you commit current thinking, dilemmas, insights and questions in writing. What you write may look naive or even wrong a few weeks later; no matter, its writing has served a purpose, if only as a marker of change when you review it. At the end of your programme you will be able to look back, re-evaluate your position on the triangle diagram and most important, be in a position to see your return to school as another opportunity for professional development which you now have the skills to use.

But let us return to the student group with which we started.

Epilogue

Four of the students find themselves together waiting to collect course materials after the examination processes are finished.

Carole: *Hi – is it really two years since we started? What a programme – I wonderd if I was going to make it. Sadly D never did sort out the demands of work on her social life. The gold stars were harder to get than she imagined. How was it for you?*

Althea: *It was great, but not what I expected. The first semester was a drag but that course with Dr. Zemenes got me thinking in a totally different way. I suddenly had some tools with which to work on the content of the courses. Not sure that it made me popular with Out-of-School course lecturers – I always seemed to be the one asking questions in classes. Still the lecturers told me in private that they knew at least one student was awake!*

Errol: *Certainly quite an achievement to stay awake in some of those lectures but, guess what, I had some of my best ideas when pondering about one idea that cropped up in the early part of a lecture. I'm dead keen on team teaching now and am going to get my principal to introduce it at our school.*

Carole: *You know this course really made me think. I panicked in the first year, because I felt I knew how to teach and I could na cope with all these new ideas. Working with a group of students on a presentation really got me going – we didn't know anything about the topic or how to tackle it. We complained about and to the lecturer for not telling us what to do, but it was amazing, we learned so much from doing it and also from the presentations of our colleagues. The course tutor seemed to have a totally different role – supporting, listening, intervening. Do you know, I tried something similar in my school based work and the students got so involved? I have some things to learn about handling it and other new ways of working but I am going to try when I get back to school and will get members of my department to try also. Althea, did the programme turn out to be a dream come true or a nightmare?*

Althea: *A bit of both actually. I found the writing so difficult. Also other students couldn't understand where I was coming from and I felt very isolated. They wanted new theories while I was trying to understand and find solutions to the problems occurring in my* *classroom. What was amazing was that through some reading on the course with Miss Prism preparing us for the school based work, I suddenly saw the connection and realised that reflective teaching requires you to relate theories, experience and yourself. Just a pity this was in my second year when I was feeling pressurised by re-sits and new courses. Still I made it and I feel that I have new ways to view my work in school plus some of the skills. I hope I can find someone else to talk to and work with back at school. I think I will try to do the MEd programme in a couple of years time.*

Errol: *Great experience but I'm exhausted. Time for one more Seacole lunch together?*

References

Hoyle, E. (1974) Professionality, professionalism and control in teaching. London Educational Review, 3(2), 13-19.

Mason, J. (1987) Only Awareness is Educable. Mathematics Teaching Vol 120, pp30-31

Mason, J. (1992) Noticing: A Systematic Approach to Professional Development Open University (informal publication)

Other reading which might stimulate thinking

Dillon J and McGuire M (1997) Becoming a Teacher Buckingham: Open University Press

Hargreaves A and Fullan M G (eds) (1992) Understanding Teacher Development, London: Cassell

Kohl H R (1986) On Becoming a Teacher London: Methuen

Lortie D (1975) School Teacher Chicago: University of Chicago Press

Schön D (1987) Educating the Reflective Practitioner San Francisco: Jossey Bass.

CHAPTER  Teaching History in Secondary Schools: Organising for Instruction

DIAN McCALLUM

Abstract

When observing Caribbean student teachers fulfilling the teaching practicum component of their degree programme, a distinction can easily be made between the lesson which was carefully conceptualized and organised and one which was hastily or thoughtlessly put together, perhaps at the last moment. Organising for instruction involves far more than reading a set number of texts, to impart such information as is contained, to students. Organising for instruction means first and foremost that one has a sound knowledge of the content of the subject, as it is this knowledge which will inform and guide the setting of meaningful and achievable instructional objectives.

Organising for instruction also means that one has a fairly good grasp - subject to continuous development and refinement - of the relevant pedagogical skills, knowledge of the most suitable strategies to be used and materials to select which will facilitate the achievement of instructional goals and objectives.

Far too often assessment of students is done in a haphazard manner without linking assessment to instructional objectives. There should be a clear link between the objectives of instruction and assessment procedures, for how else will one determine the extent to which instruction was effective? Without an understanding of the necessary elements which makes up the instructional process, one will succeed at best in conveying information to students from which they might be able to derive some meaning. At worst, the instructional period for it is certainly now not a process, might just very well be one more boring encounter to live, oops! Sleep through.

This chapter examines some of the issues involved in organising for instruction. It demonstrates that organising for instruction takes place in well-defined stages and that successful lessons are generally the results of careful planning.

Introduction

It is perhaps a grossly overstated fact that effective planning usually prefaces effective teaching. Despite this constant reiteration the cases of lack of planning for instruction are many. It is common knowledge that preparation for instruction means for some teachers the identification of a chapter in a select text for reading in class. It could also mean the finding of the relevant page from which to continue the dictation of notes - written over time perhaps and badly in need of review - or the discussion of peripheral issues ostensibly related to the topic because of the superficiality of the content knowledge.

Morine Dershimer confirms that:

> The teacher who simply writes down the page numbers in the textbook that are to be covered in the next lesson has not really planned a lesson. He or she has indicated the materials to be used in the lesson, but has evidently not determined the procedures to be used for involving students in interacting with these materials (Cooper ed. 1994, 40).

The issue of concern then is how to organise for instruction. Such organisation usually involves the setting of instructional goals and objectives, decisions as to the most suitable methods to be used to accomplish them, the selection of the most relevant and appropriate instructional materials and the use of assessment procedures, which are clearly linked to objectives of instruction.

The instructional process therefore involves a number of discrete stages, which require careful planning for the effective transition from one stage to the next.

Stages in the Instructional Process

> Instructional planning require more than information about what is included in a lesson or unit plan. To plan effectively and efficiently, a teacher needs a clear understanding of the subject to be taught, as well as information about alternative goals and objectives, productive use of classroom questions, approaches for teaching concepts, procedures for classroom management, and techniques for evaluation of student learning (Cooper ed. 1994, 46).

The foregoing might appear Herculean, but it serves to demonstrate that organising for instruction cannot take place in a vacuum, its importance should therefore not be trivialized. In fact, as Lang, McBeath and Hebert explains:

> In the teaching/learning cycle, successful lessons rarely "just happen Such lessons are generally the result of careful planning for the major phases of effective lessons ...which should flow naturally from one into another (1995, 52).

Organising for instruction involves three major phases. These phases are:
1. Planning
2. Implementing
3. Assessing

Planning

The planning phase involves the teacher in one of several of his/her decision-making roles with respect to what to teach and how to teach. Planning should begin with the setting of clear and achievable objectives, which should specify what students, should know or be able to do as a result of instruction. These objectives when formulated should be communicated to the learners.

Consider the following scenarios:
1. Students find it difficult to take notes during the lecture because they are unaware of what is important.
2. After the exam was concluded, a number of students realized they had studied the wrong content.
3. While observing the youngsters at work, it became evident they were having a lot of fun, but seemed to be learning little of value
4. The professor reported that scores on the mid-term test were very low. He had done all that he could by covering the content that he knew to be important. His conclusion: "this was probably a particularly dumb class of students" (Kemp 1985, 77).

What the scenarios above indicate is the general lack or absence of careful planning beginning with the formulation of explicitly stated learning or instructional objectives. As Kemp suggest:

> Unless the requirements are specifically defined, the learner does not know precisely what to study or what activities to perform. Also, without such definition, the instructor has difficulty in measuring the specific learning...By knowing what is expected from the stated learning objectives, learners can better structure their study procedure and prepare for examinations (1985, 78).

It has been shown that "when teachers have clearly defined instructional objectives and have shared them with their students a number of things happen"
1. Better instruction occurs
2. More efficient learning results
3. Better evaluation occurs
4. Students become better self evaluators (Cooper ed. 1994, 56).

In writing instructional objectives, teachers should ensure that they are written in the three domains of learning, that is the cognitive, skill and affective domains. The ability to distinguish objectives according to domains usually develops with repeated practice complemented of course by a sound knowledge of the subject content.

The planning phase of the instructional process also involves the selection of the most appropriate strategy and materials that will facilitate the achievement of the objective of instruction. Again the teacher can only select strategies if he/she has a fairly good knowledge of the variety of teaching/learning strategies that can be used for instruction. The ability to select the most appropriate strategy for use in a given situation no doubt comes with the development of certain skills and competencies. But if teachers have a clear idea of what they want their students to achieve, they will have a fair idea of the activities to provide from a range of possible activities given their knowledge and understanding of the strengths and weaknesses of different teaching/learning strategies.

Thus planning for teaching is a necessary first step to be taken when organising for instruction. As Jacobsen, Eggen and Kauchak states "research evidence supports the value of planning" as such evidence shows "that the actions teachers take in the classroom are influenced by the plans they make" (1999, 16).

Implementing

The next phase of the instructional process is the implementation phase. At this phase of the process, the teacher is concerned with accomplishing the objectives of instruction by means of the strategies and instructional materials selected. It should be emphasized that "in addition to considering a teaching strategy to reach a predetermined goal, teachers must also organise and manage their classrooms so learning can proceed smoothly (Jacobsen et al. 1999, 16).

The knowledge of and ability to select the appropriate teaching/learning strategy will definitely distinguish between the effective and the ineffective teacher. Gilstrap and Martin affirms this observation as follows:

> Knowledge of and ability to apply the variety of ways, patterns, or teaching strategies on the current scene is one of the crucial distinguishing differences between the lay man and the professional teacher. Within the profession, possession of a repertoire of strategies is a measure of competency that helps to separate the master teacher from his more limited colleagues (Lang et al. 1995, 268).

In the implementation phase of the instructional process the teacher can choose from two broad groups of instructional strategies. These are direct and indirect instruction. According to Lang et. al. the former tends to be teacher centered and involves methods such as lecture, practice and drills, whereas the latter is usually learner centered and involves inquiry instruction which consists of guided and unguided inquiry (1995, 268).

The implementation phase of the instructional process involves three distinct stages, the introduction, development and culmination. The introductory phase of instruction serves to provide the orientation to the lesson, to stimulate, motivate and generally to get students ready for new learning. Also referred to as set induction, this stage of instruction refers to those actions and statements made by the teacher that are designed to relate the experiences of the students to the objectives of the lesson. Its main purpose is to put students in a receptive frame of mind that will facilitate learning (Cooper ed. 1994, 91).

In the development stage of instruction, students should be actively involved in a variety of ways. It is at this stage that the principal objectives are targeted with students being engaged at different levels of operation so as to maximize learning.

This means that students should be engaged at the concrete level to promote enactive (participatory) learning. At the iconic level pictures and other visuals should be used to promote learning related to visual images while at the symbolic level symbolic learning is promoted through the use of spoken word or the written language (Lang et al. 1995, 66).

The final stage in the implementation phase of instruction is the culmination or closure. Closure is a form of review that takes place at the end of instruction. In essence closure refers to those actions or statements by teachers that are designed to bring a lesson presentation to an appropriate conclusion (Cooper ed. 1994, 101).

Assessment

The third phase of the instructional process is that of assessment. This phase is dependent on what happens in the preceding phases and serve in particular to determine the extent to which instructional objectives were achieved.

At this stage of the instructional process Kemp notes that testing instruments and materials must be developed to measure the degree to which learners have acquired the knowledge, can perform the skills, and exhibit changes in attitude as required by the objectives (1985, 160-161). It is clear then that "there must be a direct relationship between learning objectives and test items" and that being the case, "a learner must anticipate being tested in the same type of behaviour as indicated by the objective" (Kemp 1985,161).

Gronlund and Linn concurs with Kemp as according to their position:

> Instructional objectives play a key role in the instructional process. When properly stated, they serve as guides for both teaching and learning, communicate the intent of instruction to others and provide guidelines for evaluating pupils (Gronlund and Linn 1990, 23).

Despite the fact that assessment procedures should be related to the objectives of instruction W. James Popham has argued that "Far too many teachers simply stumble into an assessment pattern without giving serious consideration to why they're assessing what they're assessing." "Typically", he further observes, "teachers test students in order to dispense grades in a manner that somehow resembles the levels of academic performance that student have displayed" (1999, 85).

Given the fact that the assessment phase of the instructional process might be effected in ways which are not in keeping with sound assessment practices it is nevertheless useful to be aware of what really should take place at this phase of the instructional process.

At this phase "the teacher attempts to gather information that can be used to determine if learning has occurred" (Jacobsen et al. 1999, 17). This can be done in a variety of ways. Oral quizzes, open book test, observation, essays, interpretative exercises or by using alternative/authentic assessments such as portfolios. Assessment need not rely exclusively on traditional well-tried and tested procedures to assess progress. More attempts should be made to implement alternative/authentic assessment tasks in the classroom. This more than most forms of traditional assessments, will ensure that assessment practices in subjects such as history, will increasingly reflect the nature of the discipline. The current emphasis on alternative/authentic assessments is one way in which this can be achieved as, authentic assessment:

> Collect diverse evidence of students' learning from multiple activities. Rather than relying on single tests or narrow samples of students' knowledge, authentic assessment involves gathering evidence over time from many different academic activities (Scott and Ayres 1994, 7-8).

Organising for instruction in History

Having explored the three main phases in the instructional process, attention can now be focused on planning for instruction in a subject specific way.

Over the last three decades, history as a discipline has come under intense scrutiny with regards to its relevance and practical uses. Essentially, history had over time become stereotyped as a dull and boring subject with very little to do with the present but everything to do with the past. It became necessary therefore for practitioners to justify the continued study of history in schools and to demonstrate its relevance to society. Much has been done since then (the early 1970's) to revisit the teaching approaches used in history and to rid the subject of its association with boredom and inactivity. To this end new teaching methods were promoted in order to generate more active learning among pupils, placing more emphasis as well on the use of resources in the classroom (Haydn, Arthur and Hunt 1997, 18). Further this new approach was supported by psychological evidence, which suggest that students learn more when they are actively engaged and directly involved in the teaching/learning process. The 'new' history is the product of the movement, which sought to encourage an understanding of the nature of history and its fundamental concepts. It adopted a clearly pupil centered approach placing much emphasis on the use of evidence (Haydn et al. 1997, 18).

It is now fairly well accepted that history should be taught using the historian's mode of inquiry. For this to be accomplished proper planning is needed. There can be no doubt that the perception which developed where history was concerned resulted more from how instruction was organised than from the subject matter itself.

In view of the foregoing the issue of organising for instruction in history requires much thought and attention to details. It means that teachers of the subject should perforce be knowledgeable of the subject matter of history and possess an understanding of the nature of the discipline. This understanding will inform and guide the instructional process, as formulating specific instructional objectives, selecting appropriate teaching/learning strategies and instructional materials and developing valid and reliable assessment procedures requires an understanding of what history is as a discipline.

It has been argued and demonstrated too, that for students to know history as the historians themselves know the subject, methods of interpretation must be taught if teachers of history are to claim that they teach history. This view has been put forward by Edwin Fenton who demonstrated that students can be taught the historians' mode of inquiry irrespective of the age group to which they belong. This is especially critical as for long it was generally held that certain type of instruction was unsuited for particular age group. However, Jerome Bruner has contributed to revolutionizing this system of belief. By using research data, he advanced a counter theory. He argued that 'any subject can be taught effectively in some intellectually honest form to any child at any stage of development' " provided of course that the way in which the subject is presented suits the developmental stage of the individual child" (Garvey and Krug 1977, 12).

It is no longer acceptable at large, at least from a psychological standpoint that history is too difficult a subject for young students. It is now believed, to the contrary, that for teachers to instruct using the historians' mode of inquiry it means that they must teach for students to learn "the rules by which historians collect evidence and use it to interpret the past" (Fenton 1966, 150).

Teachers of history must therefore incorporate into their lessons the use of primary sources, which constitute the main sources, used by historians. In fact, primary source should be used alongside secondary ones in order for students to understand the differences between both types of sources especially the peculiarities of the primary source material. Primary sources facilitate the development of certain skills as students are challenged to use skills of critical inquiry by asking, certain questions of the sources.

Historians approach the sources before them dispassionately, they ask questions of them in short they are critical of the sources. Historian John Tosh argues that no source no matter how authoritative is beyond question. If students are to be trained to think and work in the same way as the historian then their skills of analysis and interpretation will improve. They will begin to demand evidence to support conclusions drawn and to begin to draw and support their own conclusions.

All of this however hinges on good planning. Nicholas in fact argues that the use of primary sources should be carefully planned. Their use in the classroom he argues "is not just a matter of enabling students to reason and think". The use of primary sources "both requires and stimulates the use of historical imagination and creativity, and carefully chosen and used, it can make a distinctive and important contribution to the historical education of children of varying ages and abilities" (1962, 232).

There is much to suggest therefore that organising for instruction is not an exercise to be taken lightly. It is in fact a complex process that if thoroughly done "allows teachers to know what students will learn, how they will learn, and the degree to which they have learned" (Jacobsen et al. 1999, 88).

Conclusion

Organising for instruction is not an easy or simple task. It is complex, intentional and focused. It is goal directed, task driven and result oriented.

The chapter examined the issues involved in organising for instruction. It revealed that such organisation proceeds in distinct phases, which are interrelated. The first phase require teachers to formulate instructional objectives, which will be used to guide the process of instruction. Instructional objectives indicate that the teacher has an idea of where he/she wants his/her students to go and the steps to be taken to get there.

The second phase in organising for instruction is concerned with implementation. At this phase the teacher's plan of action (the unit/lesson plan) is put into effect, progressing in three distinct stage from the introduction to the development through to the culmination.

The last phase in the instructional process is the assessment phase. It is at this point that the teacher will develop instruments to check the effectiveness of instruction and to evaluate the results of the teaching/learning encounter. The instructional objectives developed in the planning phase will be the benchmark used to judge or measure the overall effectiveness of the instructional design.

Organising for instruction in history is really no different than it is in other disciplines. What is different is that the entire process must be designed in keeping with the nature of the subject. There is no easy way to achieve success in instruction than to plan for it. There is therefore no harm in repeating what was said at the beginning of this chapter. Successful lessons are generally the result of careful planning.

References

Burston, W. H. 1962. Handbook for History Teachers. Methuen Educational Ltd.

Cooper, James, ed. 1994. Classroom Teaching Skills. D. C. Heath and Co.

Fenton, Edwin, 1966. Teaching the New Social Studies in Secondary Schools An Inductive Approach. Holt, Rinehart and Winston Inc.

Garvey, Brian and Mary Krug. 1977. Models of History Teaching. Oxford University Press

Gronlund, Norman and R. Linn. 1990. Measurement and Evaluation in Teaching. McMillan Publishing Co.

Haydn, Terry, James Arthur and Martin Hunt. 1997. Learning to Teach in the Secondary Schools. A Companion to school experience. London And New York: Routledge

Jacobsen, David, Paul Eggen and Donald Kauchak. 1999. Methods for Teaching. Merril

James Popham, W. 1999. Classroom Assessment. What Teachers Need to Know. Allyn and Bacon

Kemp, Jerrold. 1985. The Instructional Design Process. New York: Harper and Row Publishers

Lang, Helmut, Arthur McBeath, and Jo Hebert. 1995. Teaching Strategies and Methods for Student Centered Instruction. Harcourt Brace and Co. Canada Ltd.

Paris, Scott and Linda Ayres. 1994. Becoming Reflective Students and Teachers with Portfolios and Authentic Assessment. Washington D. C.: American Psychological Association.

CHAPTER 4
Practical Stress Management for Faculty of Education Students

ROSEMARIE JOHNSON

Abstract

One just needs to sit in the corridors of an Education department or in the commuting student lounge to hear the complaints about lecturers, the university, and fellow students. These complaints originate from a state of distress among students. Are their complaints valid? Are lecturers ogres like they are made out to be? Are students innocent helpless victims that are at the mercy of the administration and the university? It is necessary to answer these questions and to understand what stress is, how individuals cope, and what can be done to improve coping behavior. This article begins to give meaningful and useful answers to these important questions.

What is Stress?

According to the Interactive Model of Stress, stress occurs when one perceives a situation as threatening, challenging, or harmful. Additionally one also considers the outcome of the situation important to ones welfare and is uncertain if one can successfully meet the challenge or avoid the threat (Smith, 1993). This definition suggests that stress is ubiquitous because everyone encounters challenges and threats in the course of daily living that are potentially stressful. Students in the department are no exception. Almost any event can trigger stress for them. These triggers typically fall into two categories, external and internal (Roskies, 1987). External stress triggers usually involve unsatisfactory person-environment fit. For students, the department and the university make up their environment. Conflicts between a student's expectations and that of the department/university can understandably lead to stress. Additionally having too much responsibility can lead to conflicts between the person and the environment. Typically, students within the faculty are mature students with responsibilities of husband, children, and student. Some also work in addition to all their other responsibilities. These multiple responsibilities in the face of maladaptive coping strategies will inevitably lead to stress.

Another stressor for these mature students is the decision to attend college. This decision constitutes change and changes causes stress. The degree of stress will vary among students depending on their support system. Additionally, upon entering the department, students are required to take on academic responsibilities along with hearing the dos and don'ts of the different option areas. Exacerbating their heightened state stress even further is the daily hassles that inevitably come with trying to adjust to a new environment. Registration, getting information about option requirements, the misinformation from students are also issues for students. It is therefore not surprising that many become so overwhelmed that they have difficulty understanding or remembering information that is given. The state of emotional overload is so great that in order not to decompensate, they shut down. In addition to external triggers are the internal stress triggers. These involve the personality characteristics the student brings with them. That is, their unrealistic expectations about themselves and others. These are reflected in the student who believes a mistake cannot be made, or that everything should be done.

Although everyone experiences stress, variations among individuals can be seen in: (a) the stressful situations to which people are exposed; (b) the events perceived as stressful; (c) the way stress is experienced; and (d) the way one copes. Additionally, past experiences and present circumstances also influence how one evaluates situations. Most students would agree that pursuing a degree within the department was stressful. However, different things are stressful for different students. For some, it is lecturers and teaching style, the different assignments that all seem due at the same time, the inconsistency in information given, or the lack of adequate resources and passing exams.

Individual variation is going to also exist in the way students experience stress. For some, stress is going to be manifested physically. That is, chronic medical problems are going to worsen, new medical problems will emerge, including migraines, stomach aches, or acne. There will also be others who have various aches, pains, and symptoms for which there is not physical reason. It appears that for many of our students, stress is manifested in this way. A report from the Director of the Health Center suggested that students from with the department are disproportionately represented among students seeking services.

Students also have emotional stress reactions. Some become anxious or depressed. It is a frequent occurrence to see students crying because they have failed exams or after conflicts with each other and with the faculty. This emotionality then interferes with cognitive skills. Students will experience difficulty concentrating and remembering. Because the cognitive aspect of their functioning is so fundamental to success at the university, problems in this area pose serious threats to matriculation. Additionally, students also seem to lose the capacity to think and problem-solve. Typically with this manifestation of stress a vicious cycle is set up where the more interference there is with cognitive processes, the more emotional the student becomes which leads to further suppression of intellect. Finally, there is a behavioral response to stress. Students under stress become impatient and generally difficult to be around. Instead of typing to find solutions then tend to complain and whine about problems in the system. This complaining stops them for addressing the source of the stressor which causes further whining and increased stress. The problem with stress within the department is a cause for concern. Students need to be empowered to control their stress so they can reap the full benefits of their educational experiences.

What do students need to know?

First and foremost, students need to understand that although they may not be able to control the world outside, they can learn to control the way they respond. How can this be done? This can be done through awareness, developing new skills, and applying the skills (Smith, 1993).

Controlling Physical, Behavioral, and Mental Signs of Stress

Stress involves much more than tense muscles. However, effective stress management begins with bodily relaxation (Roskies, 1987). This makes sense because it is difficult to feel or behave at ease when the body is tense. Awareness of physical tension levels means paying attention to variations in bodily tension, understanding the relationship between feeling states (anger) and bodily states (pounding heart). When one is upset or overwhelmed, management of physical tension is the first step in achieving control. When we feel overwhelmed by multiple demands and insufficient time, we tend to act impatiently. This impatience is likely to cause us to yell at each other, speak curtly, interrupt, and be obnoxious. Unfortunately, such behavioral displays have a negative effect.

The very act of raising one's voice or pounding a fist increases the unpleasantness one is already experiencing. This creates within the self a negative spiral of escalating tension. Additionally it also influences others to respond in kind. There is a misconception that it is necessary to rant and rave when one is upset in order to "blow off steam." Unfortunately, by the time this ranting is finished, the eruption has created such havoc that much time and energy are required to repair the situation. What can one do in a situation that is getting out of hand?

Delay

This can be done through deep breathing or counting. This buys the individual the time to think. Secondly, engaging in behaviors incompatible with the undesirable is also useful. This could be speaking slowly to prevent shouting. The person who speaks in a calm, modulated voice assumes a relaxed body position. This will improve interactions with others, and well as one's feelings of well-being. Thirdly, expressing needs and complaints verbally in a non-hostile controlled manner stops us bottling up anger or losing control. Many people think feeling negative emotions are "bad." However, feelings of emotional upset should be used as "yellow light." A warning that special attention is required to monitor and regulate behavior. Another area in the process of stress management that requires work is our thought. To keep stress under control one needs to learn to think productively.

Thinking Productively

Productive thinking is the ability to use "self-talk" to reduce, rather than increase stress level. Everyone experiences frustrations, disappointments, and defeats in the course of ones professional and personal live. How we interpret and react to them, however, depend very much on our individual "internal programs." Two people may be in the same situations of being yelled at by someone they care about: but if one says "lecturer is having a bad day," while the other says, "I must have done something wrong," each is likely to feel very different about the situation. The point here is that external events provide the raw data for experiences, but it is one's internal program that determines how the experience is perceived and handled (Powell, 1969). What can one do?

Learn to recognize unproductive self-talk.

That is talk that increases tension and discomfort. According to Maultsby (1980), specific beliefs and habits generally underlie negative self-talk. That is, unrealistic expectations ("The world should always be fair"), catastrophizing ("If it is not perfect then, it is terrible"), putting oneself down ("I am stupid, rather than that was a stupid thing to do") and not dealing with the here-and-now ("It should not have happened"). During the state of upset an examination of self-talk is crucial to determine if it is helpful or harmful. If it is harmful, change it. Sometimes this is not so easy and a stress-crisis occurs. During a stress crisis, what can be done?

Emergency Braking

Each of us has personal signs telling us that we are out of control. When these appear, it is important to stop. There are few stress situations where an immediate response is needed. If you are upset that you cannot act in control, do not say or do anything for a few seconds. Once you are in control of yourself then you can decide how best to deal with a situation. Focusing on control first helps you avoid doing or saying things you are likely to regret. Another strategy is engaging in incompatible behavior. For example, it is impossible to shout softly. Therefore, deliberately lowering your voice will be calming. Finally, to gain mastery over stress, one needs stress resistance.

Building Stress Resistance

It is noteworthy that when one is feeling particularly good about self and the world, the irritants of life do not seem such a bother. Feelings of well-being makes you more relaxed and more tolerant and better able to cope with the stresses of daily living. Additionally, adequate rest, sensible diet, regular exercise and pleasurable activities go a long way in bolstering your ability to manage stress. Remember, "A pleasure a day keeps the stress away" (Smith, 1993).

Stress is here to stay and to be better adjusted and receive the most out of the university experience, students need to recognize they are not helpless victims. However, there are things that lecturers can do to improve the learning environment. First, manage their own stress so they will be more patient and understanding with students. Additionally, lecturers can try to understand the experience from the perspective of the student and not be judgmental when students become overwhelmed.

References

Maultsby, M. C. (1980). Your guide to emotional well-being: The handbook of rational self-counselling. Rational Self-Help Aids: Kentucky.

Powell, J. (1969). Why am I afraid to tell you who I am: Insights into personal growth. Tabor Publishers: Texas.

Roskies, E. (1987) Stress Management for the health Type A. Guildford Press: New York.

Smith, J. C. (1993). Creative stress management: The 1-2-3 cope system. Prentice Hall: New Jersey

CHAPTER 5
The Teacher and Instructional Management in the Classroom

AUSTIN EZENNE

Abstract

Classroom management skills are of primary importance in determining teaching and learning successes in Caribbean schools. Classroom management includes all the things teachers must do to foster effective learning and good behaviour in our classrooms.

Caribbean teachers must motivate their students to learn effectively, create conducive learning environments and use effective methods of teaching to make students learn in the classroom. Instructional methods such as concept attainment, mastery learning, inquiry, projects and cooperative learning can be used effectively in classrooms to facilitate students learning.

Introduction

Classroom management is getting more attention in educational research in recent times than ever before. This is because no other topic in education receives greater attention or causes more concerns for teachers, parents and other stakeholders than classroom management. Lack of effective classroom management is a major obstacle to effective teaching and learning in our schools today. School management and parents contribute to ineffective classroom management when they fail to provide necessary facilities for teaching and learning. Many studies on teacher effectiveness indicate that classroom management skills are of primary importance in determining teaching success, whether it is measured by student learning or by other rating methods. A teacher who is inadequate in classroom management skills is not likely to achieve much in the classroom and therefore basic management skills are crucial to the achievement of classroom objectives in the school. Students' learning is adversely affected if teachers fail to do their work well in the classroom.

The concept of classroom management is wider than the notion of student discipline. Classroom management includes all the things teachers must do to foster effective learning and good behaviour in the classroom. Teachers should approach classroom management as a process of establishing and maintaining effective learning and not just for eliciting students' obedience to classroom rules and procedures. Effective classroom management should be used as a vehicle for the enhancement of student self-understanding and control and for effective learning. Student learning and behaviour go hand in hand, and problems arising from these activities have for many years been a major concern of teachers, administrators, parents and members of the society at large. Teachers face the task of educating many students who may have problems from their homes. It has been established through researches that teachers' skills in creating supportive classrooms are a major factor influencing students' motivation to learn, achievements and behaviour in the school. Wagner (1993) identified classroom management as the most important factor affecting students' learning and behaviour in the school. The problems of students' misbehaviour and increasing students' achievement in the school, can be tackled by creating classroom communities in which students' physiological, psychological, social, and academic needs can be met.

Classroom management is a broad and important area of school management. Evertson et al (1989) identified a variety of subsidiary concerns of classroom management as planning, organisation, environment, materials, procedures, directions, feedback, communication, record keeping and instructional dynamism. Planning for instruction contributes to efficiency through laying out in advance what is to be done everyday and how to do it well. Organisation contributes by arranging the classroom so that it functions more effectively with students ready to learn and materials ready for use. Both physical and psychological environments influence learning in the classroom. Materials are the tangible objects such as books, papers and teaching aids and other instructional materials used to enhance teaching and learning in the classroom. Feedback refers to responses teachers make as students attempt to learn and this helps the teacher to know the strengths and weaknesses of individual students. Communication refers to the exchanges among teachers, students, parents and administrators. Ineffective communication leads to misunderstanding. Proper record keeping provides a profile of student accomplishment and helps to reveal the strengths and weaknesses of the students and this enables the teacher to work more effectively with students and to communicate better with parents. Classroom management is very broad and cannot be adequately treated in a chapter of this nature. The focus of this chapter is therefore on instructional management in the classroom.

Managing Student Motivation to Learn

Many teachers derive happiness from working with well behaved students who are trying hard to learn but teachers are unhappy with students misbehaviour and inability to motivate some of their students to learn, in the classroom. Jones and Jones (1998) pointed out that many students meet their personal needs by successfully completing classroom activities and assignments. Other students who are not interested in school work, find the school to be an anxiety producing and stressful place. Teachers should understand the importance of motivation in student learning, and should not be frustrated by students' failure to pay attention complete assignments, attend class punctually or misbehave in the classroom.

Very often, teachers blame the family and the community for students' lack of motivation to learn in the school. Teachers should understand that students may show lack of motivation to learn when they do not see classroom work as interesting and useful, or when the learning activity is very difficult to master. Teachers should strive to create a learning atmosphere in which students and teachers feel respected and connected to one another. By so doing they can attract students' interest and engage them more meaningfully to classroom work. Jones and Jones (1998) made a study of motivation in a classroom setting and they concluded that students become actively involved in lessons to the extent they expect success in those lessons.

Managing Instruction in the Classroom

Many students believe that effective learning means doing better than many of their classmates in class. But for students to understand the meaning of effective learning, they must first of all understand the learning process, and the functional definition of an effective learner.

Teachers can use effective management to forestall or reduce the occurrence of problems in the classroom. A peaceful classroom environment will help both the teacher and the students to concentrate their energies on learning and instruction. Instructional management does not refer to skills peculiar to teaching a particular subject, but rather to those skills that cut across subjects and activities and it involves gaining and maintaining the cooperation of students in learning activities. Glasser (1990) pointed out that students who are willing participants are not likely to create disturbances in the classroom. Meaningful student engagement can be increased if the teacher uses a variety of teaching and learning activities to occupy the students in the classroom. These learning activities should be tied to student interests and should be aimed at achieving specific educational aim.

Lectures, group instructions, discussions, role plays, independent and group projects are some of the common activities used in the classroom today. Each of the activities is used to help students to acquire some skills. Kounin (1970) has identified three clusters of instructional management skills, as Movement Management which refers to the teacher's effectiveness in maintaining momentum, and making movement from one topic to another. Group Focus which refers to the ability of the students to maintain group concentration. The third management skill concerns avoiding boredom by both the teacher and the students in the classroom. These skills are independent of the subjects and contents associated with instruction. The management skills influence the extent to which students participate in activity related behaviours, maintain a high level of involvement, and preclude the occurrence of disciplinary problems in the classroom.

Effective Room Management

Many provisions for learning are usually made by the teacher before students arrive in the classroom for instruction. Teachers spend time getting the classrooms ready for instruction, by organising teaching and learning materials, testing equipment, and planning the procedure that will be used to support the instructional programmes. The importance of planning, that is operating according to a schedule and distributing activities according to predetermined objectives and allocation of time are all important planning activities carried out by the teacher for classroom instruction. There are some instructional rules about how a classroom should look like. The general appearance of the classroom can convey teacher's dedication or indifference in his classroom responsibilities. Teachers should try to make the classroom a place where students feel at home, and therefore conducive for effective learning.

Careful student seating arrangements can help to maintain attention and facilitate monitoring of student behaviour during instruction. Research indicated an increase in work completion by student with row and column seating arrangement. But having rows of seats may not be an effective way to promote group discussions and therefore teachers should design a classroom arrangement that permit greater visual contact with the teacher such as arranging the seats in groups, circular or in semi-circular forms. Effective seating arrangements are made on the understanding that the school and the classrooms are social institutions where socialization among students should be taken into consideration. The spaces between the seats should be freed of obstacles and should be wide enough to accommodate the movement of students.

Teachers can ensure the availability of instructional materials by checking well in advance whether the materials and equipment are available and in good condition for instructional activity. It is important to keep a list of all instructional materials and equipment and there should be careful and resourceful management of instructional materials. Teachers should devise methods for using and storing instructional materials. Classroom instructional materials should be stored in safe places where students will not damage or remove them and where they will be readily available for use in the classroom. Classroom rules and procedures are necessary for the smooth management of classroom teaching and learning. Classroom rules may be viewed as oppressive and stripping away students' rights by some students. The rules and procedures should be reviewed by the teacher with students at the beginning of the term.

Managing relationships between school and home, teacher and student and student and student are important aspects of classroom management. Effective management of these relationships relies heavily on communication skills of the teacher and the school administration, positive school-home relationship is very vital to school administration and should be encouraged by the teacher through school-home contacts.

Methods of Creating Conducive Learning Environments

Teachers can easily create a more conducive learning environment to many students by adjusting the classroom environment and some instructional methods, to be more conducive to students' unique learning needs. Jones and Jones (1989) suggested the following methods for creating more conducive learning environment in the classroom:

1. When presenting your lessons, use visual displays such as writing on the overhead projector to assist students who are visual learners.
2. Allow students to select where they will sit. This is because students vary in the amount of light, sound, and heat they prefer and may, in fact, self select seats that

provide more conducive learning environments for them.
3. Permit students to choose where they wish to study because some students work most effectively at a table and others in soft chairs.
4. Be sensitive to individual students' needs to block out sound or visual distractions. The teacher should discuss the different learning styles with students and then allow them to select the learning style they like best.
5. The school can make good quality snacks for the students or allow them to bring their own. It has been observed that many students do not eat an adequate breakfast before coming to class and they should be given ample time to have snacks during the break.
6. Provide opportunities for students to select whether they will work alone, in pairs or with a small group. Students can work with peers to complete assignments, study for tests or work on long term projects.
7. Give students instructions in study skills which will help them to concentrate on their work. They should also be instructed on how to organise materials using an outline format.
8. Learning centres that incorporate a variety of learning modalities can be developed to assist students to learn visually, and auditorially. Learning centres also enable students to make decisions concerning light, sound, and design preferences.

Students differ in their approaches to learning because every student has a cognitive or learning style he or she takes to learn. Teachers can increase students' motivation and success by responding effectively to students' learning styles.

Instructional Methods for Motivating Students to Learn

Teachers' instructional methods constitute an important factor in learning in the classroom. Charles and Senter (1995) identified two broad instructional approaches which can lead to a variety of outcomes in the classroom. These are Direct and Facilitative teaching approaches. The direct teaching approach is used to advantage when goals of instruction are stated very precisely and when content coverage is extensive as in many science courses. The two main strategies used in Direct Instruction are Concept attainment and Mastery learning.

To help students attain concepts in school, teachers should ask them to categorise objects and ideas on the basis of their important attributes and students refine their concepts about these objects and ideas as they compare and contrast examples. For example, a student can refine his concept of an apple by contrasting apples' characteristics with those of oranges and bananas.

Mastery Learning came into focus in the 1970s because of the concern that, while many students in a given class learned what was intended, many others did not, Charles and Senter (1995). Based on the belief that all students could learn well, given proper instruction and adequate time, mastery learning was developed as an important instructional strategy. In mastery learning no student is allowed to move ahead to the next unit of the subject matter until the previous unit has been mastered. To facilitate the process, the subject matter is broken into small parts and carefully sequenced and students are given extra help and time by the teacher until mastery is attained.

In the Facilitative Teaching Approach, the main role of the teacher is to facilitate students' effort and progress in learning. First students are encouraged to make inputs in what they are learning and to explore problems and come up with their own solutions. The three strategies frequently used in facilitative teaching are: inquiry, projects and co-operative learning.

The major purpose of inquiry is to teach students how to learn on their own and this method can be used to explore topics, find information and reach conclusions. Inquiry teaches students to confront problems, gather information about it and to compose conclusions. Projects are activities carried out over periods of time and usually result in a product or a presentation from the student.

Cooperative learning involves groups of two or more students working together to complete specific tasks. This strategy is used to facilitate teaching because it encourages good cooperation, requires positive give and take, and shows the value of collective wisdom. Consequently, students learn to think for themselves and show resourcefulness and creativity. Cooperative learning is a popular and effective method for meeting students' varied learning styles.

The Peer Tutoring Method strategy encourages cooperation among students and thereby creates a more supportive, safe learning environment. The opportunity to instruct another student can provide a student with a sense of competence and personal worth. By allowing students to serve as resources for other students, the teacher increases the availability of individual attention and this can help in reducing students frustration in the classroom.

Conclusion

The concept of classroom management includes all the things teachers must do to foster effective learning and good behaviour in the classroom. Classrooms are social settings in which many young people are expected to spend harmonious time together in a very small space. Parents' expectations of teachers should be shaped by the unique, demanding realities of the classroom. They can be helped to understand and appreciate these realities when teachers point out the similarities and differences between home and school management conditions.

Classroom management formerly focused on how to increase on task behaviour with little attention paid to whether the curriculum and instructional methods motivated students to learn or not. Recently, educators are becoming aware of the relationship between student motivation to learn and students' behaviour. When motivational factors are ignored, teachers find themselves spending much time attempting to control students behaviour. Many students make effort to complete their learning tasks when their needs are met, in the classroom and in the school.

References

Charles, C.M. and Senter, G.W., (1995) Elementary Classroom Management. 2nd Edition. New York: Longman Publishers.

Evertson, C., Emmer, E., Clements, B., Sanford, J. and Worsham, M., (1989) Classroom Management for Elementary Teachers. New Jersey: Prentice Hall.

Foot, M. and Hook, C.,(1996) Introducing Human Resource Management. London and New York: Longman Publishers.

Froyen, L.A. and Iverson, A.M., (1999) Schoolwide and Classroom Management: The Reflective Educator-Leader. 3rd Edition. New Jersey: Merrill and Prentice Hall.

Glasser, W., (1990) The Control School: Managing Students without Coercion. New York: Harper and Row.

Jones, F.J. and Jones, L.S., (1998) Comprehensive Classroom Management. 5th Edition. Boston and London: Allyn and Bacon.

Kounin, J., (1970) Discipline and Group Management in Classrooms. New York: Holt, Rinehart and Winston.

Wagner, R.W.,(1993) "No More Suspensions: Creating a shared Ethical Community", Journal of Educational Leadership No. 8, Vol. 4 pp. 34-37.

SECTION 2

LANGUAGE EDUCATION

Chapter 6
Promoting Language Awareness through Language Study
Beverley Bryan   43

Chapter 7
Two Contrasting Foreign-Language Teaching Orientations
Hazel M. Salmon   49

Chapter 8
Foreign Language Teaching Strategies and Students' Performance in Spanish
*Joycelyn Barton and
Hazel M. Salmon   61*

Chapter 9
Revisiting Methodological Approaches to Foreign Language Teaching: From Communicative to Actional Language Teaching
Béatrice Boufoy-Bastick   77

Caribbean Perspectives

CHAPTER  # Promoting Language Awareness through Language Study

BEVERLEY BRYAN

Abstract

The twin goals of competence in the official language and pride in the mother tongue are part of policy directions within the Caribbean region. The task of the language teacher is how to engender both. This article discusses the promotion of a stance within language teaching known technically as metalinguistic awareness but more generally as language awareness. The aim is to make language visible for play and investigation, and to develop in learners the ability to talk about such language behaviour. A strong content area would be the dynamic language environment of the region. Ideas for a programme of language study and the findings of one local study, based on the notion of metalinguistic awareness, are presented.

Promoting Language Awareness through Language Study

The nature of language teaching in Jamaica, has meant that we must continually evaluate the twin goals of encouraging proficiency in Standard English (SE) without denigrating the vernacular language, as laid out in the Barbuda proposals of CARICOM Ministers of Education in 1993. Historically, approaches to the first language have been pathological, seeing it as a shadow to be removed from the learner's horizon (Craig, 1978). Replacing rather than adding to the mother tongue is almost impossible. So the question must be how to include the vernacular language within a conceptual framework for language teaching. This is the topic now for discussion.

The approach that I will discuss is not new (Bryan, 1982) and is not meant to replace the emphasis on Communicative Language Teaching (CLT) now being promoted in the Reform of Secondary Education (ROSE). CLT is a particular Teaching English to Speakers of Other Languages (TESOL) methodology which focuses on meaning and which has a sound base in language acquisition theories. Somewhere in the ROSE curriculum, there is a hint of the orientation I want to propose to help in accomplishing the twin goals that were laid out at the beginning of this piece. As a reminder they were the goals of competence in the official language and pride in the mother tongue. The direction I want to take is to consider the concept of language awareness. This is not such a strange notion because the principles drawn from the different second language teaching methods suggest that some level of language awareness is already recognised as a necessity in all language environments and with all methods.

Alternative notions of language awareness

The term "language awareness" has some currency in second language teaching but it has been strongly associated simply with linguistic knowledge and something that primarily teachers should possess. (Wright and Bolitho: 1993) attempted to develop this notion with a teacher education programme that allowed participants to explore language and reflect on their discoveries. Yet Hales (1997) echoed the earlier notion with the exploration of recorded conversations used with trainee teachers. The emphasis here, though, is still primarily of analysis of structures.

THE FOUNDATIONS OF LANGUAGE AWARENESS: METALINGUISTIC AWARENESS

In further understanding language awareness, Cazden (1973) has defined the more fundamental and specific term, metalinguistic awareness:

> The ability to make language forms opaque and attend to them in and for themselves" (p. 29)

The ability to discern the shape, sound and boundaries of units of language is named as a precondition for literacy. Piper (1993) who cites recent research linking children's rhyming and alliterative skills with the development of reading supports this assertion. However, although Cazden focuses on the benefits of language awareness for young children developing literacy, it is a concept that can be given wider application. In facilitating metalinguistic awareness we are going further, drawing attention to the form language takes, rather than just the meanings of words. For young children the purpose is playful manipulation in rhymes, puns, jokes and nonsense words. Cook (1997) takes this play notion further linking it to Bakhtin's notion of "carnival reality", a rule-governed, form-driven "exuberance of the mind". Such exuberance can take the form of playing with sounds to create alternative rhymes and rhythms. It can also take the form of playing with meaning to create the alternative worlds we call story/fiction. For other adults it might be more cognitive: an attempt to evaluate and analyse words with other words. In each case it is about noticing language behaviour, being conscious about what language is doing: making language visible and nameable. Thus metalinguistic awareness takes language awareness further by including not just new consciousness but the metalanguage to discuss the new concept.

METALINGUISTIC AWARENESS IN A PROGRAMME OF LANGUAGE STUDY.

The concept of metalinguistic awareness I am developing has, at its base, an awareness of the different uses of language, a conscious knowledge of its different forms and an ability to control its use. I therefore propose to discuss it in three main ways, which I will call the sociolinguistic, linguistic and stylistic or textual aspects. These are the different features that I believe can be brought together in a programme of language study to promote language awareness.

The sociolinguistic aspect is concerned with the use of language in society. This is not of course, a new suggestion. Rosen and Burgess (1980) suggested that language diversity should be the core of language study, drawing on the use of dialects, group language, anti-language and the language associated with sex, race and class. Our environment would allow for an added dimension in this area. It provides rich resources for the study of language in society because we live in a dynamic and changing linguistic situation. Mapping the changes and developments in English and Creole is a good source of knowledge about language behaviour. Equally rich would be capturing the cultural artifacts as they combine the play and fictive elements: the oral literature of stories, songs, riddles and proverbs so that they too can become serious objects of study.

This is one possible outcome of a language study programme but more than that language study should increase critical awareness of the effects and consequences of particular types of language use. My emphasis is on the dialectical relationship between language and society. It is about the influences on the individual and the way the individual and community influences change. As a programme of language study, to develop language awareness, it includes issues of power and discrimination. With one group of students I have taught, we have made a comparison between the development of language in two colonized societies: Britain under the Normans; Jamaica under the English. We were able to examine the languages in a historical and political context. We looked at the changes forced on a subject people invaded by a powerful army and those forced on a people who had no common means of communicating and who were forced to develop a new language. The theme was of people involved in creating language out of a particular experience. The other part of the dialectic was of attitudes and practices sustained by language and reinforcing the social situation.

This means going on to examine the way the language of race and sex discrimination in particular is used to underscore and legitimize certain attitudes in society. It would have to be a study in the ideological function of language, examining the part language plays in reinforcing what are accepted views in the dominant ideology. The potential for developing this area is enormous and depends on the level of maturity amongst the students. With older students it is possible to examine more closely the ideological construction of media messages, and the linguistic structures that determine their effects. This would go past some of the very limited work around advertising. It would be more closely aligned with what is being contemplated by the CXC CAPE syllabus.

The second point of metalinguistic awareness is conscious knowledge of the forms language takes. This might be termed the linguistic aspect. By this I am envisaging a study of the way languages are often interlinked. In my work with students, after we had looked at the way Standard English and Jamaican Creole languages had developed. We compared the two varieties, exploring the differences and similarities between them. We compared the verb system of Jamaican Creole and Standard English; we looked at the way English drew on French forms and Jamaican Creole drew on West African forms. The students own language experience came into play. In one instance a Mauritian student who spoke French was able to make the French links with English. In another, a Greek student was able to make another language link with English; a Black South African who spoke several varieties from that region was able to illustrate, by her own experiences, reasons for West African multi-lingualism (Bryan, 1982).

Languages have rules and introducing the language rules of the different systems of Jamaican Creole and Standard English on an equal footing, pointing to the validity of each, makes the enterprise a serious study in language structures. Bearing in mind the central concern of acquiring formal English, this could be a very useful study and could be developed according to the linguistic resources of the students. There are suggestions for this kind of work in the ROSE programme. Translation work has been carried out with parts of the Bible and Shakespeare being translated into Creole.

We know that language study has been used in the classroom simply as a prescription for denying one form of language and promoting another but if we use contrastive techniques, an uncomfortable term but the best at the moment, the structure of language forms become more meaningful. The student can then see where there are differences between her own writing and the standard form. This is the strategy behind the process approach. How can children really revise if they do not have the competence to make a choice? We have to help them. Direct teaching in language forms them becomes directed towards the students' own generated needs.

A source for the study of language could also be found in literature – the natural habitat. When the writer can see experienced writers using these contrasting structures effectively, they will be greatly encouraged. There is a vast difference between the Jamaican Creole pattern in the poetry of Louise Bennett, Linton Kwesi Johnson, Dennis Scott and Mervyn Morris. There are also many differences between the novels of de Lisser, set in Jamaica at the turn of the century, the work of Selvon (post-war Trinidad) and the stories of Olive Senior set in rural Jamaica. Comparisons will pull in the students' own resources. The importance of this kind of comparative study is that it ensures linguistics a place as a proper area of study, a vital resource in the classroom.

The idea that language study, focusing on structures, can be fun might seem novel but it seems to me to be only a few steps away from Cazden's and Cook's emphasis on language play as a means of encouraging metalinguistic awareness. Linguistic study can be compared to taking a machine apart with the intention of exploring its structure, to examine each part and its connection with all other parts. Such an activity in language can be very exciting for students who might never have thought of their work as made up of separate elements. This revelation helps to demystify the written language and enables the writer to bring it under conscious control.

This leads to the third aspect of this developing concept of metalinguistic awareness in a programme of language study. The stylistic or textual aspect draws on the two previous areas discussed and would be integrated with the other strands in any teaching unit. The sociolinguistic theme allows the student to see how language develops and how meanings are socially constructed; it can also alert them to how they can produce their own meanings. The linguistic strand draws on their own language experience to show that language structures exist in many forms from which they can choose. The third part should therefore be about the techniques used in creating their own meanings and seeing themselves, first and foremost, as writers.

Writing can seem an extremely conclusive activity where commitment to paper is not as negotiable as it can seem for experienced writers. The students need to become aware that in writing they can make false starts and begin again; they can go back afterwards and alter what they have written. It is the first step in acknowledging the editing process that comes after composing but which is integral to writing. Realisation means seeing the language as something that can be constructed and re-constructed. These acts of re-structuring, of draft and re-draft are now basic tenets of the craft of writing, acts that can give any writing activity as much pleasure as the first creative urge.

The writing process now demands that every piece of work does not have to be rushed off for a deadline at the end of the lesson. Students are able to take the writing away to consider new ways of creating its effects. In the beginning the teacher was the first and main audience but now they are encouraged to share and show the writing to other students. Class magazines, newspaper outlets, class workshops helped some to see writing as having a wider audience. Some who said they found it difficult to pick out errors in their own work could often do so in others. The whole practice encouraged the stance of writing as a measured activity. By testing the product on friends the process becomes a collective and shared learning experience.

Language awareness across the curriculum: moving to genre-based teaching

If the textual aspect remained with the writing process it would not really be moving the debate forward. However, in making a link between language awareness and textual features we are moving to genre-based approaches to writing. The distance that is part of the act of writing, which by its very nature relies on a high level of attention to forms. Genre-based approaches stress the type of recurring features generated by the link between language, society and communicative intent/purpose. Halliday has contributed much to this debate with his ideas about the tripartite division of context into field, tenor and mode. Field refers to the content of the text; tenor refers to relationship between text sender and receiver; mode refers to the type and purpose of the text. Together, the three areas of constraints determine discourse structure and articulation (Flowerdew: 1993). The full import of these notions does not have be exposed to children but some teaching which is related to such as the writing required in different school subjects is of considerable benefit e.g. the science report or the literary response.

It would be legitimate to ask if any of language awareness work has been recorded in Jamaican schools. Williams (1997) implemented such a programme with a group of Grade 10 students in a, then, recently upgraded urban school. At the beginning of the programme she described the group as Creole speaking, willing to talk but finding writing "hard". They were bored and uninterested in English, seeing it as just as a subject to pass. The teacher-researcher implemented a unit, which aimed at sensitising students to the differences between Creole and English vocabulary and the use of the verb in expressing past and present tense. She used transcripts of spoken language, stories and songs. Activities included research, translations, contrastive work and personal/expressive writing.

Through error analysis and observation Williams (1997) found that students were able to deal with the level of abstraction required of the work. She found that the unit was most successful when students had to work out the rule for themselves and that they made some improvement in verb use when they used the language they had acquired in re-drafting their writing. She also found that the knowledge thrived in a culture of writing, where perhaps a unit on writing preceded language study work. So there was a measure of success when the work was actively discovered and then applied. Such a finding supports the view that communicative competence rests on the foundation of metalinguisitic awareness (Wright and Bolitho: 1993). Additionally, she felt that there was improvement in student's attitude to English: students developed a greater curiosity about language; they wanted to know the reasons why things might or might not be wrong. However,

Williams also felt that some direct teaching was helpful in paying attention to structures from the two languages that apparently seemed similar.

Concluding Remarks

The concept of metalinguistic awareness as I have expanded it, can I believe answer the central question posed at the beginning of this article, namely how can we promote competence on English without undermining the students' first language? We can facilitate acquisition of Standard English by exposing the students to language as visible forms, which they can choose; this is conscious knowledge. My language study programme for language awareness suggests that the learner needs to pay attention to language behaviour on a social, cultural and personal level. With the sociolinguistic base the students can analyse their own responses to Standard English with a clear perspective of how and why they need it. He/She needs to know what s/he needs to use; why s/he needs it; how s/he can control it; how it came about; what are the contrasting structures in his/her own repertoire. Language awareness is crucial in any situation where more than one language system is in use competitively with another. Choosing implies knowing.

References

Bryan, B (1982) Language, dialect and identity: an examination of the writing of bi-dialectal adults in a London FE college. Unpublished MA thesis, Institute of Education, University of London.

CARICOM, (1993) Report on the Special Meeting of the Standing Committee of Ministers Responsible for Education and Culture (S.C.M.E.) in Antigua and Barbuda. 9-10 September 1993.

Cazden, C. (1973) Play and metalinguistic awareness. In: Urban Review, 28-38

Cook, G. (1997) Language play, language learning, ELT Journal, 51 (3) 224-231

Craig, D. (1976) Bidialectal Education: Creole and Standard in the west Indies. In: International Journal of Sociology of Education, 9, 93-134.

Flowerdew, J. (1993) An educational, or process, approach to the teaching of professional genres. In: ELT Journal, 47 (4) 305-316

Hales, T. (1997) Exploring data-driven language awareness. In: ELT Journal, 51 (3) 217-223

Ministry of Education and Culture, (1992) Reform of Secondary education (ROSE) Curriculum Guides/ Teaching Materials. Kingston: MOE&C

Piper, T. (1993) Language and Learning: The home and school years, New Jersey: Merrill

Rosen, H and Burgess T. (1980) Languages and Dialects of London School Children, London: Ward Lock Educational.

Williams, J. (1997) An examination of the effects of a programme of Language awareness on the writing of Grade 10 students. Unpublished B. Ed Study, School of Education, University of the West Indies.

Wright, T. and Bolitho, R. (1993) Language awareness: a missing link in language teacher education? ELT Journal, 47 (4) 292-304.

CHAPTER 7
Two Contrasting Foreign-Language Teaching Orientations

HAZEL M. SALMON

Abstract

This chapter examines two diverse approaches to foreign-language pedagogy, namely the 'formalist' which is grammar-based, and the 'activist' which focuses on the acquisition of functional (communicative) skills. Each approach represents a distinct view of language and language learning. The teacher is perceived as occupying a central role, in that, she directs learning through practice which is driven by her conceptualisation of the nature of language and her consequent orientation towards teaching and learning.

A major divergent factor between the two approaches is presented as the language of classroom instruction, that is, L1 versus FL. Following two examples of non-traditional teaching, the chapter concludes with statements of the advantages of contextual teaching and learning, and makes recommendations for further consideration.

Introduction

Foreign-language (FL) classrooms are known to differ in a diversity of ways, and in all likelihood no two classrooms are similar even if they are served by the same teacher, the same methods and the same materials. The differences may be significant or insignificant. Insignificant differences may go unnoticed, but major ones do attract the attention of educators and investigators primarily because of the negative or salutary effects exerted on learners' lives. A century or more of FL teaching and learning has clearly differentiated between classroom types by virtue of the major pedagogical or methodological characteristics which they exhibit and, in particular, the results they achieve. This chapter focuses on the learning experiences consonant with two widely divergent methodologies.

Textbooks designed for FL teacher preparation typically offer descriptions of and commentaries on the methodological practices that have been and are adopted to foster learner competence. Among the popular textbooks are **Teaching Foreign Language Skills** (Rivers 1981) and **Teaching Language in Context** (Omaggio Hadley, 1993).

From the vantage point of current pedagogical thinking and practice these authors look backwards to survey theoretical and practical developments in the field as a salient means of creating an informed profession. Although not explicitly stated, a motivation

for retrospection may be deduced from such prevailing conditions and views as:
(i) the continuity and vigour of ineffective teaching approaches deriving from the distant past and detached from present realities.
(ii) the interconnectedness of past and developing concepts and practices, preserving what Omaggio Hadley refers to as the wealth of knowledge and understanding which we have inherited.
(iii) the perpetuity of methods resulting from teachers teaching the way they were taught (Rivers in conversation with Rehorick 1990) and experiencing in very many instances extreme difficulty in transcending habit and tradition.

The consequences of the teacher's posture, relative to the achievement of learners, consistently obligate the teacher educator to provide trainees (and certainly practising teachers) with the opportunity to examine and reexamine the pedagogical options to the end that informed selection or adaptation may be made. An optimism of this training task resides in the belief (strengthened by observation) that debilitating traditions can be softened, ameliorated, or resisted altogether, to liberate teachers towards practice consistent with communicative language-learning goals.

The foregoing discussion places the teacher at centre, functioning as a kind of engineer who conceptualises, plans and then executes the plans. After reviewing the research, Long (1983) expresses his approbation that instruction (and by implication, the instructor) does make a difference.

Underlying the teacher's practice must be a conceptualisation, implicit or explicit, of what language is and how it should be learned or acquired. Thus the teacher adopts an orientation towards the classroom which results in the kind of practice that dominates her work. Figure 1 illustrates the interrelationship between conceptualisation, orientation and practice.

Figure 1. Interrelationship of teacher's FL conceptualisation, orientation and practice

To elucidate, the teacher believes, for example, that language is a compendium of grammatical and lexical elements (conceptualisation); she makes decisions based on her belief, e.g. materials to select, how to sequence them, the kinds of classroom activities and techniques to devise (orientation); the decisions are put into operation in the classroom (practice or behaviour). The teacher is clearly then not a non-thinking person, whether she is simply conforming to tradition or habit or whether she is explicitly applying her critical faculties to select from among the options. Her importance is evident. Against this background we may begin to examine two FL teacher orientations which the history of pedagogical developments highlights.

FL Teacher Orientations

Rivers (1981) classifies teacher types as ranging between two distinct positions, formalist and activist, both representing "two main streams of thought" (p. 25). Rivers observes that teaching emphases "swing from a preference for one approach to a growing attraction to the other" (p. 25), in an attempt to correct previous imbalance. A teacher who may be predominantly formalist in thinking may, however, from time to time, elect to do activities which reflect activist thinking, but on the basis of observation of classroom practice the distinction, formalist and activist, is convincingly valid.

Formalist Orientation

The formalist teacher, as implied in the term, is preoccupied with, and therefore focuses on the forms or grammar of the language. Language is perceived as functioning with a set of rules which form the basis of teaching and learning. The study of language is an intellectual activity encompassing:
- knowledge of the rules, their variations and exceptions
- practising the rules in sentences which are usually disconnected
- learning by rote and practising paradigms; for example, the preterit form of the Spanish verb "tener" (to have) produces

    Yo   tuve   (I had)
    Tu   tuviste   (You had)
    El, ella, usted   tuvo   (He, she, you had) Etc.

- discriminating and learning in turn the forms of verbs with the infinitive endings of 'ar' 'er' 'ir', in that order
- learning copious vocabulary items glossed to ensure meaning, e.g.,

    El muchacho   the boy

- familiarity with textual materials of a literary kind, doing reading comprehension exercises and translating into L1
- concentrating first on present tense verb forms, then adding other tenses in a linear fashion, ending up in the subjunctive
- constructing discrete sentences to demonstrate knowledge of the rules
- translating into the foreign language and writing compositions as the ultimate test of ability to synthesise the grammatical knowledge acquired.
- reading and writing skills

(See Rivers and Omaggio Hadley for descriptions of grammar-translation lessons). Accuracy in language production is held at a high premium. Thus, error correction, designed to achieve a high level of performance, is a major teacher-student activity.

The methodology, as described, reflecting a heavy concentration on reading and writing, offers a rationale for the non-recognition of the development of the oral communicative skills of listening, speaking and pronunciation. Intimately associated with inattention to these skills is the neglect in using the target language as the principal means of teacher-student interaction. A strong correlation is assumed between classroom language and teacher orientation. The predominance of the first or shared language (L1) is typical of a grammatical focus.

Duff and Polio (1990), researching the quantity of FL input in the FL classroom, argue that the amount of FL used by the teacher is critical for acquisition of the language. Salmon (1986) found that between grade 7 and grade 9 teachers in a representative sample of Jamaican high schools were reducing the quantity of Spanish used for instruction, with grade 9 students receiving the least input.

Figure 2 symbolises the nature of teacher-student interaction when the teaching orientation is of a formalist nature.

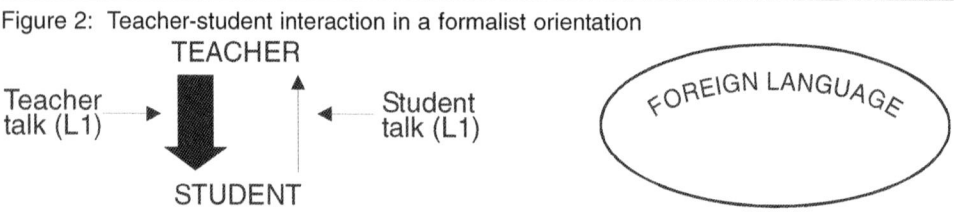

Figure 2: Teacher-student interaction in a formalist orientation

L1 is the language mode. Teacher dominates talk, presenting and explaining rules and giving instructions, etc. The student plays a relatively passive role, answering convergent type questions, initiated by the teacher, with minimal amount of the foreign language – a sentence, a phrase or a vocabulary item.

The principal observation here is that students are deprived of direct interaction with, or experience in the FL. Often the teacher's rationale for the predominant use of L1 is students' stated resistance to the FL because of inability to understand what is heard. Teacher trainees on teaching practice sometimes fall into the same trap when they are confronted with students unaccustomed to learning and speaking the FL even though common sense suggests that the more they hear, given comprehensible language, the more they will come to understand. Covering material for examinations was another reason found for excessive L1 use (Duff and Polio).

PERSISTENCE OF THE FORMALIST ORIENTATION

The grammar-translation method (GTM) prevails in many school systems (Finocchiaro and Brumfit 1983). Foreign-language education students at the University of the West Indies reported in 1998 and 1999 that their classroom observations (a course assignment) showed a preponderance of purely grammar-based teaching. Further, micro teaching (1999) of some of those same students revealed, after much emphasis on the need to shift the FL teaching-learning paradigm to one of 'bringing learners inside of the FL', that a number of trainees were stating lesson topics such as **¿Qué hora es**? (What's the time?), **¿Qué tiempo hace**? (What's the weather like?) and **¿Dónde está...**? (Where is...?) True to expectation, these topics were played out in class participants (their peers) responding in the typical discrete and complete sentences to the questions posed. Here is an example.

T: ¿Dónde está Pedro?
S: Pedro está delante de la mesa.
T: ¿Dónde está el bolígrafo?
S: El bolígrafo está sobre la mesa.

The deceptiveness of this kind of teacher-student exchange is the appearance of students' communicative involvement through responding in the FL to questions asked in the FL. The 'hybrid' nature of the presentation (topics are reminiscent of grammar-translation textbooks, or a lingering attachment to a grammar focus, and the question-answer exchange of the structural and audio-lingual method) depicts a step away from extreme GTM, but falls short of contextual communicative behaviour, and the practice of functional grammar.

EFFECTS OF A FORMAL ORIENTATION ON LEARNING

Evidence of, and references to the profoundly adverse psychological and academic effects on students of traditional teaching and learning abound in the research literature and in the experiences of countless numbers of teachers. The success of the method among the small percentage of highly intellectually capable students tends to camouflage the devastating effects on the majority of learners. Success of the few comes from the ability (and no doubt, the motivation) to close the gap between inert grammatical knowledge and functional language use through opportunities sought after to practise speaking the language.

It should not be wondered at that a great majority of our learners cry 'difficult!' or 'impossible!', suffer failure and frustration, lack confidence in their ability to learn and become alienated from the programme. Salmon's (1988) statistics reveal that, with respect to eligibility for advanced study in Spanish (G.C.E. advanced level), only 2.58 per cent of grade 7 enrolment in Jamaica emerged from the system. From the typically small cohort of grade 11 and subsequently grades 12 and 13 students it is logical that the teacher-trainee cohort in the Department of Educational Studies of the University of the West Indies in Jamaica would remain consistently small, and that language skills and practice reflect the traditional grammar methodology.

Tradition tends to hold firmly and deeply, as witness the long life of GTM. However, the evidence of some teacher trainees attempting to engage their peers in real-life experiences in the FL (as in the case of the student whose context was a visit to the dentist after a road accident), and of some practising teachers reportedly employing communicative techniques indicates what was previously alluded to as the 'softening' of tradition. In this there is much optimism.

The Activist Orientation

Rivers portrays the activist approach as one which, contrasting with a focus on form, engages students in a FL learning experience towards communicative attainment. Beyond GTM there has been increasingly a multiplicity of methods, approaches and strategies with a communicative focus undergirded by theory.

Among these methods and approaches are:
- the direct method (see Rivers, Omaggio Hadley)
- the audio-lingual method (see Rivers, Omaggio Hadley)
- the situational method (see Finocchiaro and Brumfit 1985)

- the cognitive code-learning method (Chastain 1976)
- the total physical response approach (Asher 1977)
- the silent way (Gattegno 1972)
- the natural approach (Terrell 1985)
- the proficiency movement (Omaggio Hadley, Higgs 1984)

An examination of these and other methods and approaches reveals the common thread of a communicative teaching-learning orientation, despite wide variations among them concerning, for example, the organising of the syllabus, the teaching/learning strategies to be employed, and the role of grammar. As an example, the total physical response adopts a wholly kinaesthetic approach whereby learners listen to and perform commands during a comprehension phase, then begin themselves to give commands to their peers when speaking is introduced. In technique this approach is unique.

In the early decades of the twentieth century the direct method took the lead in providing a sharp contrast to the grammar-translation method, introducing into teaching and learning fundamental features essential to the acquisition of oral communication skills. A principal and drastic change was the involvement of learners in listening to and speaking the FL. With this innovation, notwithstanding the observed limitations and ineffectiveness (see Rivers and Omaggio Hadley), foreign-language pedagogy took a turn which, from the evidence and the increasingly pressing societal needs for functional language ability, is not likely to be reversed. Communication has become the primary established goal of FL teaching and learning, involving all the modalities.

One must hasten to state, however, that teaching/learning for communication is not a simple notion, but one fraught with tremendous complexity, the discussion of which is outside the scope of this chapter. Suffice it to say that in the quest over the many decades to understand the nature of language and how it is really learned (Gass, Mackey and Pica 1998, Swain and Lapkin 1998, Long 1997, Ellis 1985, Krashen 1982) and then to devise strategies to achieve successful learning in the 'unnatural' FL language setting of the classroom, numerous positions have been adopted, different emphases have emerged, and strategies have been endless. In the words of Omaggio Hadley we do have a rich FL heritage. Instead of being overwhelming, this diversity can provide a rich source of information to make the FL classroom a busy and productive place.

Fundamental to the acquisition of communicative skills is 'bringing learners inside of the FL' as illustrated in Figure 3 which must now be seen as a contrast to Figure 2.

Figure 3. Teacher-student interaction via the foreign language

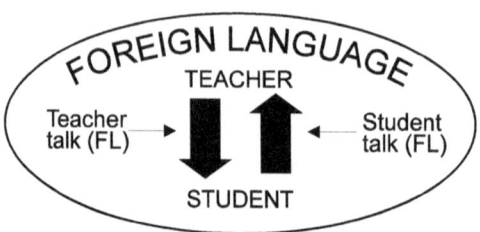

This model achieves a distinct operational shift in which the language of instruction is the FL being learned (unmediated by L1 except where communication in FL breaks down). The student assumes a most important role in the interaction, experiencing the language in activities which integrate listening, speaking, reading and writing, with culture. Interactive language receives strong focus.

In a previous study Salmon (1996) proposed a three-dimensional model of FL acquisition/learning tapping three principal domains: the cognitive, socio-cultural and affective, proposed as the dominant elements of semantics or meaning. In the present context semantics may be extended to incorporate learner experience which more explicitly takes into account the whole person, and this has strong implications for language acquisition.

IMPLICATIONS OF THE L1 ACQUISITION FOR THE FL CLASSROOM

The process of first and second/foreign language acquisition, as a cognitive – socio-cultural – affective phenomenon, has been viewed to be similar in many respects (Chastain, Krashen, Terrell). Despite obvious differences which may be attributed to maturation (McLaughlin 1987, Met and Galloway; Swaffer 1989) it is feasible to explore a common element which is that of experience as the basis for language acquisition.

First language acquisition is intimately and fascinatingly experiential. The young child, situated in the normal and affectively healthy socio-cultural environment, interacts with adult speakers around him, listening, observing, processing sense impressions, mentally accommodating and assimilating input, attempting to speak, involved in trial and error, and gradually emerges as a competent communicator in the language community (Berk 1997). The adult speaker-guide, the family, and 'extended' family, the society, now interacting normally in the socio-cultural setting of the home and beyond, now adjusting language to the developmental level of the child, provide, in the Vygotskian sense, a zone of proximal (or potential) development in which, the child is gradually "pulled up" beyond his present level to an increasingly higher level of understanding and functioning (Berk).

This account of L1 development, highly abridged, can be paralleled to a degree in the FL classroom setting. The teacher can take advantage of the vast experiences of students and of her own knowledge and experience of the FL by providing context-content-rich real-life materials through which the students will interact – listen, speak, read, write, assimilate the sound system, and acquire vocabulary, grammar and cultural understanding. As in L1 acquisition, room must be made for trial and error. Learners must explore content first for its own sake by focusing on the experience contained in it, thus providing opportunity for interactive and meaningful practice activities. The acquisition of grammar and vocabulary embedded in context will be an easier undertaking. Contextual teaching and learning offers a wide spectrum of advantages (see Salmon 1996).

Frantzen's (1998) experience that

> **Few [persons] propose a return to the meaningless** decontextualized centered practice of earlier days that treated the process of language acquisition as if it were merely a case of mastering a series of component **parts (p. 134)**

hardly accords with our local FL experience, as discussed earlier, of persistent grammar-dominated teaching. However, the cases to be visited below are encouraging from the perspective of the observed pedagogical shift.

Two Cases of a 'Softened Tradition': From Formalist to Activist

I now make brief reference to two practising teachers, recent graduates of the foreign-language teacher-education programme of the University of the West Indies, Jamaica.

TEACHER A

Profile
- teaches Spanish in a rural high school
- while in training became aware of the contextual (real-life) approach to FL teaching/learning
- showed signs of understanding and commitment to this approach
- displayed high level of motivation throughout the programme
- adopted the approach in teaching practice
- demonstrated good facility in Spanish
- obtained good grades, emerging with distinction

Telephone conversation with Teacher A (May 15, 1999)
- continues contextual teaching
- undertakes classroom innovations and experiments
- treats grade 9 as a special group needing motivation
- has instituted a system of teacher-student collaborative teaching, teacher being a member of the class which student teaches
- promotes collaborate student learning and encourages much classroom interaction
- has devised a functional syllabus
- collaborated with the Spanish department head of a high school in Kingston to create a similar syllabus for her school
- is enjoying, with students, the teaching/learning experience
- students express how much they remember from previous year's work

Brief outline of a unit of work
Contextual theme: Travelling Overseas (interactive)
- Content: (1) family makes preliminary plans (2) interacts with travel service – details of time, place, cost, picking up tickets (3) family preparation for departure (4) arrival at airport, checking in (5) going through immigration, boarding (6) in-flight conversation (7) arrival at destination, immigration, customs.
- Week 1 spent in teaching/learning, dialogue writing in preparation for –
- Week 2: role play – each scene confined to an area of the classroom – a hub of activities

Result: a thoroughly rewarding and enjoyable experience.

TEACHER B

Profile
- teaches Spanish in an urban high school for girls
- while in training appreciated the difference between formalist and functional approach
- was honest in reporting previous formalist style
- was motivated by training programme
- was an alert student, making valuable contribution to class life
- decided to return to previous school and previous class for teaching practice
- wanted to test effects of contextual teaching on oral performance of students previously tied to grammar
- selected for study, the topic of strategic competence, i.e. finding one's way out of a difficulty when speaking to allow listener(s) to understand (other competencies are grammatical, socio-linguistic and discourse (see Canale and Swain 1980, Omaggio Hadley)
- competent speaker of Spanish
- emerged from programme with distinction

Brief outline of unit of work
Contextual theme: Travelling – Sub-theme: giving and receiving directions
- aim: helping students to see how speech adapts itself for the speaker to express what she wants to say and the listener to understand, e.g. circumlocution
- understanding: "if you can't say it one way, stop, think, adjust, restart, find another way, using the language that you have
- practice: situations set up, at the school, in vicinity of school
- acquisition of necessary tools – vocabulary phrases, sentences, questions, answers while experimenting with the language
- slow beginning (students did little speaking before)
- improvement with time
- students aware that much of burden is on language
- gradually becoming braver, less inhibited

Result: a successful and encouraging beginning, an eye-opener to teacher and students. "Oh! There are several possibilities, not just one right sentence!"

Conclusions

These two episodes encapsulate the implications of an activist (communicative/interactive) approach for classroom teaching and learning. Their concreteness speaks for itself, but allows room for further comments.

Within a contextual situation content is potentially expansive, leading into a variety of other related experiences. "In an uncontextualized exercise, once the particular structure is practiced, little more can be done with the exercise because the elements in focus occur within a set of isolated thoughts or are limited because there is only one correct answer" (Frantzen, p. 135). Experiences are "tangible", being immediate referents giving meaning to learning. They provide opportunity for both explicit (conscious) and implicit (unconscious) learning.

Cognitively, students are functionally, meaningfully and actively exposed to the necessary linguistic elements: syntax, morphology, lexis, phonology. These are not isolated, but are repetitively embedded in all of the language skills being acquired. Students exercise their creative abilities in writing and speaking.

Socio-culturally, contextualisation accommodates the dynamics of group interaction (Rivers 1996, Kramsch 1996). The classroom setting is student-centred, allowing interaction (with the expert guidance of the teacher) which facilitates students learning from each other. In the Teacher A classroom students were relating to each other discussing, exploring, adjusting their ideas, accepting, rejecting, making decisions – collaboratively and amicably – to achieve a common purpose.

Collaboration tactically excludes competition and its attendant tensions, and promotes joint responsibility. Our children need to develop good social skills – interdependence, respect and esteem for each other, sharing and concern. These are values and attitudes which an activist approach to FL study can promote.

Affectively, contextual teaching/learning has the potential to stimulate and motivate students towards a high level of interest, enthusiasm, participation, and achievement. As they are engaged in enjoyable, yet challenging activities, self-concept of ability to learn the language is being strengthened. In this most important respect also the activist approach will prove itself superior to a form-based approach.

Recommendations for Further Consideration

The critical role of the language of interaction in the FL classroom recommends the practical exercise of observing oral language use in a number of classes. This exercise could involve the recording of instances of language used by teacher and students – English and the foreign language. The expressions could then be examined for (i) purpose (e.g. asking and answering questions, expression of personal ideas), (ii) length (e.g. single words, phrases, sentences) and (iii) source of initiation (e.g. teacher, student, tape).

This recommendation could be modified to form the basis of an action study in which the classroom teacher records a series of his/her own lessons which would then be evaluated along the parameters indicated above. These lessons would be contextualised, with the language of instruction being purposefully the target language. The teacher would also be alert to note (i) the events which necessitated the use of English (ii) possible alternatives to English use and (iii) opportunities provided students to use the FL to express their own meanings.

References

Asher, James J. 1977. Learning Another Language Through Actions: The Complete Teacher's Guidebook. Los Gatos, California: Sky Oaks Production.

Berk, Laura E. 1997. Child Development, 4th ed. London: Allyn and Bacon

Canale, Michael and Merrill Swain. 1980. "Theoretical Bases of Communicative Approaches to Second Language Teaching and Testing." Applied Linguistics 1, 1-47

Chastain, Kenneth. 1976. Developing Second Language Skills: Theory to Practice. 2nd ed. Chicago: Rand McNally College.

Duff, Patricia and Charlene Polio. 1990. "How Much Foreign Language is There in the Foreign Language Classroom." Modern Language Journal 74(2): 154-166.

Ellis, Rod. 1985. Understanding Second Language Acquisition. Oxford: Oxford University Press.

Finocchiaro, Mary and Christopher Brumfit. 1983. The Functional-National Approach: From Theory to Practice. Oxford: Oxford University Press.

Frantzen, Diana. 1998. "Focusing on Form while Conveying a Cultural Message." Hispania 81 (1): 134-145

Gass, Susan M., Alison Mackey and Teresa Pica. 1998. "The Role of Input and Interaction in Second Language Acquisition." Modern Language Journal 82(3): 299-307

Gattegno, Caleb. 1972. Teaching Foreign Languages in School the Silent Way. New York: Educational Solutions, Inc.

Higgs, Theodore V. (ed) 1984. Teaching for Proficiency, the Organizing Principle. Illinois: National Textbook Company.

Kramsch, Claire J. 1996. "Interactive Discourse in Small and Large Groups." In Rivers (ed). Interactive Language Teaching. New York: Cambridge University Press.

Krashen, Stephen D. 1982. Principles and Practice in Second Language Acquisition. Oxford: Pergamon Press.

Long, Michael H. 1983. "Does Second Language Instruction Make a Difference?" TESOL Quarterly 17(3): 359-382

_____. 1997. "Construct Validity in SLA Research: A Response to Firth and Wagner." Modern Language Journal 81(3): 318-323

McLaughlin, Barry. 1987. Theories of Second Language Learning. London: Hodder and Stoughton.

Met, Miriam and Vicki Galloway. 1992. "Research in Foreign Language Curriculum." In Philip W. Jackson, ed. Handbook of Research on Curriculum: A Project of the American Educational Research Association. New York: Macmillan Publishing Co.

Omaggio Hadley, Alice. 1993. Teaching Language in Context, 2nd ed. Boston, Mass.: Heinle and Heinle

Rehorick, Sally. 1990. "A Conversation with Wilga Rivers." Canadian Modern Language Review 46 (2): 284-288

Rivers, Wilga M. 1981. Teaching Foreign-Language Skills. 2nd ed. Chicago: University of Chicago Press.

_____(ed.) 1996. Interactive Language Teaching. New York: Cambridge University Press.

Salmon, Hazel M. 1986. Factors in Achievement and Attrition at Grade Nine in Jamaican High Schools. Unpublished Ph.D. Thesis, University of the West Indies, Jamaica.

_____ 1988. "Foreign Language Achievement and Student Attrition in Jamaican High Schools." Caribbean Journal of Education 15(3):231-239

_____ 1996. "The Case for a Modified Pedagogy in the Foreign-Language Classroom." In Dennis Craig (ed). Education in the West Indies: Developments and Perspectives, 1948-1988. University of the West Indies: Institute of Social and Economic Research.

Swaffer, Janet. 1989. "Competing Paradigms in Adult Language Acquisition." Modern Language Journal 13(3): 301-314.

Swain, Merrill and Sharon Lapkin. 1998. Interaction and Second Language Learning: Two Adolescent French Immersion Students Working Together. Modern Language Journal 82 (3): 320-337

Terrell, Tracy D. 1985. "The Natural Approach to Language Teaching: An update." The Canadian Modern Language Review 41(3): 461-479.

CHAPTER  # Foreign Language Teaching Strategies and Students' Performance in Spanish

JOYCELYN BARTON AND HAZEL M. SALMON

Abstract

Based on a sample of 368 traditional and upgraded high school students and 10 teachers in Jamaica, this study investigated the relationship between students' performance in Spanish and teachers' self-reported instructional strategies. The Specific aims were to determine (1) the levels of performance of grade 7 and grade 9 students in five skills, namely, listening, reading, conversation, cloze and writing and (2) whether there were significant differences in performance linked to teaching strategies. Grade 7 was found generally to perform at a higher level than grade 9. Grade 7 scores showed significant differences, the highest scores associated with the best teaching strategies. The findings point to the need to revisit grade 9 learning difficulties and to consider teaching strategies for best effect.

Introduction

Teaching strategies constitute an essential component of FL study. The pedagogical practices which teachers employ often reflect their attitude toward the students and their beliefs about teaching and learning processes. The level of effectiveness of the teachers' instructional practices is often reflected in the students' performance. Although there are many factors which are associated with FL achievement, this discussion deals only with the teachers' classroom practices.

The description provided by Dudley-Marling and Searle (1991) about the role of the teacher in creating environments for learning language is of great significance for FL classrooms. These authors note that effective teachers provide situations in which students are immersed in the language. They ensure that students are exposed to varied settings which drive them to make optimal use of their linguistic abilities. Dudley-Marling and Searle express the view that in order to promote in students the willingness to use language, teachers must create an environment where students feel safe enough to experiment without being ridiculed by teachers or peers. This is because language development will be hindered if they are made to feel uncomfortable when practising their language skills.

Purcell (1993) recommends role play, especially for younger learners, as a desirable teaching-learning technique since it contributes to making classroom experience comfortable and enjoyable. Purcell observes that teachers have found that role play enhances students' personal development and motivation, reduces inhibition. Omaggio-Hadley (1993) perceives role play as a valuable means of bringing real-life situations into the FL classroom to provide context to aid acquisition.

Lightbown and Spada (1996), in describing some of the theoretical bases for second language learning in the classroom refer to the interactionist model which emphasises the importance of learners' exposure to meaningful and comprehensible input through conversational exchange with teachers and peers. The view is that conversations provide the avenue through which students can negotiate meaning as they attempt to explain their intentions, thoughts, and views in a manner which leads to mutual understanding. In the process learners are helped to acquire the L2 words and grammatical structures which contain the meanings.

It is useful to examine empirical data to judge the extent to which there is support for claims about the relationship between pedagogy and foreign language achievement. In a sample of schools in the United States of America Hatfield (1993) conducted a survey in an effort to describe good pedagogy and to discover factors associated with successful learning and with poor work.

Data gained from the survey revealed that for successful learning, teachers created an environment in which students perceived language learning as a serious, important, and often pleasurable undertaking. The students were able to master their work and gain a sense of accomplishment. Positive teacher attitudes and competent display of teaching skills were crucial for student success.

The good teachers had high but realistic expectations of the students. They acknowledged students' effort and good work by the judicious use of praise and encouragement. Such teachers practised thoughtful lesson planning, a thematic approach to content, and the use of many activities which all helped to promote students' learning. In the classroom widespread use of the target language incorporated a large number of appropriate questions. Students thus developed comprehension skills and positive attitudes toward speaking the language. The teachers who facilitated students' learning engaged also in creative use of audio-visual and other resources which supplemented commercial texts, tapped students' interests, and promoted their active involvement in classroom activities.

Hatfield reports that, in contrast, one of the most outstanding factors which was related to students' poor foreign language performance was teachers' low expectation of students. This led them to set unchallenging tasks for them. There was also limited use of the target language in the classrooms. This retarded students' ability to comprehend and practise the foreign language outside a set of prescribed situations. Many of the activities in the lessons were not clearly focused because they were developed from unclear objectives. In addition, the teachers' delivery of classroom activities failed to tap students' interest and active participation.

Information from the literature and observations of students' low Spanish achievement, dwindling interest in Spanish study, and the constraints on learning associated with a lack of meaningful, real-life opportunities for practising Spanish have prompted this investigation into the relationship between Spanish achievement and teachers' classroom strategies. This consideration is particularly timely in view of the many arguments in favour of foreign language teaching. Some benefits for students include: the enrichment of students' personalities through exposure to other cultural practices, norms and manner of thinking; greater communication with speakers of other languages, promotion of intellectual development, enhanced job opportunities, and commercial advantages (CXC Modern Language Syllabus, 1996; Met and Galloway, 1992; Van Els et al, 1984; and Rivers, 1981).

Methodology

The purpose of the study was to investigate the relationship between the teaching of Spanish and the achievement of Spanish among grades 7 and 9 secondary high school students in Jamaica. The study sought to determine (1) the levels of Spanish performance and (2) the significant differences in students' Spanish performance related to teaching strategies. The language skills tested were listening, reading, and writing. Speaking was omitted because of the enormity of testing the sample on an individual basis.

STUDENT SAMPLE

The student sample comprised 368 students: 194 from grade 7, 90 males and 104 females; and 174 from grade 9, 66 males and 108 females. The ages of the students ranged from 11 to 13 and 13 to 15 years respectively for grade 7 and grade 9. One intact grade 7 and one grade 9 Spanish class were randomly selected from each of eight schools. High schools in Jamaica are mainly traditional and upgraded, hence the sample of students was chosen from both categories to effect a realistic representation of high schools. Four traditional, and four upgraded schools were selected.

Traditional high schools are viewed as prestige institutions which focus on an academic curriculum, so entry to such schools is much desired (UNESCO Report, 1983). The report defines upgraded high schools as those which were not high schools from their inception and which place less emphasis on academic subjects.

Another salient consideration was the location of schools. The eight schools were chosen on the basis of urban-rural criteria. Four co-educational schools were chosen from the corporate area of Kingston and St. Andrew, and four from the rural areas (two from the parish of St. Catherine, and one each from St. Ann, and Westmoreland). In the schools selected Spanish was a compulsory subject for all students in grades 7 to 9. Beyond grade 9 students could choose to continue or discontinue the study of Spanish.

TEACHER SAMPLE

A sample of 10 high school teachers of Spanish spanning 16 classes participated in the study. The number of years in which the teachers were involved in foreign language instruction ranged from 1 to 33 years. The teachers' qualifications ranged from pre-trained to trained with a Masters degree.

INSTRUMENTS

(1) Questionnaire for Teachers

A 17-item questionnaire for teachers was developed primarily to gather information about teaching strategies (Appendix C). The first three items sought background information about years spent in teaching in general, as well as the number of years spent in the teaching of Spanish. Professional qualifications attained by teachers was an item. The last question, item 17, sought information about levels of Spanish achievement in grades 7 and 9. All other items dealt with the specific pedagogical practices which the teachers employed to effect student learning.

Included among the questions which covered classroom pedagogy were items geared to determine the roles of the teacher and the student. Questions concerned classroom grouping strategies, teacher's presentation of content, feedback procedures and the orientation of the classroom. Classroom orientation was in terms of whether or not the teacher subscribed to the traditional philosophy where the teacher had sole control over selection and organisation of classroom learning experiences.

In this questionnaire, scores ranging from *1* to *5* were used to measure the item which dealt with the teachers' qualifications. The lowest scores were assigned to the pre-trained teachers while the highest scores were attributed to the trained graduates. For other items, for example, those dealing with teaching strategies, the range carried maximum points of 4 or less. In all instances, the highest score represented the best teaching strategies. Some sample items are:
(i) *Give examples of the kinds of practice activities which follow the presentation of each new concept.*
(ii) *What kinds of project work does your class do?*

The instrument was piloted on a sample of grade 7 and 9 teachers of Spanish. The reliability coefficient (Cronbach alpha) calculated was 0.60.

On the basis of information from the questionnaire teachers strategies were categorised into three groups: least effective, moderately effective, and most effective. The teachers in the most effective category engaged in class activities involving role play, project work, co-operative groups, and much use of the target language.

(2)   Spanish Achievement Tests

Before attempting to describe the Spanish achievement tests it is important to explain the process involved in constructing the tests. The content and structure of the tests were within the boundaries imposed by the modes of testing suggested in the literature and the learning experiences of the student sample obtained from questionnaires completed by the head of the Spanish department in each school.

The structure of the grades 7 and 9 Spanish achievement tests was the same. The tests assessed students' competence in executing various tasks. These tasks included listening comprehension, reading comprehension, a cloze exercise, conversation and writing. However, the content of each category differed in keeping with the length of exposure to the language and the content covered in each grade. The grade 7 test contained 25 items and the grade 9 comprised 30 items. The tests consisted of multiple choice items, sentence completion exercises, and open-ended items.

The overall test score for grade 7 was 50 while that for grade 9 was 66. For grade 7, every item on each component of the test was assigned 2 points. For the grade 9 test, the only component which was assigned 3 instead of 2 points was the writing exercise. Points were subtracted for answers containing spelling errors.

Description of Components of the Tests

Listening Comprehension

The grade 7 listening comprehension test comprised 5 multiple choice items. The items consisted of five sets of pictures. Each set contained three pictures. The students were required to listen while the name of one picture in the set was called, then tick on answer sheets the letter which matched the one beside the correct picture, for example, *los libros* (the books). Each correct answer was awarded two points. The total possible score was 10 points. The grade 7 listening comprehension test was similar to that used for grade 9. In the latter case, there were six instead of five items and students listened to statements about the pictures instead of the names of the pictures, for example, *El es futbolista* (He is a footballer).

Reading Comprehension

This exercise also contained multiple choice items for both grades, five items for grade 7 and six for grade 9. The students in each grade were instructed to read a passage, then tick on answer sheets the letter which matches the correct answer for each question. Some questions were written in English while others were written in Spanish, for example, *What is the father's name?* (grade 7) and *From which country is Miguel?* (grade 9).

Conversation

Conversation in each grade was a reading and writing task like that described by Omaggio-Hadley (1993) as partial conversation which involves a dialogue completion exercise. In the present study, students were required to complete a dialogue by choosing from various options provided, for instance, *¿Cuántos años tienes?* (How old are you?) was the question expected to match the statement, *Tengo once años* (I am eleven years old). The response options comprised questions and answers and the dialogue was illustrated with pictures. The students were first allowed to do choral reading of the incomplete dialogue and the response options in order to nullify possible confounding effects of reading ability. They were then instructed to indicate their individual choices without corresponding with each other. The tasks for grades 7 and 9 both contained five items. Two points were awarded for each correct response.

Cloze

For the cloze exercise, the grade 7 students were instructed to complete five sentences by choosing the most suitable words from a list provided, for example, *Carlos tiene muchos amigos* (Carlos has many friends). The missing word was *tiene*. The task for the grade 9 students was to complete a passage with seven missing words by choosing the most suitable words from options provided. In both grades each correct response was worth two points.

Writing

The grade 7 writing task had an open-ended format. The students were required to write the Spanish and English words for any five classroom objects. Each correct response was awarded two points. The grade 9 writing exercise was based on situations. Students were given six situations written in English. Their task was to write in Spanish what they would say in the situations outlined, for instance, *Tell your friend that you like to watch television*.

The tests were piloted for reliability and validity resulting in minor adjustments being made to them. The internal consistency reliability coefficient (Cronbach alpha) of the tests were 0.60 and 0.78 for grades 7 and 9 respectively.

Rivers states that one of the more valid forms of testing reading comprehension is by choosing the correct answer from multiple choice items, in the foreign language, on a reading passage. In this instance, the student demonstrates his ability to comprehend the foreign language and to determine the fine distinction between the choices offered him.

With regard to listening comprehension, Rivers explains that at earlier stages listening comprehension can be conducted with aids such as pictures. The teacher may make three statements about the picture, with two of them being inappropriate. The student will then indicate A, B, or C on paper to show which one he believes is the fitting statement

It has been advocated that students' FL speaking skills are best tested through their speech production (Omaggio-Hadley, 1993; Rivers, 1981; Valette, 1977). However, Omaggio-Hadley also recommends a useful reading and writing exercise which she describes as partial conversation. This activity involves an open-ended format where students supply the missing half of a conversation based on what they see

With respect to a cloze exercise, Rivers explains that the *fill-in-the-blank* type of test may have a multiple choice format or it may call upon the student to supply a suitable FL word. Tests of this nature are good for assessing knowledge of language structure, use of tenses, and vocabulary.

Data Analysis

Descriptive statistics were used to derive means and standard deviations and frequency distributions of students' scores on all the variables. The mean is described as the most widely used measure of central tendency (Gay, 1996; Neuman, 1991). Spanish total scores were assigned to three groups according to the teaching strategies which students experienced. The strategies were designated 'most effective', 'moderately effective', and 'least effective. Analysis of variance (ANOVA) was used to determine whether there were significant differences among the scores as they relate to teaching strategies.

RESULTS

Question 1: What are the levels of Spanish performance of grade 7 students, and grade 9 students?

Tables 1 and 2 respectively present a summary of grade 7 and grade 9 performance on each component of the tests, and the total scores. The tables suggest that students in both grades performed best on the listening comprehension task. The mean scores show values of 93.2% and 86.7% for grades 7 and 9 respectively. The listening comprehension exercise involved identifying pictures which corresponded to the words and sentences which students listened to. For grade 7 the second best performance is evident for conversation followed by reading. The pattern was reversed for grade 9. Conversation in each grade was a dialogue completion exercise while reading involved prose passages followed by multiple choice questions. The tables also indicate that both grades show the least competence in the Cloze exercise and the productive skill, writing. The overall test score for grade 7 was 63.2% compared to 53.0% for grade 9.

Table 1: *Means & Standard Deviations of Grade Seven Spanish Scores (n =194).*

Variables	Maximum Score	Mean	Percent	Standard Deviation
Listening Comprehension	10	9.32	93.20	1.41
Reading Comprehension	10	6.92	69.20	2.67
Conversation	10	7.07	70.70	2.28
Cloze	10	4.24	42.40	2.82
Writing	10	4.05	40.50	3.09
Total	50	31.60	63.2	7.86

Table 2: *Means & Standard Deviations of Grade Nine Spanish Scores (n = 174).*

Variables	Maximum Score	Mean	Percent	Standard Deviation
Listening Comprehension	12	10.14	84.5	2.05
Reading Comprehension	12	7.98	66.5	3.04
Conversation	14	6.51	46.5	3.90
Cloze	18	6.13	34.1	4.09
Writing	10	4.19	41.9	3.06
Total	66	34.95	53.0	11.95

Question 2: Are there any significant differences in students' Spanish performance as linked to teaching strategies?

Descriptive statistics were used to determine whether or not there were significant differences in students' Spanish performance in grades 7 and 9 as linked to teaching strategies (See tables 3 and 4). To determine whether or not there were any statistically significant differences among students' mean test scores an, analysis of variance (ANOVA) was carried out. ANOVA data show the significance of F and the critical values.

Table 3 indicates that the students whose teachers used the most effective strategies attained the highest mean Spanish test score (**35.95**). The moderately effective and least effective strategies corresponded with low (**29.24**) and middle (**30.75**) scores respectively.

Table 3: *Means, Standard Deviations, and Analysis of Variance of Grade Seven Students' Spanish scores by TeaStr.*

Variable	Categories	Mean Test Scores	Standard Deviation	Number of Cases (n)	F	Significance of F
Teaching Strategies (TeaStr)	Least Effective	30.75	6.24	36	17.75	P=.001<.01
	Moderately Effective	29.24	7.75	98		
	Most Effective	35.95	7.21	60		

ANOVA computed for grade 7 (Table 3) yielded statistically significant differences among the students' overall Spanish scores (F = 17.75, p < .01) in favour of students taught by the most qualified teachers who used the most effective teaching strategies.

The analysis of data for grade 9 students (Table 4) showed that students whose teachers used the most effective strategies obtained the highest mean score (37.70). The moderately effective, and the least effective strategies corresponded with low (32.52) and middle (33.98) scores respectively. Although the performance of students who had the most effective teachers was better than that of the less effective ones, ANOVA showed no significant difference.

Table 4: *Means, Standard Deviations and Analysis of Variance of Grade Nine Students' Spanish scores by TeaStr.*

Variable	Categories	Mean Test Scores	Standard Deviation	Number of Cases (n)	F	Significance of F
Teaching Strategies (TeaStr)	Least Effective	33.98	11.67	51	2.120	.124 n.s.
	Moderately Effective	32.52	11.24	56		
	Most Effective	37.70	12.34	67		

Discussion

The performance in both grades in listening comprehension reveals that students in the sample could comprehend much more Spanish than they could produce in writing and speech. This finding is in keeping with much of the literature. For instance, Lowe (cited in Omaggio Hadley, p. 163), found that native English speakers performed better in French and Spanish listening comprehension activities than in speaking on the ILR (Interagency Language Roundtable) Proficiency Scale.

The students' better performances on the listening, reading and conversation exercises than on cloze and writing may be partially explained by the use of pictorial cues included in these tasks. These cues were likely to have filled gaps in the students' linguistic command of the language.

The disparity in the level of overall performance between the two grades reflects the reports which teachers provided through a questionnaire administered to them by the researcher. Teachers were asked to indicate in percentage form the level of Spanish achievement exhibited by students in grades seven and nine. All teachers but one, reported higher achievement levels for the grade seven students.

The superior Spanish test performance of grade 7 over grade 9 may be explained by the less complex nature of the grade 7 task. It is possible that other issues may have accounted for the better Spanish test performance demonstrated by the grade 7 students over their grade 9 counterparts. For instance, information gathered in this study from the questionnaire administered to the teachers indicates that they attributed to the grade 7 students greater interest and enthusiasm for learning Spanish. Further, some grade 9 students had already indicated their intention to discontinue Spanish study at the end of the grade 9 year.

Three other components of the Spanish test for grade 9 proved to be so challenging that students obtained mean scores below 50%: conversation (mean score = 46.5%), cloze (mean score = 34.1%), and writing (mean score = 41.9%). The students' mediocre performance on conversation was unexpected because students did not have to generate spontaneous responses, instead, they had to complete a dialogue by selecting appropriate responses from various options provided. Moreover, the exercise included content which the students would have practised while they were in lower grades. The unsatisfactory performance suggests that students lacked the strong vocabulary base necessary to execute the task successfully. This comment applies to the cloze exercise.

In the writing exercise, the students were required to write appropriate Spanish statements to correspond to various situations presented to them in English. The content incorporated every-day themes such as time, greetings, days of the week, and leisure time activities presented in the context of a telephone conversation with a friend. Some of the errors which were evident in students' responses were in respect of concord, spelling, and inability to differentiate between the correct use of the verbs *ser* and *estar* (to be). For example, students were expected to generate the question, ¿Cómo está tu mamá? (How is your mother?). In many instances, *es* instead of *está* was used. To a lesser extent, *su* (his/her) was used instead of *tu* (your).

The results revealed best performance for students exposed to the best teaching strategies. These strategies included:
- group work
- real-life learning situations
- project work
- extensive use of target language
- role play
- the use of a variety of audio-visual resources
- and student input in the selection of classroom activities.

IMPLICATIONS AND RECOMMENDATIONS

The better Spanish test performance of grade 7 students, unlike the relatively lower performance of the grade 9 students, implies that the grade 9 students had more problem recalling their Spanish knowledge than had the grade 7 students. This could be due to the fact that some features of the language tested were what some students had learned and used in grades 7 and 8, and rarely used in grade 9. This explanation was based on anecdotal reports of some of the teachers that some students attributed their poor Spanish test performance to forgetting Spanish features which they learned in earlier grades, but which they did not use for a long period of time.

The teachers also reported that grade 9 students often complained that Spanish at that level was much more difficult than at lower levels. Many students cited Spanish grammar as a major area of difficulty. Studying the language thus became less appealing and enjoyable to them.

To improve Spanish performance, it is recommended that teachers embark on a shift away from teaching Spanish exclusively as a core entity, with strongest emphasis on grammar (See Salmon, this volume) and textbook exercises as reported on by teachers in the sample. Yalden (1987) recommends a balance between task-based and situation-based frameworks to foreign language learning. Situation-based frameworks encompass real life situations and may explore topics such as: 'Eating in a Restaurant,' and 'At the Airport.' Task-based frameworks include activities such as 'Reading for Information,' and 'Making Inquiries'. Yalden explains that there should be preliminary units on social skills and management of discourse. These recommendations lend themselves to a communicative approach to teaching and learning, integrating all the skills and making provision for revisiting vocabulary and grammatical structures which are soon forgotten by students if not repeatedly practised. With reference to other subjects on the school curriculum, for example, the target culture art, music, social studies, and dance, students can use Spanish as an additional tool for effecting a deeper understanding of these subjects.

Such an approach would address the difficulty of Spanish grammar as the teacher would structure classroom activities so that the grammatical features are embedded in communicative activities. In this way, foreign language experiences which place the focus on grammar also place the focus on meaning. Fotos and Ellis (cited in Fotos, 1994), recommend grammar-consciousness raising tasks as a method of incorporating formal instruction within a communicative framework. In this approach, they explain, learners are presented with grammatical problems to solve interactively. Even though the learners attend to the form of the grammar structure, they are simultaneously pursuing meaning-focused uses of the target language as they solve the grammar problems.

In order to provide optimal use of the target language and to compensate for the time constraint associated with Spanish study, the teachers can introduce various extracurricular activities. One such avenue is a Spanish club. Such a club could organise class and school-wide activities such as Spanish quiz competitions, concerts featuring various aspects of Spanish culture, (e.g., their food, dance, dress, drama, art, political structure, films, and native Spanish speakers). Students can also use their knowledge of Spanish to conduct routine activities such as devotion and purchasing from the school's canteen . Before the latter could be attempted, students and teachers should embark on a project of attaching Spanish labels to all the goods which the canteen has to offer. A major advantage of the pursuits described is that students are relieved of the burden of examinations while pursuing enjoyable activities. It is advantageous also that students would be putting into practical use the foreign language skills which they would have acquired in the classroom. Moreover, the students would be charged with various roles and responsibilities. The language-learning opportunities provided through students' involvement in the various pursuits are likely to promote their interest, motivation, self-confidence and communicative competence in Spanish. The teacher is expected also to strive to make language learning in the classroom a motivational experience. Activities such as dance, song, and other forms of music, and role play are usually regarded by students as welcome deviations from teacher-fronted activities followed by textbook exercises.

The researchers of the present study suggest that one of the ways in which the school can tap the interests of the students is to adopt a learner-centred approach to the teaching of Spanish. This approach should help to bridge the gap between what the teachers teach and what the students learn (Nunan, 1995). Nunan proposes that a "mismatch" between learners and teachers in the pedagogical process occurs when the teacher teaches one thing, but the learner focuses on something else. In the local context, if foreign language teachers were to adopt the learner-centred approach, students should have opportunities to choose learning activities relevant to their unique learning styles and their personal goals for learning the language. According to Nunan and McCombs and Whisler (1997), the main difference between a learner-centred classroom and traditional ones is that the learner is afforded an input concerning decisions about what he wants to learn; how he wants to learn ; and when such learning activities should take place.

The finding that there were significant differences in grade 7 students' test performance based on the effectiveness of their teachers' strategies has many implications for second and foreign language education. One of the pictures which emerges is the role of the teachers' grouping strategies in the education process. The most effective teachers used grouping strategies more regularly than the least effective ones. Group work is associated with co-operative learning. McManus and Gettinger (1996) describe co-operative learning as a process whereby learners work together in groups to learn materials which were given by the teacher. Evidence which supports the effectiveness of co-operative student learning was derived from a study conducted by McManus and Gettinger. The study revealed that teachers and students reported positive academic, social, and attitude outcomes.

Overall, foreign language teachers need to use a variety of teaching techniques to promote Spanish achievement in their students. The techniques should include group work, real-life learning situations, a variety of audio-visual resources, optimal use of the target language, and students' input in the classroom by nominating classroom learning experiences.

References

Caribbean. Examinations Council Modern Languages Syllabus. French and Spanish (1996).

Dudley-Marling, C., & Searle, D. (1991). *When Students Have Time To Talk. Creating Contexts For Language Learning*. Portsmouth, N H: Heinemann.

Fotos, S. S. (1994). Integrating Grammar Instruction and Communicative Language Use Through Grammar-Consciousness Raising Tasks. *TESOL Quarterly, 26*(2), 323-344.

Gay, L. R. (1996). *Educational Research. Competencies for Analysis and Research*. U.S.A: Merril, an imprint of Prentice Hall Inc..

Hatfield, W. N. (1993). Creative Approaches in Foreign Language Teaching. *Selected Papers From the Central States Conference*. ERIC Document Reproduction Service. No. ED352481.

Lightbown, P. M. & Spada, Nina (1996). *How Languages are Learned*. U.K: Oxford University Press.

McCombs, B. L. & Whisler, J. S. (1997). *The Learner-Centered Classroom and School. Strategies for Increasing Student Motivation and Achievement* (1st ed.). San Francisco: Jossey-Bass Publishers.

McManus, S. M, & Gettinger, M. (1996). Teacher and Student Evaluations of Co-operative Learning and Observed Interactive Behaviours. *The Journal of Educational Research, 90*(1), 13-22.

Met & Galloway, V. (1992). Research in Foreign Language Curriculum. In Philip W. Jackson (Ed.) *Handbook of Research on Curriculum. A Project of the American Educational Research Association.* New York.: Macmillan Publishing Co., 852-890.

Neuman, L. W. (1991). *Social Research Methods. Qualitative and Quantitative Approaches.* U.S.A: Allyn and Bacon, A Division of Simon and Scuster, Inc..

Nunan, D. (1995). Closing the Gap Between Learning and Instruction. *TESOL Quarterly, 29*(1), 133-158.

Omaggio Hadley, A. (1993). *Teaching Language in Context.* Boston: Heinle and Heinle Publishers.

Purcell, J. M. (1993). Livelier FLES Lessons Through Role Play. *Hispania, 76*(4), 912-918.

Rivers, W. M. (1981). *Teaching Foreign Language Skills.* (2nd ed.) U.S.A: The University of Chicargo Press.

Valette, R. M. (1977). *Modern Language Testing.* (2nd ed.) New York: Harcourt Brace Jovanovich, Inc.

Van Els, T., Bongaerts, T. Extra, G., Van Os, C., Janssen-van Dieten, A. (1984). *Applied Linguistics and the Learning and Teaching of Foreign Languages.* London: Edward Arnold.

Yalden, J. (1987). *Principles of Course Design for Language Teaching.* London: Cambridge University Press.

Report

Jamaica Development of Secondary Education UNESCO Report. Paris, (1983).

APPENDIX A

SPANISH ACHIEVEMENT TEST FOR GRADE SEVEN
STUDENTS : SAMPLE ITEMS

- **Listening Comprehension**

    There are five sets of pictures. Each set has three pictures. I will call the name of one picture in each set. When you hear the name tick the letter on your **answer sheet** which matches the letter beside the correct picture.

2. A.   B.   C.

[1]

- **Reading Comprehension**

    Read the following passage. On your **answer sheet** tick the letter which matches the correct answer for each question which follows.

    ### La Familia García

    La familia García es grande. El padre de la familia se llama Enrique y la madre se llama Marta. Alicia y Antonio son los hijos. Alicia y Antonio son hermanos. Alicia tiene doce años y Antonio tiene nueve años. Roberto y Ana son los abuelos.

    El padre de la familia es profesor. Trabaja en una escuela pequeña. La familia vive en una casa blanca.

    6. What is the father's name?

        (a) Roberto

        (b) Enrique

        (c) Antonio

    8. Which statement is correct?

        (a) Alicia is older than Antonio.

        (b) Alicia is younger than Antonio.

        (c) Alicia and Antonio are the same age.

- **Conversation**

    Kevin is talking with Sharon. Choose the expression below which best completes each blank space in the dialogue. Write your answers on your **answer sheet.**

    There are more responses than what is required, so choose carefully.

        ¿Dónde estás?   Buenos días   ¿Cuántos años tienes?

        Me llamo Sharon.   ¿Cómo estás?   Adíos   Buenas tardes

    (Followed by items with pictures)

- **Writing**

Write on your **answer sheet** the Spanish and English words for five objects which you usually use in the classroom. Remember to use *el* or *la* before each word.

---

[1] Refer to authors for complete tests. The grade 9 test in listening comprehension, reading comprehension and conversation are similar in form to the grade 7 test.

APPENDIX B

SPANISH ACHIEVEMENT TEST FOR GRADE NINE STUDENTS: SAMPLE ITEM

Writing

On your answer sheet, write in Spanish what you will say in the following situations.

Y ou are speaking with your friend over the telephone. He asks you about the weather where you are. Tell him it is sunny.

APPENDIX C

QUESTIONNAIRE FOR SPANISH TEACHERS OF GRADES AND NINE: SAMPLE ITEMS

The purpose of this questionnaire is to gather information about the teaching strategies of grade seven and nine Spanish Teachers.

Please respond to the following questions.

4. On average, out of ten typical lessons, in how many do you provide opportunities for students to work in groups?

7. Give examples of the kinds of practice activities which follow the presentation of new concepts.

9. W hat kinds of project work does your class do?

12. W ith each new unit of lessons, in how many lessons do students engage in role play?
    (a) Almost all   (b) About 50%   (c) About 25%   (d) None

CHAPTER 9

Revisiting Methodological Approaches to Foreign Language Teaching: From Communicative to Actional Language Teaching

BÉATRICE BOUFOY-BASTICK

Abstract

This chapter gives personal perspectives on international trends in foreign language teaching. It positions Caribbean language teaching relative to these global trends. These trends are illustrated by giving a brief overview of language teaching methodologies, from around the world, that are most representative of these trends. These summary impressions are mainly derived from extensive experiences of foreign language teaching in Britain, the Caribbean, Australia, US, France, Singapore and Fiji. To these descriptions, a brief presentation of current pedagogical developments in Europe has been included. This chapter describes how the specific environmental conditions of these regions and the social values underpinning their language education policies and practices influence their preferences for *Communicative Language Teaching* (COLT) and determine the different ways they use *Situated Language Teaching* (SLT) methodologies. The SLT influences that are described here span over two decades from Wilkins' (1976) notional syllabus to Bastick's (1999) subjectivism. The chapter concludes with an introduction to *Actional Language Teaching* (ALT) for the XXIst century.

International overview of diverse applications of Situational Language Teaching (SLT).

Communicative language teaching (COLT) is a methodological approach which has profoundly influenced modern foreign and second language teaching (Stern, 1983, p. 473). The pedagogical COLT methodology began to emerge in the late 1970's from a preoccupation with developing the foreign-language learner's communicative competence. COLT-based methodologies were then developed more fully in the 1980's (Breen & Candlin, 1980; Canale & Swain, 1980; Ek & Alexander, 1980; Hymes, 1972; Littlewood, 1981; Richards & Rogers, 1986; Spolsky, 1989; Yalden, 1981; Wilkins, 1976) . These methodologies view language learning as a process of developing the ability to use the language rather than learning about the language (Nunan, 1988, p. 78). Situated Language Teaching (SLT) is one of the COLT methodologies which aims at communicating appropriately and effectively in specific contexts.

SLT is a communicative language teaching methodology which presents language in situations similar to those the learner may encounter in the foreign country. The language is presented in different types of cultural situations because "culture is the paradigm of situation types" (Halliday, 1991, p. 11). These situational contexts are used as contextualised frameworks for teaching the foreign-language structures (Munby, 1978; Shaw, 1977).

This approach to language teaching is a move away from traditional language teaching approaches which view language as an intricate system of grammatical and syntactic rules to be studied, understood and internalised by the student. In contrast to this traditional approach, SLT advocates a context-based language teaching methodology in which the language learner experiences some aspects of the culture of the target language, participates in simulated situations and acts both verbally and behaviourally in culturally appropriate ways.

The global trend towards COLT has resulted in the developments and uses of different SLT methodologies that vary greatly across the world. This diversity is a result of the specific environmental conditions of the countries where the languages are taught and the current social values underpinning their language education policies and practices. We now illustrate this diversity in the development of SLT methodologies by using examples from Britain, Singapore, Australia, France, the USA and Fiji. We then describe one of the most recent developments in SLT methodologies which is an application of Bastick's Subjectivism (Bastick, 1998, 1999a, 1999b, 1999c).

SLT in British secondary schools

Foreign language curricula in British secondary schools is primarily geared to preparing secondary school students for the national examination taken in the 5th Form (grade 10). Over two decades ago the examination changed from the GCE to the GCSE. The GCSE examination differs markedly from the old GCE O' level and the change in examinations marked a major change in pedagogy. The emphasis changed from linguistic accuracy to the production of *meaningful* language utterances.

Meaningful utterances, in sociolinguistic terms, are those utterances which are appropriate to a specific situation. The GCSE examination also differs from the GCE in that it assesses all four linguistic skills of speaking, listening, reading and writing; whereas the former GCE O' level emphasised reading and writing.

The old GCE was developed for university selection. The main social conditions that precipitated the change from an 'elitist' GCE grammatical pedagogy to an 'equitable' GCSE production of 'meaningful' utterances were (i) the move to mass tertiary entrance and (ii) increased mass travel and commercial interchange with European Union countries, most of which are now less than two hours from England.

The primary objective of the GCSE five-year course is to develop the necessary social and linguistic skills to successfully communicate when in France or in Spain. The learner initially aims to 'Get by' in the language and then progressively develop both social and linguistic proficiency.

The first objective of 'Getting by' is achieved by placing the language learner in diverse daily social situations which he/she is likely to meet in the foreign country. This SLT pedagogy views "language ability as being developed through activities which actually simulate target performance" (Howatt, 1984, p. 279).

Language patterns are taught in these contexts and the learner memorises these set patterns and re-uses them in similar socially and culturally appropriate situations. Examples of this situational language use are: greetings, ordering drinks at the café, asking for directions, shopping, booking a hotel room or a table at a restaurant, buying stamps etc. The GCSE foreign language syllabus owes much to Wilkins (1976)'s notional syllabus as it is organised on semantic rather than grammatical principles; emphasis is placed primarily upon the acquisition of communicative functions and notions of time, space and quantity.

The five main features of the GCSE foreign language syllabus are:

(i) A common syllabus taught to all students irrespective of their linguistic abilities
(ii) Language Is taught in simulated contextualised situations (examples of situations are given above)
(iii) Real-life situational language practice in the country of the target language - which is most often a European language (examples are one-day trips to Boulogne/Calais for French, student home exchanges).
(iv) Teacher/student negotiated profile assessment through the 4 language skills of listening, speaking, reading and writing (in this order).
(v) Use of 'equitable' non-academic criteria are also part of the language profile assessment (motivation, attitude, participation, etc.)

GCSE foreign language learning is not an 'elitist' activity - high percentages do not 'fail' as assessment is by 'profiling' and all students should be able 'to get by' to some extent in the target language. Students wishing to pursue foreign language studies can take the AO'level a year after GCSE and the A'level two years later. The new A'level syllabus gives students the choice between the study of literature or the study of French civilization.

SLT in the Caribbean

Most foreign language syllabi in the Caribbean are modelled on the British ones. At the time when Britain developed the GCSE to replace the O'level, Caribbean governments set up the Caribbean Examinations Council (CXC) in 1979 to devise local curricula for secondary education. Foreign language CXC curricula, i.e. French and Spanish, show extreme similarities with the GCSE and recommend an SLT approach to language learning. Like the GCSE, the CXC French and Spanish examinations, the CSEC, are taken after five years of study and are also offered at two competency levels: Basic proficiency level and General proficiency level. The CSEC examination assesses sociolinguistic competence in each of the four language skills and students are expected to express themselves confidently and adequately in ordinary situations.

The Caribbean Advanced Proficiency Examinations (CAPE) replace the British-based 'A' and AO' levels as CSEC replaces the GCE: like the AO'level CAPE functional French is taken after six years of study and like the A'level the CAPE 2-unit is taken after seven years of study.

The following descriptions of the CAPE show that SLT is a major methodology of these Caribbean examinations.

Functional French is one of the six core courses contributing to the total French CAPE certificate. It was developed with the intent "to contribute to regional integration and co-operation" (CXC A14/U1/98, p. 1). This explains the emphasis on developing communicative ability in the four language skills of: listening, speaking, writing and reading in content areas such as: personal identification; home, family and daily routine; occupation and education; free-time, leisure and sports; food and drink; shopping; travel, holidays and weather; business transactions; francophone cultures and customs; and current issues (CXC A 14/U1/98, p. 3). Learners are assessed at the end of the 120-hour course both internally and externally. Internal assessment carrying 25% of the total mark consists of an oral examination in the form of a role play and a written project report. External assessment of 75% of the mark has three components, two written papers and the oral: listen/respond (50%), read (25%) and write (25%) (CXC A14/U1/98, p. 17).

The CAPE 2-unit French course replaces the former A'level French course and it is open to students having passed Grade 1 or 2 French General Proficiency CXC examination. The French CAPE syllabus differs from the traditional A'level in that it includes not only the study of literary texts but also a wider range of communicatively-based language activities as part of the 2 three-module units. These communicative language activities include listening to radio and TV broadcasts, oral presentations and debates, dramatisation, speech writing and delivery, preparing press releases and announcements as well as reading and discussing newspaper and magazine articles and literary texts and conducting group and individual research projects (CXC A13/U2/98, p. 11, p. 18). Each of the two units is assessed separately both internally (25%) and externally (75%). The internal assessment consists of a three-part oral examination which includes the delivery of prepared topic, topic conversation followed by general conversation on current issues (CXC A13/U2/98, p. 19). The external assessment comprises three papers for each of the two units: a listening comprehension paper making up 20% of the 75% of the total examination mark for each of the two unit levels, a reading and writing paper making up 30% and a literature paper making 25% (CXC A13/U2/98, pp. 20-22).

The CXC foreign language syllabi content thus closely follows SLT methodological objectives of communicating clearly, appropriately and effectively in various sociolinguistic contexts.

SLT in Singapore

SLT methodology is not used. The Singapore government paid Cambridge University to keep producing the antique GCE format. The foreign language students are highly selected for their intelligence and politically correct attitudes. These elite students, less than 1% of the student population, are trained to a high proficiency in writing and grammar for the GCE with minimum conversation. The examination training, developed over decades of unchanged format, has become highly effective and efficient, guaranteeing the highest passes for the few students selected. This application of Confucian teaching fits the Singaporean policy of 'investing' educational resources in those who will bring most benefits to the country, benefits that maintain the values of its 'permanent' Chinese government (Boufoy-Bastick, 1997, p. 64; Lim, 1991, p. 84).

SLT in Australia

SLT in Australia is currently task-based. Project work is a fundamental part of the 'second language' classroom. Students are encouraged to work in groups towards completing a set activity. This task-orientation to SLT can be explained by the remoteness of the foreign country where the language is spoken and the lack of contact with native speakers. The guiding theoretical assumptions are that language is a communicative activity hence language learning is interactive. Interaction has to be between teacher and students and among students because of the comparative remoteness of the country.

The values that Australia currently places on community and on enhancing internal multiculturalism (Arnot, 1985; Barcan, 1980; Boufoy-Bastick, 1997a; Crittenden, 1982; Keeves, 1990; Rivzi, 1986) is reflected by :

(i)   no distinction between foreign and second language learning
(ii) students working in groups
(iii) teaching language in its cultural context
(iii) highlighting those cultural aspects of the foreign country that are absent, different or less pronounced in Australian society (different greetings, table manners, cooking etc.).

SLT in France

SLT in French foreign language curricula prioritises sociolinguistic accuracy. It differs from the UK and Australian SLT orientations in that it views second language learning basically as an intellectual problem-solving activity. The learner is expected to develop his or her ability to express himself or herself accurately in the target language. Language accuracy is demonstrated by the learner's appropriate use of linguistic patterns in given social situations. Strong emphasis is placed upon teaching speech acts and sensitising the learner to linguistic nuances. The theoretical basis for this pedagogical approach is that speech acts help in determining the situations in which the foreign language learner receives meaningful input (Schmidt & Richards, 1980).

The contextualised pattern-learning is claimed to help in developing the learner's communicative competence. This follows from Austin (1962), Grice (1975) and Searle (1969)'s influential speech act theory. This theoretical 'rationale' accommodates the fact that, although travel throughout Europe is very convenient from France, language teachers in France are unlikely to have the communicative skills of native speakers because of bureaucratic requirements to employ French nationals as teachers. This is now changing with ERASMUS, COMENIUS, GRUNDTVIG AND LINGUA teacher exchanges and training programmes, and with other participations of France in the European Union - this is discussed in the last section of this article on Actional Language Teaching. Nonetheless, up to the end of the XXth century in France, the guiding theoretical assumption has been that foreign language learning is an intellectual activity which aims at developing both linguistic and sociocultural competence.

SLT in the US

A wide variety of SLT methodologies have been developed in the US. The variety of American language learning methods spring from the variety of American social influences and foreign policies. Like Australia, the USA population is composed of mainly recent immigrant populations and for similar reasons promoting social unity the US also do not make the foreign language / second language distinction that is made in European language teaching.

The audiolingual methodology was developed in the 1960's (Brooks, 1960; Chastain, 1971; 1976; Lado, 1964; Moulton, 1963; Rivers, 1964; Stack, 1960). It prioritised the aural/oral skills of listening and speaking. This method aimed at developing fluency in the foreign language without reference to the mother tongue. Foreign language learning was fundamentally conceptualised as the acquisition of practical communicative skills. We now briefly describe some of the recently more popular language teaching methodologies in the US.

ASHER'S TOTAL PHYSICAL RESPONSE (TPR)

Asher's (1981) foreign language teaching approach is based upon prioritising the development of listening skills over speaking in the early learning stages. This approach parallels first language learning where the child listens to the language and does not speak. Asher claims that foreign language learning failure is due to the stress put on the learner to produce language before he/she is ready to do so. He explains that children are ready to talk only when they have acquired an intricate map of how language works. He underscores the role of the home as "an 'acquisition-rich environment' in which there is a maximum understanding of the spoken language in transactions between the caretakers and the child... these transactions do not demand speech from children" (Asher, 1981, p. 325). By contrast, Asher claims that foreign language teaching is 'acquisition-impoverished' and requires the learner to speak before he/she has developed the skills to do so. TPR is a SLT methodology using semantic contact which is related to physical reality. Thus, the teacher tells the student what to do; this is followed by students contextually-appropriate response. TPR has been influenced by American behaviourism and by American foreign policy funding - equipping 'our boys abroad' with a command register.

KRASHEN AND TERREL'S NATURAL APPROACH

The Natural Approach is based upon the principle that "comprehension precedes production" (Krashen & Terrel, 1983, p. 20). This methodology is influenced by Asher's silent period. Krashen and Terrel's contribution to language learning theory is their distinction between acquisition and learning. Krashen and Terrel (1983, p. 18) explain that "acquiring a language is 'picking it up', i.e. developing ability in a language by using it in natural, communicative situations" whereas "language learning is 'knowing the rules', having a conscious knowledge about grammar". Language acquisition takes place when language is used for "communicating real ideas" and "people understand messages in the target language" (opus cit, p. 19). Hence, they maintain that comprehensible input is a necessary condition for language acquisition. This, they describe as: "Comprehensible Input condition...: The learner is expected to understand; therefore the speaker makes an effort to see that language is comprehensible" (Spolsky, 1989, p. 193). Another of their necessary conditions for language acquisition is the creation of stress-free learning environment by lowering the "affective filter" (Krashen, 1978).

The hallmarks of the Natural Approach are simulating the natural environment in the classroom (Terrel, 1977), and lowering the learner's affective filter (Krashen, 1978; 1981). The Natural Approach is promoted by the same social reverence for ecological validity that values the 'correctness' of nature, the 'great outdoors', the National Parks, natural vs artificial foods, etc. The theoretical assumptions are that learning occurs best in the same natural way that a first language is learnt - input first (listening and reading). The only initial output required is 'yes/no'. The learners then gradually develop their ability in small comfortable stages (Krashen, 1985). Krashen's 'i+1' approach models Vygotsky's 1930's description of natural development via small comfortable stages within the zone of proximal development that became popular with the Americans in the 1980's via translations in the 1960's (Vygotsky, 1962).

SUGGESTOPAEDIA.

This is a psychiatrical approach to SLT, developed in 1979 by a Bulgarian psychiatrist, Lozanov, and it gained popularity across America and in Europe (Rose, 1985, pp. 116-125).

Suggestopaedia is like learning on the psychiatrist's couch. Language is to be learnt in relaxed conditions mainly subconsciously and thus with less conscious effort (Lozanov, 1979). An atmosphere conducive to such learning is created through listening to baroque music, dimming lights, sitting in large comfortable armchairs, etc. (Rose, 1985, p. 217). The appeal of Suggestopaedia has its roots in the nostalgia and diffidence many Americans had for their European cultural roots - as epitomised by Freudian psychiatry, fuelled by introspective doubt arising from claims to being the biggest and best. The death of the Protestant work ethic adds to the appeal of learning through relaxing. This low-effort method is paradoxically promoted as Super Learning and Accelerated Learning.

In a typical lesson development, the teacher reads a dialogue and students listen with their eyes closed. Then students listen a second time to the text and follow with their scripts (with translation on the right hand page). Students read, choose and play a role. This process-oriented language teaching alternative became extremely popular in California in the late 1980's.

SLT in Fiji

Fiji is a small island state like those of the Caribbean. English is the language of instruction in Fiji and it is taught in Fiji as a second language. For some students English is actually a foreign language, for others it is a second language and for urban students it may be their first language (Boufoy-Bastick, 1997b, 2001). The current language curriculum was developed in the late 1970's and it was implemented in the early 80's. Language curriculum developers from metropolitan countries - mainly Australia and New Zealand - helped local educators to design a localised language curriculum. Hence, the English as a Second Language curriculum reflects the language teaching methodological trends of the late 70's. The ESL curriculum is based upon the notional-functional syllabus developed by the Council of Europe.

The three guiding theoretical assumptions of the English curriculum are:
(i) Language curriculum is organised on semantic principles as opposed to grammatical principles.
(ii) Language is presented in contextualised situations and
(iii) Hierarchical classification of meaning is the essential component of the language syllabus.

In metropolitan countries the notional-functional syllabus involved teaching how to communicate their cultural notions, e.g. time, space, and quantity (Wilkins, 1976). However, ethnographic research has found (Boufoy-Bastick, 1997b, 1997c, 1999a, 1999b) that many of these 'notions' are for communicating through writing across contexts and do not exist in Fijian which is traditionally an oral language for within context-referenced communication (1 metre approximates 1 arm length, 1 kg approximates 1 heap). Hence, the Fijian notional-functional syllabus consists of teaching both the notions as well as the communicative functions that learners need to acquire, e.g. informing, requesting, enquiring, greeting, etc.

In the classroom, although the methodological assumption is that language teaching is based upon communication, actual interaction is limited to teacher questions and student answers (often chanted by the whole class). Teachers and students plod through the language textbook, completing the written exercises which are then corrected. The language exercises aim at teaching L2 patterns which are likely to occur in an interactive oral situation. However, these interactive oral communication patterns are learnt and practised through written exercises, which is a contradiction between the communicative curriculum objectives and its written practice.

Subjectivist teaching approach to SLT: A new dimension to SLT

One of the most recent developments in SLT is the application of Subjectivist Psychology to language teaching. Subjectivism focuses on the subjectivist experience of the learner and because it uses enculturation processes within social learning environments it is ideally suited to SLT. Subjectivist Psychology explains how SLT can create affective learning milieu to arouse students' emotional feelings which act as affective multiplying factors in the learning activity (Bastick, 1998, 1999a, 1999b, & 1999c). See also chapter 21 of this book.

GUIDING THEORETICAL ASSUMPTIONS

Subjectivist SLT is the application of Subjectivism to teaching languages. It is an affect-structured constructivist language teaching methodology (Boufoy-Bastick, 1995). Its fundamental theoretical assumption is that each student constructs his or her own understanding from the bricks of his or her own experience. 'Understanding' is the links within and between the student's experiences - both affective links as well as traditional cognitive links. Hence, each student understands differently to the extent of his or her different experiences. Subjectivist teaching recognises the indivisibility of *cognition* and *affect* in all experiences and so structures both the affective and cognitive aspects of learning experiences to optimise each student's understanding vis. choreographing the motivation, intention, curiosity, confusion and the energy of the learning experience as well as the associated cognitive content.

TEACHING METHODOLOGY

Subjectivist teaching methods utilise developmentally appropriate cognitive/affective techniques of enculturation. That is, the teacher uses teaching methods equivalent to those through which a student socially learns his or her own language and culture, e.g. through needing to communicate, through peer pressure, through modelling others, through seeking rewards and avoiding disappointments, etc.

AIMS AND ASSESSMENT

The two aims of Subjectivist teaching are 'Empowerment' and 'Enculturation':

(i) Empowerment is a humanistic intent of Subjectivist teaching to help students become autonomous, successful self-directed learners, i.e. developing a justified confidence in choosing what is best to learn as well as how best to learn it. Empowerment is assessed by evidence that the students are focused on their own activities and not on the teacher's management of their pedagogic processes.

(ii) Enculturation is the processes of learning the culture of the subject through. These are the natural age-appropriate learning processes of students' own socio-cultural sub-groups. In the case of language teaching, the culture of the subject includes the guiding attitudes and motivating values of the linguist as well as the culture of the users of the target language.

Enculturation is assessed through its three learnt abilities:

(a) 'objective' assessment of student's reproductions, just as used in the assessment of traditional transmission teaching
(b) assessment of student's justifications of novel transfer (usually through peer group acceptance) and
(c) student's demonstrations of appropriate values/attitudes (through needs-driven communication).

CHARACTERISTICS OF THE CLASS

Subjectivist SLT utilises the multi-age and multi-ability range within a class, which contrasts with traditional FL language teaching. Traditional FL language teaching is usually done in a streamed single aged class. Even in streamed classes there is individual diversity, a range of abilities and a range of mental age/maturity. However, the traditional teacher tries to ignore this diversity so as to more effectively 'go at the speed' of the average students. From the Subjectivist view, suppressing individual diversity and ignoring different abilities is very much to the detriment of the teaching/learning relationship. The utilisation of this diversity, even extreme diversity, shows clearly how Subjectivist teaching can be used to positively utilise the 'problematic' diversity of the traditional classroom. The methods used in streamed single aged classes are less effective because they do not utilise the diverse characteristics of the class.

LESSON CHARACTERISTICS

The 'deep' purpose of the lesson is learning language as required by the syllabus and course objectives. However, in common with Suggestopedia, in the Subjective lesson students are unaware of much of the management, effort and processes of learning that are necessary to achieve the deep purpose. Suggestopedia achieves this by 'relaxation', whereas Subjectivism achieves this by 'distraction'. Students are actively distracted from the efforts involved in the 'deep' purpose of the lesson by the design of needs-driven activities that totally involve them. These activities are the 'surface' purposes of the lesson. To create these surface-purpose activities, the lesson has to fit the needs and aspirations of the students - like the glove fits the hand. The lesson has to build on students' expectations, using their interests and experiences. The activities of the lesson fit the cultural values, experiences and expectations of the students. For example, the activities require the students to organise themselves to work in groups and to take communicative roles which are very acceptable to them. These may be roles such as investigative journalists questioning official spokespersons to reveal hidden agenda for the public good (Boufoy-Bastick, 1995).

DESIGNING ACTIVITIES THAT LINK AFFECT AND COGNITION:

A typical subjectivist SLT lesson is comprised of communication activities that increasingly integrate each student's individual contribution into a final event that is given approval by the whole class. Each activity, and the lesson as a whole, uses three Subjectivist teaching techniques to synergise affect and cognition: (a) an Emotional anchor, (b) Motivation and (c) Cognitive direction.

(a) Emotional anchor:

The Emotional anchor sets and captures the students' feelings for the duration of the activity so that whatever students choose to think or do during the activity will be related to the activity. The emotional anchor ensures the relevance of all learning states during the activity.

(b) Motivator:

The motivator has three purposes (i) to imply that the students can be successful at the surface purpose, (ii) to link their feelings of involvement to the activity so that they own the activity and (iii) to give them an entrance to the activity so they can start doing it.

(c) Cognitive Direction:

The Cognitive Direction identifies a course of action (what to do) within an information context matching the emotional anchor. It directs the students' awareness to information that is relevant to the lesson. The Cognitive Direction does this using three processes: (i) The Cognitive Direction describes the scenario, suggests an appropriate organisation, sources information and other resources for the activity. (ii) The Cognitive Direction situates the surface purpose within information related to the emotional anchor. This is how it directs the students' awareness to information that is relevant to the activity. Hence, students will be able to judge which information is relevant and can be used, and which information is peripheral and may be ignored. (iii) The Cognitive Direction also guides their organisation of the tasks involved in the surface purpose such as social bench-marking of standards, role responsibilities, etc.

In theory, the Motivatior reinforces the Emotional Anchor and the Cognitive Direction which then reinforces the Motivator. This is because, Emotional anchor + Cognitive direction = Intrinsic motivation. The affective multiplying factor for cognitive learning is achieved by the positive feedback loop created between these three subjectivist techniques. In practice, students are emotionally involved and need to take action, they own the activity. This cognitively directed emotion generates intrinsic motivation to participate. In the classroom, student's intrinsic motivation is further augmented by Motivation tokens during the activity. This motivation is covertly managed by the teacher so as to develop students as self-directed language learners, e.g. the teacher implicitly sets-up, or taps into, student's communication needs in ways that guarantee the student will be successful and will take the credit for his or her own success - thus building a self-perpetuating process.

SLT in Europe

ACTIONAL LANGUAGE TEACHING (ALT)
ALT FOR AN INTEGRATED MULTILINGUAL EUROPE

As European integration makes it imperative for Europeans to speak one or more European foreign languages European governments make significant strides in expanding foreign language (FL) courses at all levels of education, from kindergarten to university level, and developing domain-specific modern language courses (Socrates language actions, such as Comenius, Erasmus, Grundtvig, Lingua). The rationale for these modern European language developments is to guarantee democratically-rooted linguistic diversity in a politically and economically integrated Europe.

European determination to maintain a linguistically-diverse integrated entity has resulted in several significant language initiatives since the last two decades of the XXth century, these being impulsed by the Council of Europe in Strasbourg and the European Commission in Brussels. This section only reviews only one of many current pan-European FL-promoting initiatives, the European Language Portfolio (ELP).

ELP as a common European FL accreditation

The European Language Portfolio was officially launched on February, 19th, 2001 in Lund, Sweden, following a three-year trial (1998-2001) in the 15 European member countries. This coincided strategically with the official launching of the '2001 European Year of Languages' – a policy decision which publicised the shaping of a multilingual Europe. The purpose for implementing the ELP is twofold: (i) to ensure linguistic democracy by promoting the acquisition of one or more European languages by all European citizens and (ii) to provide a document identifiable in all European countries (Halberstadt, 2001; Scharer, 2000). This document is being introduced in several European schools, and this, in parallel with existing national FL certification. As opposed to national qualifications whose primary objective is to give summative evaluations through formal examinations, the ELP is a document in which all language experiences are entered. These experiences include formal FL educational qualifications, linguistic exchanges, visits and travels in the FL country as well as work experience in institutions where FL is used. ELP also supports learner-centredness and assumes that the learner owns and constructs his/her ELP according to his/her perceived evolving FL needs throughout his/her life. To this effect, ELP is used to record developing FL proficiency and attest life-long FL learning.

ELP assessment procedures

ELP assessment differs from traditional assessment methods. It is characterised by a novel approach to assessing FL competence based upon self-evaluation. This self-evaluation is reported in the portfolio under three rubriques: (i) the passport, (ii) a linguistic bibliography and (iii) the Dossier (Puren, 2001, p. 45). The following brief descriptions of the three rubriques are intended to shed some light on the self-evaluation instrument.

(i) The passport is used by European FL learners over the age of 16 years of age. This first ELP section shows the learner's self-evaluation which he/she has entered into a six-level grid. The passport takes into account the learner's FL experiences both in and out of school in the evaluation.

(ii) The linguistic bibliography has two functions. First, the linguistic bibliography indicates the diverse language learning experiences of the learner, such as FL training, films, books and lectures/presentations in FL, as well as interactions with FL speakers. Secondly, the linguistic bibliography provides a ten-level self-evaluation grid, the six levels from the European passport and four supplementary levels which allows for finer evaluation. This evaluation is concretely carried out against a list of descriptors. The learner assesses his/her developing FL proficiency by ticking the descriptors which correspond to his/her current FL competence. A competence level is reached when the learner has ticked two thirds of the descriptors. These descriptors are expressed in terms of positive concrete actions such as "I understand when people greet me" (Puren, 2001, p. 46).

(iii) The 'Dossier' is the third ELP section. It is a blank section which acts as the learner's journal. The learner can record his/her own reflections on his/her own FL learning experiences (courses, awards, internships etc.). This can serve as a useful tool for the learner to reflect on his/her learning strengths and weaknesses, needs and requirements. Thus, the 'Dossier' is expected to enhance learner's autonomy and life-long learning (Kohonen, 2000).

It is interesting to note that ELP assessment procedures starkly differ from those used in national educational systems in Europe. They provide an 'emic' self-evaluation, hence promote increased learner's responsibility for his/her FL actions and outcomes.

ELP socio-pedagogical functions

The ELP serves two major functions: (i) social and (ii) pedagogical.

(i) The ELP social function is twofold: socio-professional and socio-political. The ELP socio-professional function is to facilitate professional mobility within Europe. This pan-European FL document records an individual's FL history, highlighting FL educational and professional experiences, hence providing an indication of an individual's FL competence and ability to act in a FL environment. The ELP socio-political function is to foster a European civic identity. As opposed to national FL qualifications, the ELP is a supra-national document recognised throughout Europe. This language initiative demonstrates attempts at converging ideologically-diverse European education systems within existing national educational structures.

(ii) The ELP pedagogical function is to promote learner autonomy. This has implications for both the FL learner and the teacher. The FL learner, on one hand, is expected to be in charge of his/her own learning – although this not a novel methodological teaching conceptualisation, this may be considered as a concrete application. The learner's responsibility for FL acquisition is hence to be demonstrated in his/her identification of his/her specific FL needs and the actions to be taken to fulfil these needs. As opposed to traditional school-based learning, the ELP allows the student to choose what materials (textual, audio-visual, electronic), activities and actions are best suited to progress to the next ELP competency level. The FL learner is aware of what competencies need to be developed to graduate to the next ELP level – each of the six is described in the learner's ELP. The teacher, on the other hand, is expected to relinquish his/her didactic authority to support autonomous learning. His/her role shifts from delivering prescribed FL content – as in national syllabi - with a view to assist and direct the learner in his/her FL experiences. The implicit constructivist pedagogical strategies are embedded in the supporting ELP learner-oriented teaching. It should be noted, however, that there exists diverging approaches within Europe in operationalising the ELP given country-specific pedagogical conceptualisations (Bertochhini & Puren, 2001, p. 38). Some European countries stress student-centred *teaching*, such as France with *'la pédagogie différenciée'* (differentiated teaching), Italy with *'l'insegnamento individualizzato'* (individualised teaching), Spain with *'atención a la diversidad'* (diversity awareness), others focus on 'open *learning*', such as the UK and Austria (*'offenes Lernen'*). These divergences reflect the teacher's degree of influence on directing the student's learning – that is his/her culturally-defined interpretation of Actional Language Teaching.

The ALT teacher as an interactional facilitator

A significant aspect of ALT pedagogy is its culture-specific interpretation and implementation. In other words, teaching behaviours may differ between European countries. However, ALT rests on a common underlying educational ideology stressing the learner's accountability for his/her own learning actions and on a synergy between the teacher's and the learner's actions (Gannac, 2001; Puren, 2001). The latter is crucial to ALT. The ALT teacher uses learner-responsive pedagogical strategies geared to assist – motivate or enhance – FL learning. He/she helps the learner to become 'a social actor' (Council of Europe, 1996). Tavares (2001, pp. 48-49) points out that: "La perspective actionnelle implique non seulement le développement de compétences par l'action, mais aussi par la réflexion sur l'action..." (The actional perspective not only implies the development of competencies through action, but also through reflection on action...).

'Action', a buzz word among European FL policy-makers, highlights this redefinition of FL objectives. These objectives, in contrast to COLT, are not simply communicational, but inter-actional, that is FL learning is expected to facilitate 'action' between European speakers of different languages and to enable Europeans to live and work together, that is 'to act' together (Council of Europe, 1996). In sum, European ALT conceptualises FL as a requisite tool for 'common action'; it goes beyond 'reciprocal communication' which is central to SLT. ALT pedagogy provides a new dimension to FL communicative language teaching.

References

Arnot, M. (1985). *Race and Gender. Equal Opportunities Policies in Education.* Potts Points, Australia: Pergamon Press.

Asher, J.J. (1981). The total physical response (TPR): theory and practice. In H. Winitz (Ed.) *Native and Foreign Language Acquisition* (pp. 324-331). New York: The New York Academy of Sciences.

Austin, J.L. (1962). *How to Do Things with Words.* Cambridge, Mass.: Harvard University Press.

Barcan, A. (1980). *A History of Australian Education.* Melbourne: Oxford University Press.

Bastick, T. (1998, November). *Constructivist pedagogy and student-centred learning: the Subjectivist paradigm.* Paper presented at the 8th Annual Conference of the , Ellenville, NY.

Bastick, T. (1999a, January). *Subjectivism - A learning Paradigm for the 21st Century.* Paper presented at the 3rd North American Conference on the , San Diego, CA.

Bastick, T. (1999b, May). *Subjectivist psychology: an affective-constructivist pedagogy.* Paper presented at the 1999 Irvine, CA.

Bastick, T. (1999c, July). *Enculturation and Empowerment in the Subjectivist classroom.* Paper presented at the 9th Biennial Conference of the International Study Association on Teachers Thinking : Teachers & Teaching: Revisioning Policy & Practice for the 21st Century, Dublin, Ireland.

Boufoy-Bastick, B. (1995). *Multi-Cultural, Multi-Ability French Teaching: A Constructivist Perspective.* Teacher Training video. Suva: University of the South Pacific, Pacific Collection.

Boufoy-Bastick, B. (1997a). Using language policies to highlight and contrast the values that shape multicultural societies: Examples for Singapore and Australia. *Australian Journal of Education* 41,(1), 59-76.

Boufoy-Bastick, B. (1997b). *An exploratory study of the theory-practice interface of the English language policy in Form III and Form IV in nine rural secondary schools in Fiji.* Paper presented at the . The University of the South Pacific, Suva, Fiji, July 13-19th, 1997.

Boufoy-Bastick, B. (1997c). *Cultural influences on the teaching of English in Fiji's secondary schools: The construct of event horizon.* Paper presented at the . The University of the South Pacific, Suva, Fiji, July 13-19th, 1997.

Boufoy-Bastick, B. (1999a). *Allocating educational funding to maximise academic attainments.* Paper published in the proceedings of the Fifth Biennial cross-campus conference on , Trinidad and Tobago, April 7-9th, 1999. ERIC ED453117.

Boufoy-Bastick, B. (1999b). *Social values as a determinant of teaching behaviours: The Fiji example.* Paper presented at the International Study Association on Teacher Thinking conference, Dublin, July 27-31st, 1999.

Boufoy-Bastick, B. (2000). *Storying cultural specificities of ESL teaching in Fiji: A grounded composite narrative.* Paper presented at the 29th Annual Meeting of the , New Orleans, February 22-27, 2000. ERIC ED452722.

Boufoy-Bastick, B. (2001): *Conflicting goals: Promoting social inequality by supporting cultural diversity in second language learning.* Paper presented at the XXth Fédération Internationale des Professeurs de Langues Vivantes, Paris, July 22-26.(http://cvlium.univ-lemans.fr:8900/indexdess.html).

Boufoy-Bastick, B. (2001): *A methodological approach to the study of socio-cultural influences on the teaching of English in Fiji.* Unpublished doctoral thesis, the University of the West Indies, Jamaica.

Bertocchini, P. & Puren, C. (2001). *Les Langues Modernes,* 95(4), 38-44.

Breen, M.P. & Candlin, C.N. (1980). The essentials of a communicative curriculum in language teaching. *Applied Linguistics* 1, 2.

Brooks, N. (1960). *Language and Language Learning.* New York: Harcourt, Brace and World.

Brumfit, C. (1984). *Communicative Methodology in Language Teaching: The roles of Fluency and Accuracy.* Cambridge: Cambridge University Press.

Caribbean Examinations Council (1998). Caribbean Advanced Proficiency Examinations: Functional French Syllabus. CXC A14/U1/98.

Caribbean Examinations Council (1998). Caribbean Advanced Proficiency Examinations: French Syllabus. CXC A13/U2/98.

Chastain, K. (1971). *The Development of Modern Language Skills: Theory to Practice.* Philadelphia: Centre for Curriculum Development.

Chastain, K. (1976). *Developing Second Language Skills: Theory to Practice.* Chicago: Rand McNally.

Council of Europe (1996). *Les langues vivantes: apprendre, enseigner, évaluer. Un Cadre Européen Commun de Référence. Projet 2: Langues vivantes* (Modern languages: Learning, teaching, evaluating. A Common European Frame of Reference. Project 2: Modern languages). Strasbourg: Conseil de la Coopération Culturelle.

Crittenden, B. (1982). *Cultural Pluralism and Common Curriculum.* Carlton, Melbourne: Melbourne University Press.

Gannac, N. (2001). Travail autonome… pédagogie différenciée: d'où venons-nous? *Les Langues Modernes,* 95(4), 26-31.

Grice, H.P. (1975). Logic and conversation. In P. Cole and J. Morgan (Ed.) *Syntax and Semantics 3. Speech Acts.* New York: Academic Press.

Halberstadt, W. (2001). Le portfolio européen des langues. (European Language Portfolio). *Les Langues Modernes,* 95(2), 38-47

Halliday, M. (1991). The notion of "Context" in language education. In T. Le and M. McCausland (Eds.) *Language Education: Interaction and Development* (pp. 1-26). Proceedings of the international conference held in Ho Chi Minh City, March 30-April 1, 1991.

Howatt, A. (1984). *A History of English Language Teaching.* Oxford: Oxford University Press.

Hymes, D. (1972). On communicative competence. In J.B. Pride and J. Holmes (Eds.) *Sociolinguistics.* Harmondsworth: Penguin Books.

Keeves, J.P. (1990). The expansion and rationale of Australian education. To the 1990's and beyond. In L.J. Saha and J.P. Keeves (Eds.) Schooling and Society in Australia. Sociological Perspectives (pp. 49-68). Rushcutters Bay, Australia: Pergamon Press.

Kohonen, V. (2000). *A European Language Portfolio. Developing the Pedagogic Function of a European Language Portfolio: The "Dossier"*. Council of Europe.

Kramsch, C. (1993). *Context and Culture in Language Learning.* Oxford: Oxford University Press.

Krashen, S.D. (1978). The monitor model for second language acquisition. In R. Gringras (Ed.) *Second Language Acquisition and Foreign Language Teaching.* Washington: Center for Applied Linguistics.

Krashen, S.D. (1981). *Second Language Acquisition and Second Language Learning.* Oxford: Pergamon Press.

Krashen, S.D. (1985). *The Input Hypothesis: Issues and Implications.* London: Longman.

Krashen, S.D. & Terrell, T.D. (1983). *The Natural Approach: Language Acquisition in the Classroom.* Oxford: Pergamon Press.

Lado, R. (1964). *Language Teaching: A Scientific Approach.* New York: McGraw Hill.

Lim, C. (1991). The role of English in the development of a national identity in a multilingual setting: The Singapore dilemma. *Vox 5*, 83-86.

Littlewood, W. (1981). *Communicative Language Teaching.* Cambridge: Cambridge University Press.

Lozanov, G. (1979) *Suggestology and Outlines of Suggestology.* New York: Gordon and Breach.

Moulton, W.G. (1963). Linguistics and language teaching in the United States: 1940-1960. *IRAL 1*, 21-41.

Munby, J. (1978). *Communicative Syllabus Design: A Sociolinguistic Model for Defining the Content of Purpose-Specific Language Programmes.* Cambridge: Cambridge University Press.

Nunan, D. (1988). *The Learner-Centred Curriculum. A Study in Second Language Teaching.* Cambridge: Cambridge University Press.

Puren, C. (2001). Observation, conception et mise en oeuvre de séquence de pédagogie différenciée. *Les Langues Modernes, 95*(4), 10-25.

Richards, J.C. & T. Rodgers (1986). Approaches and Methods in Language teaching. New York: Cambridge University Press.

Rivers, W.M. (1964). *The Psychologist and the Foreign Language Teacher.* Chicago: University of Chicago University Press.

Rivzi, F. (1986). *Ethnicity, Class and Multicultural Education.* Deakin: Deakin University Press.

Rose, C. (1985). *Accelerated Learning.* Great Missenden, UK: Topaz Publishing Ltd.

Scharer, R. (2000). *Draft Final Report: A European Language Portfolio.* Pilot project, phase 1998-2000. Council of Europe.

Schmidt, R.W. & Richards, J.C. (1980). Speech acts and language learning. *Applied Linguistics 1*, 129-157.

Searle, J.R. (1969). *Speech Acts: An Essay in the Philosophy of Language.* Cambridge: Cambridge University Press.

Shaw, A.M. (1977). Foreign-language syllabus development: Some recent approaches. *Language Teaching and Linguistics: Abstracts 10*, 217-233.

Spolsky, B. (1989). *Conditions for Second Language Learning.* Oxford: Oxford University Press.

Stack, E.M. (1960). *The Language Laboratory and Modern Language Teaching.* New York: Oxford University Press.

Tavares, C.F. (2001). Former des enseignants plurilingues pour l'enseignement précoce: des enjeux aux propositions d'action. *Les Langues Modernes, 95*(1), 47-53.

Tavares, C.F. (2001). Former des enseignants plurilingues pour l'enseignement précoce: des enjeux aux propositions d'action. *Les Langues Modernes, 95*(1), 47-53.

Stern, H.H. (1983). *Fundamentals Concepts of Language Teaching.* Oxford: Oxford University Press.

Terrell, T.D. (1977). A natural approach to second language learning. *Modern Language Journal, 61*, 325-337.

van Ek J. & Alexander, L.G. (1980). *Threshold Level English.* London: Longman.

Wilkins, D. (1976). *Notional Syllabuses.* London: Oxford University Press.

Yalden, J. (1983). *The Communicative Syllabus: Evolution, Design and Implementation.* Oxford: Pergamon.

Vigotsky, L.S. (1962). *Thought and Language.* (Translated by E. Hanfmann and G. Vakar). Cambridge, Mass.: The MIT Press.

SECTION 3
SCIENCE EDUCATION

Chapter 10
Planning Lessons for Science Teaching
Kola Soyibo   97

Chapter 11
Questioning Techniques in Science Teaching
Kola Soyibo   111

Caribbean Perspectives

CHAPTER 10
Planning Lessons for Science Teaching

KOLA SOYIBO

Abstract

This article discusses and suggests ways in which Caribbean teachers could effectively (a) use a science syllabus and prepare a science teaching schedule; (b) write appropriate objectives for teaching specific topics; and (c) prepare unit lesson plans and detailed daily lesson plans on specific topics using different formats. Specimen detailed daily lesson plans on theory and practical lessons are provided as guides. These guides can be used by science teachers and also by teachers of other school subjects.

After reading this article, you should be better able to
(a) use a science syllabus and prepare a science teaching schedule;
(b) write appropriate objectives for teaching given topics; and
(c) prepare unit lesson plans and daily lessons plans on specific topics.

The Science Syllabus and Science Teaching Scheme

A *syllabus* is a general outline of the objectives, and contents/topics on a particular subject. It is usually developed and prescribed for a given category of learners who are expected to cover it completely within a specific period of time so they can write theory and practical examinations set on it. For example, the Caribbean Examinations Council (CXC) has a syllabus for each of biology, chemistry, integrated science and physics and other school subjects. Each CXC science syllabus is expected to be taught in the last two or three years of the five-year secondary education for students being prepared to sit the secondary education certificate examinations (SECE) at the general or basic proficiency levels.

Each of the four CXC science syllabuses is an examination syllabus. Hence, the contents of the syllabuses are not arranged in a teaching sequence. Science teachers are therefore expected to develop their own teaching schedules or schemes of work based on the syllabuses. Each science syllabus is divided into sections. Each section has *general* and *specific objectives* as well as explanatory notes which indicate the scope of the content including practical work on which the examination will be based. You must therefore have a copy of the most current edition of the CXC syllabus on the subject you teach and be familiar with its format and contents including the list of recommended textbooks and reference materials you require for your teaching.

The teaching schedule (or scheme of work) on each science subject is derived from the relevant syllabus. The science teaching schedule (STS) is the breakdown of the syllabus into units and topics. Normally, the topics to be taught weekly in each term for a given class are expected to be arranged logically and sequentially. However, there is some evidence indicating that in some Caribbean high schools the STS produced by some teachers are often not properly prepared and logically arranged. See Table 1.1. Some science teachers tend to regard the teaching schedule as synonymous with a unit plan. Yet, a unit plan is a series of lessons related to a theme/topic that can be taught during a given period of time. Details of unit plans are discussed in a later section of this chapter.

The following are some of the guidelines you will find useful when preparing a teaching schedule from a syllabus.
1. Begin with the simpler topics and arrange related topics sequentially.
2. Arrange the topics relative to the students' age, intellectual ability and prior knowledge.
3. Specify the time needed to teach each topic.
4. Specify relevant student practical activities on each topic.
5. In sequencing the content of the biology teaching schedule, give due consideration to the time of the year when certain specimens will be readily available.
6. Adequate time must be made for revision and examination as well as school time that is likely to be wasted because of unforeseen circumstances.

Table 1.1 Part of a Jamaican Grade 10 Biology Teaching Schedule 1997-98

Month	Christmas Term September - December Topic	CXC Objectives
Sept.	1. Revision of Section A	A 1.1 - 4.2
	2. Life processes and structures	B 1.1 - 1.2
	3. Cells and cell specification	C 1.1 1.3 B 1.3
Oct.	4. Soils	E 1.1 - 1.4
	5. Osmosis and diffusion	B 3.6
	6. Respiration	B 3.1 - 3.4
Nov.	Respiration cont'd	B 3.5, 3.7 - 3.9
	Complete unfinished topics, Revision and Exam begin	
Dec.	Examination ends, Review of examination	
	Start nutrition if time allows	

Objectives in Science Teaching

The CXC's science syllabuses contain two types of objectives: *general* and *specific*. *General objectives* are those that might take a fairly long time to achieve. On the other hand, *specific objectives* (also called behavioural, instructional or performance objectives) are statements that specify definite, observable tasks or actions a student/learner is expected to be able to display or perform during or at the end of a lesson. *Action verbs*, such as those exhibited in Tables 1.2 -1.4, are used for formulating *specific objectives* for a given lesson.

Specific objectives can be classified into three types: *cognitive, psychomotor* and *affective*.

Cognitive objectives are statements that specify the particular knowledge (intellectual) skills learners are expected to have acquired and display visibly during or at the end of an instruction. *Psychomotor objectives* are statements which specify the manipulative skills learners are expected to demonstrate when performing scientific activities with scientific tools (devices) or materials. *Affective objectives* are statements that specify the particular attitudes, emotions, feelings, interests, values etc. learners are expected to develop and visibly show during or at the end of a lesson.

In Tables 1.2-1.4 are examples of some words (*action verbs*) that are used for stating specific objectives in each of the three domains (UNESCO, 1986, pp. 183-185). You may need to use some of them in stating objectives for your lessons in addition to those in your CXC science syllabus.

Table 1.2 Some Useful Words for Stating Specific Objectives - Cognitive Domain

Level	Verbs to use
Knowledge	define, identify, label, list, name, mention, state
Comprehension	convert, describe, explain, illustrate, interpret, measure, summarize
Application	apply, construct, demonstrate, draw, perform, solve, use, appropriate procedures
Analysis	analyze, conclude, deduce, determine, differentiate, distinguish, generalize, organize, predict
Synthesis	create, compile, design, develop, justify, plan, produce
Evaluation	appraise, compare, conclude, contrast, decide, develop criteria, evaluate

Table 1.3 Some Useful Words for Stating Specific Objectives - Psychomotor Domain

Level	Behaviour
Perception	detect, feel, hear, listen, observe, recognize, see, smell, taste, view, watch
Set	assume a body stance, position the body, sit, stand, station
Guided response	copy, duplicate, imitate, operate under supervision, practise, repeat
Mechanism	conduct, demonstrate, execute, improve efficiency, make, produce
Characterization	act upon, defend, display, exemplify, expose, maintain, serve, support

Table 1.4 Some Useful Words for Stating Specific Objectives - Affective Domain

Level	Behaviour
Perception	detect, feel, hear, listen, observe, recognize, see, smell, taste, view, watch
Set	assume a body stance, position the body, sit, stand, station
Guided response	copy, duplicate, imitate, operate under supervision, practise, repeat
Mechanism	conduct, demonstrate, execute, improve efficiency, make, produce
Characterization	act upon, defend, display, exemplify, expose, maintain, serve, support

Unit Plans

A *unit plan* is a workable aspect of the larger teaching schedule within which the subject matter of a discipline can be organized for instruction during a specific period of time. It may be organized around concepts (e.g. the cell, photosynthesis) or around principles or themes (e.g. homoeostasis, balance of nature) (UNESCO, 1986). A reason for producing *unit plans* derives from the theory that learning by wholes is more effective than learning in bits. Moreover, a unit plan provides an overall view which enables the teacher to anticipate problems that may arise, particularly in relation to prerequisite content, concepts and skills (Ornstein, 1990).

UNIT PLAN COMPONENTS

The unit plan consists of six basic components. These are objectives, content, skills, learning activities, resources and materials, and evaluation (Ornstein, 1990).

Objectives can be behavioural or nonbehavioural (topic, problems, questions).

Content should be outlined to show its scope; it often includes three main categories: knowledge, skills and values.

Skills   A list of cognitive and social skills to be developed is occasionally optional. The skills should be based on the content to be taught but occasionally they may be listed as separate from the content. Among the vital basic skills to develop are critical reading , reading graphic materials (charts, diagrams, tables) composition and reporting skills, note-taking, study skills, cooperative and competitive skills and leadership skills.

Learning activities - sometimes called *student activities* - should be based on implementing objectives and student activities (e.g. guest speakers, field trips, debates, projects, experiments, and summative examination) should be listed. The common recurring activities can be shown as a part of the *daily lesson plan*.

Resources and materials - are included in the plan to guide the teacher in assembling the various materials (e.g. reading, audiovisuals) needed to carry out instruction. A list of resources is often covered in the listing of learning activities. Hence, it is sometimes considered as an optional component of a unit plan.

Evaluation   Procedures and culminating activities should be included. These include formative and summative evaluations, student exhibits and demonstrations, debates and discussions, quizzes and examinations. The main purpose is to ascertain whether the objectives have been achieved and to obtain information for improving the unit plan.

APPROACHES TO UNIT PLANNING

There are two basic approaches to unit planning which you may consider as a teacher.

Taxonomic approach   Table 1.5 illustrates parts of a unit plan based on the taxonomy of educational objectives in three domains of learning: cognitive, affective and psychomotor skills, modified from Peterson et al. (1994). The unit plan usually states a problem that leads to the objectives and indicates the corresponding activities and the materials and resources. Evaluation is not listed separately but is included as a part of the activities suggested at the tail end of the unit (e.g. the tenth lesson in Table 1.5).

Table 1.5 Part of a Unit Plan on 10th Graders' Ecological Studies Using the Taxonomic Approach

Problem	Cognitive process	Attitudes and values	Psychomotor skills	Learning activities	Resources and materials
1. Identifying habitats	To identify habitats based on physical features	To explore social and scientific issues; to ask questions	Manipulation of equipment	Observation of specimens; discussions	Filmstrip, handlenses, bioviewers
2. Comparing habitats	To recognize different habitats	To discuss alternative viewpoints; to debate responsibility for the health and welfare of others	To use tools that call for fine adjustment and discrimination	Debates and discussions	Pictures, replicas, models, hand lenses, bioviewers
10 Summarizing and evaluating	To show proficiency in facts, concepts and principles of the content	To argue, appraise, and judge based on scientific standards		Unit examination	

Topic approach Table 1.6 shows an example of the topic approach based on Ornstein's (1990) example. The unit plan is organized by topics and objectives. The objectives introduce the lesson while the topic serves as the main basis for outlining the unit. The objectives are in accord with the suggestion that the content should focus on concepts, skills and values. The objectives are not separated into general and specific objectives. The topics are arranged in the order in which they would be taught. The topics are used to write the daily lesson plans. The activities listed are non-recurring, special activities; repeated activities can be listed at the lesson plan level. The activities are listed in the order in which they will be carried out, but there is no one specific activity listed for each topic (as in Table 1.5). The evaluation component is separate and includes formative and summative tests, discussions and feedback.

Table 1.6 Unit Plan on 10th Graders' Biology Concepts Using the Topic Approach

Objectives
A. Knowledge
1. To lead learners to investigate the relationships among organisms living in terrestrial, aquatic and arboreal habitats using specific inquiry techniques
2. To encourage them to hypothesize, design and carry out investigations to test their hypotheses and draw conclusions from the data obtained
3. To assist them to critically evaluate the evidence they obtain
4. To enable them to recall basic ecological concepts accurately

B. Skills
1. To develop the learners' science process skills
2. To improve their experimental and investigative skills
3. To facilitate their ability to use tables, graphs and diagrams in assessing, interpreting and drawing conclusions from the biological data
4. To improve their reporting skills

C. Values
1. To enable learners appreciate the importance of using appropriate techniques during investigations
2. To enable them develop an awareness of the similarities and differences in the habitats inhabited by different organisms
3. To sensitize them to need for them to develop a commitment to the accurate reporting of findings from their investigations

Topics
I. Basic ecological concepts
1. Types of habitats
2. Adaptations shown by organisms living in different habitats
3. Similarities and differences among organisms living in different habitats
4. Feeding relationships in a given habitat
5. Food chains and food webs in different habitats
6. Energy flow in different ecosystems and the cycling of materials in ecosystems

II Geochemical cycles in nature
1. Carbon cycle
2. Nitrogen cycle
3. Water cycle
4. Forms of energy and interconversion
5. Evaluation
1. Short quizzes and essay tests on I 1-6, II 1-4
2. Graded reports with specific feedback for each student - half a lesson.
3. Unit test

Activities
1. Field work on I 1-5
2. Class discussion on each topic
3. Homework on each topic
4. Film show on forms of energy

Guidelines on the Writing of Daily Lesson Plans

To be able to teach any subject or science topic properly, teachers are expected to prepare daily lesson plans on the specific topic/topics they intend to teach their students. To be able to do this, either of two formats are used. An example of each is given so you could consider which one you prefer. The suggested features of the format of a daily lesson plan for a theory lesson is now outlined (Soyibo, 1992).

1. General Information (a) Name of school (b) Date (c) Subject (d) Class (e) Time (f) Duration (g) Period (h) Topic (i) References (j) Teaching Aids

2. Objectives Here, you are expected to state what you expect your students to be able to do during and at the end of a lesson by using appropriate action verbs and phrases for cognitive, psychomotor and affective objectives discussed earlier in Tables 1.2 - 1.4. The objectives should include tasks that would help in developing high level cognitive, psychomotor and affective skills in your students. Your must not state too many objectives for a lesson but must ensure that you would be able to achieve all your lesson's objectives. This is because it is a n indication of bad planning if you have five objectives for a lesson but succeeded in attaining only four! Of course, the number of objectives for a 35-minute lesson (single period) will be less than that for a 70-minute lesson (double period).

3. Entry Behaviour Clearly state the knowledge your students already possess (prior knowledge) that is relevant to the topic you are to teach.

4. Content This is a summary of the vital facts on the topic of a lesson. It should be treated under appropriate subheadings and numbered, if possible. To ensure that the content of the lesson is accurate, appropriate and up-to-date, you should consult, at least, two current science textbooks on any topic you plan to teach. Misleading terms, misconceptions or alternative conceptions and erroneous drawings and labels in such texts must be discarded from your lesson plan. You must draw in your lesson plan, accurate, well-labelled diagrams or drawings on your lesson's topic.

5. Introduction This should be based on your students' previous knowledge. It may be in the form of the revision of a previous lesson you have taught using oral questions, or it may be in the form of a teacher demonstration etc. It should be brief, appropriate and interesting so that your students will be alert and eager to know the purpose of the lesson. In general, by using well prepared introductory questions based on your students' previous knowledge (in an orderly and logical fashion) you are likely to succeed in leading them to mention the topic of the lesson from their responses. Then, tell them the objectives of the lesson as you have written them in your lesson plan. Avoid starting your lessons with the opening remarks similar to the following one that many teachers are fond of, "Good morning class.. (Students answer:.. 'Good morning Miss/Sir'). Today, we are going to learn about the topic, "Photosynthesis". "What did I say ? ...Photosynthesis (Students will repeat the word". Such remarks often dampen students' enthusiasm to learn.

6. Presentation For effective lesson presentation, you need to have spent reasonable quantity of time beforehand to plan what you and your students are to do at every stage of a lesson. You ought to have taken some time to revise thoroughly your lesson's content, and get ready the materials and equipment, and teaching aids you need for the

lesson. By using carefully prepared questions asked sequentially, starting from *known to unknown* and from *simple facts* to *principles*, you should lead your students step by step to discuss a lesson's content. Unless you have mastered your lesson's content and instructional strategies properly, you may be compelled to look at your lesson plan endlessly before you could do the right thing. Nevertheless, you should not feel shy to occasionally check up in your lesson plan some facts that you forget.

The questioning technique is an effective way to make students participate actively in your theory lessons. Hence, a golden rule of teaching is, *do not tell students what they can tell you*. Instead, ask them relevant questions to this end. It is when none of them can answer your questions correctly that you should supply the answers. Of course, allow your students to ask you questions at every stage of a lesson. Other strategies of keeping students actively involved in your theory lessons is to teach them how to use the *portfolio* or *journal* during your lessons. After teaching them how to use these tools, you can score them on their portfolio and journal's content as alternative assessment methods (AAMs) in addition to the traditional assessment methods (TAM) - i.e. the paper and pencil test and oral quiz that you may also give them as the summative evaluation of a lesson.

7. Evaluation   This is usually done by the use of oral questions or written exercises towards the end of a lesson to ascertain the extent to which your lesson's objectives have been attained. Evaluation should, nonetheless, occur at each stage of your lesson. This could be done via the use of the (a) TAMs (e.g. by using carefully prepared thought-provoking questions for students to answer orally or in written form) and (b) AAMs (e.g. scoring your students' portfolio or journal writing on a given lesson, performance-based assessment or the use of practical activities) to assess your students' learning experiences on a lesson.

8. Chalkboard summary As your lesson progresses, write on the chalkboard the important points and new terms. You might ask your students to form notes on the lesson taught on their own. Some teachers allow their students to copy on the chalkboard contents of their lesson plans during their students' free periods. Their students then copy the chalkboard notes in their science notebooks.

9. Homework   Before the end of a lesson, you should ask your students to bring certain materials from home for the next lesson, or read the next topic or do certain exercises on the lesson you have just taught them. In science teaching and learning, asking students to find out information about certain topics from the library or from resource persons is regarded as an aspect of *practical work*.

10. Students' Written Work Always ensure that you score all the written exercises you give your students to do in class or from their homes and discuss their errors etc. with them in the class. Their practical notebooks must also be marked. Never give your students any written work if you would not mark it.

11. Teacher's Personal Evaluation of a Lesson   After you have taught a lesson, write in your lesson plans what you feel went wrong in the lesson that you should correct if you have to teach the topic again or what you ought to have done but failed to do. Score yourself on the extent to which you think you have attained or have not attained the objectives of your lesson and think about what you need to do to improve the teaching of a topic in future or in another class.

Specimen Biology Daily Lesson Plan

    Subject: Biology
    Grade   9
    Date   2 /3/99
    Topic   Parts of a flower and their functions
    Time   8.10 - 8.50 am (40 minutes)
    Period   1st
    Objectives At the end of the lesson, the students should be able to
                          (a) identify the parts of a flower;
                          (b) state the functions of the flower's parts; and
                          (c) explain what a flower is.
    Entry behaviour   The students can identify parts of a flowering plant and state
                          their functions.
    References *CXC biology* by Chinnery, et al. 1992
                          Caribbean biology by Soper et al. 1991
    Teaching aids   Live specimens of Pride of Barbados flower, an unlabelled chart
                          of the LS of Pride of Barbados flower.

Procedure	Teacher Activities	Student Activities	Teaching Method
Step 1	Ask the students to name some plants that produce flowers.	Students answer	Questioning
Step 2	Give each student a live specimen of Pride of Barbados flower and ask students to name it.	Students observe and answer	Questioning
Step 3	Hang on board the chart of LS Pride of Barbados flower.	Students observe	Display of teaching aid
Step 4	Using the chart, point to the pedicel, receptacle, sepal, petal, stamen, pistil, etc and ask students to identify these parts in their own specimens and name them. Ask the students the function(s) of each part as soon as it is named.	Students observe and answer	Discussion
Step 5	Tell them the names of the parts they cannot name.	Students listen	Lecturing
	Ask the students to ask you questions on the parts discussed with them.	Students ask you questions	Facilitation of student questions
Step 6	Tell the students the names and functions of the parts if they cannot.	Students listen	Lecturing
Step 7	Ask the students to explain what a flower is.	Students answer	Questioning
Summary	Summarize the main points	Students jot them	Lecturing

		on the board as the lesson progresses.	in their jotters Students can also journal or use their portfolio	Use of alternative assessment tool
Evaluation		Number all the parts of the unlabelled flower on the chart and ask students: (a) What are the names and functions of each part of the flower numbered in the chart ? (b) What is meant by a flower ?	Students answer questions orally	Questioning
Homework		Students to bring to the next lesson 4 live specimens of P of Barbados, Hibiscus and Kingston buttercup.		
Summary		Summarize the main points on the board as the lesson progresses.	Students jot them in their jotters Students can also journal or use their portfolio	Lecturing Use of alternative assessment tool
Evaluation		Number all the parts of the unlabelled flower on the chart and ask students: (a) What are the names and functions of each part of the flower numbered in the chart ? (b) What is meant by a flower ?	Students answer questions orally	Questioning
Homework		Students to bring to the next lesson 4 live specimens of P of Barbados, Hibiscus and Kingston buttercup.		

As the above lesson plan shows, there is no provision for content or subject matter. But, this author is of the view that any lesson plan that omits content from its format is worthless. This format assumes that a teacher should know and remember off-head all the facts, and other details about a lesson. But in reality, only few teachers can easily do this. It is therefore suggested that if you decide to use the above format for your daily lesson plan, you should include content after Previous knowledge. Note that a good lesson plan (with content) is necessary but inadequate to guarantee the success of a lesson. For your lesson to be effective, you must have mastered its content and relevant teaching strategies coupled with adequate preparation and a high sense of commitment (Soyibo, 1992).

Specimen Practical Biology Daily Lesson Plan

Grade	9
Date	4/3/99
Topic	Practical work on the structures of flowers
Time	9.30 - 10.50 am (80 minutes)
Period	3rd

Objectives   At the end of the lesson, the students should be able to
(a) identify and draw the parts of different dicotyledonous flowers; and
(b) state the similarities and differences among their parts.

Entry behaviour   The students can name the parts of some dicotyledonous flowers.

References   Macmillan biological drawing for tropical schools 1977
Practical biology, by Sands & Bishop 1984

Teaching aids   Four live specimens each of the flowers of Pride of Barbados, garden Hibiscus, Kingston buttercup, razor blades, handlenses or bioviewers

Procedure

Step 1   Give each student four live specimens each of the flowers of: (i) Pride of Barbados, (ii) garden Hibiscus, and (iii) Kingston buttercup.

Step 2   (1) Ask each student to record on a worksheet his/her observations on the listed features of the named flowers (using handlenses /bioviewers where necessary).

	i	ii	iii
Name of flower			
Colour of			
(a) sepal			
(b) petal			
Number of sepals			
Number of petals			
Number of filaments			
Number of anthers			
Number of stigma			
Number of style			
Number of ovaries			

(2) State two similarities between Pride of Barbados and Hibiscus flowers.
(3) State two similarities between Pride of Barbados and Kingston buttercup flowers.
(4) State five differences between Pride of Barbados and Hibiscus flowers.
(5) State five differences between Pride of Barbados and Kingston buttercup flowers.

Step 3   Draw and label fully in your drawing books (a) a stamen, and (b) a pistil of (i) Pride of Barbados flower, (b) Kingston buttercup flower, (c) LS ovary of Pride of Barbados flower.

Evaluation   Collect the students' worksheets and drawing books and mark

Homework   Students to read from home pollination and fertilization in flowers .
Note: In Step 2 , sufficient spaces will be provided in the worksheets for students to write on.

Specimen Physics Daily Lesson Plan

        Date   4/4/99
        Grade   10
        Time   8.10 - 9.30 am. (80 minutes)
        Period   1st
        Topic   Motion: its meaning and types

Objectives   At the end of the lesson, the students should be able to
        (a) define what motion is;
        (b) explain the causes of motion;
        (c) mention four types of motion;
        (d) classify the different types of motion and give examples of each class; and
        (e) explain what relative motion is.

Entry behaviour The students are familiar with moving objects or bodies such as motor vehicles, birds, and electric fans.

References   *Physics for the Caribbean* by Duncan and Onac (1985)
                 Physics for CXC by Avison (1988)

Teaching aids   Iron or snail cones, empty milk tins, pieces of paper or inflated balloons, ceiling or table fan and the simple pendulum.

Content

1. *Definition* **Motion** is the change in the position of an object from one place to another along the line and direction of applied force. Hence, the cause of motion is called *applied force*. The force could be from within or outside the object.
2. *Types of motion* Motions can be linear, rotational/circular, oscillatory, random or relative.
(a) *Linear motion* is the movement of a body or an object along a straight line with the applied force (e.g. motor vehicles moving on roads, airplanes moving on runways, birds flying straight in definite directions and athletes running 100m).
(b) *Rotational or circular motion* is the movement of an object in circular direction or around a fixed point (e.g .the movement of electric fan blades, the movement of motor vehicle wheels about their axles and the movement of a cone). W hen an empty milk tin is given a push on the floor, it could show linear and rotational motions.
(c) *Oscillatory motion* is the movement of an object to and from a fixed point (e.g. the clock's pendulum, simple pendulum, and the movement of the head of electric fans (standing or table type).
(d) *Random motion* is the zig-zag, indefinite movement of an object to no particular direction. (e,g. the movements of dust particles, pieces of paper or dried leaves blown about by strong winds and the movement of saw-dust particles in water containers).
(e) *Relative motion* is the movement of an object in relation to another object.(e.g. the movement of a train as observed by a driver of a moving car).

Introduction
The teacher introduces the lesson by asking students the following oral questions:
(a) What happens when you put some dry, face powder on your palm and blow air on it?
(b) What causes the powder to be blown off?
(c) Name some objects that move on their own or when pushed.

Procedure

Step 1 From the introductory questions, the teacher leads the students to the concept of motion and what causes motion. Furthermore, he/she leads them to define *motion*.

Step 2 Ask a student at the back of the class to walk straight to the chalkboard and back to his/her seat. Ask students to describe and name this type of motion and then ask then to give you more examples of linear motion.

Step 3 To demonstrate rotational motion, put an empty plastic bowl or empty tin of milo/milk on the floor and ask a student to move round it. Then, ask the student or another student to describe and name this type of motion. The students should then be asked to mention other objects that show rotational motion.

Step 4 Tell the students to watch you as you demonstrate how a pendulum works. Ask them to describe their observations and to name this type of movement shown by the pendulum. Ask them to name other objects that show oscillatory motion. At this point, you can also demonstrate the motion of an iron or snail cone.

Step 5 Ask the students to take and throw up into the air some pieces of paper or balloons they have inflated and describe what happened. Ask them to name this type of motion and to name other examples of objects that show random motion.

Step 6 To illustrate relative motion, call two students to stand in front of the class. Let one of them remain in a fixed position and ask the other one to walk or run past the fixed point. Ask the other students to describe what happened between the stationary student and the one who moved past the former. If the students cannot explain, you should do so. Ask students to name examples of objects that show relative motion.

Evaluation
About 20 minutes before the lesson ends, ask the students to write their answers to the following questions on a piece of paper:
1. Explain the term *motion*.
2. What causes motion?
3. Describe briefly four types of motion and give two examples of each type.
4. Name two objects that can perform more than one motion at the same time.
5. Briefly explain what you understand by the term *relative motion*.

Note: You can ask students to exchange their sheets of paper to mark their answers, return the sheets to their owners and discuss their performance on the short quiz or you can ask them to write their names on their sheets of paper, collect them and mark at your spare time.

Homework
Students should read from home the relationships among speed, velocity and acceleration.

Study questions

1. Carefully examine the biology teaching schedule in Table 1.1. List the defects you identify in it. What could be done to rectify these defects?

2. Select three topics in your teaching subject on which you can write exclusively (a) cognitive objectives, (b) psychomotor objectives, and (c) affective objectives.

3. Prepare a unit plan of 5-10 lessons on aspects selected from relevant, current CXC science syllabus on your area of specialization using any approach of your choice.

4. Prepare a detailed daily lesson plan on any science topic of your choice to be taught in a named grade level lasting 40 or 80 minutes (theory or practical lesson). You can use any lesson plan format but ensure that you include the topic's content (for a theory lesson) and relevant illustrations.

References

Ornstein, A. C. (1990). *Strategies for effective teaching*. New York: Harper & Row.

Peterson, R. et al. (1994). *Science and society: A source book for elementary and junior high teachers*. Columbus, Ohio: Merill.

Soyibo, K. (1992). *CUS708/4-6 Biology Methods*. Lagos: Correspondence and Open Studies Institute, University of Lagos, Nigeria.

UNESCO (1986). *UNESCO handbook for biology teachers in Africa*. Paris: UNESCO.

CHAPTER  Questioning Techniques in Science Teaching

KOLA SOYIBO

Introduction

This article focuses on (a) some of the reasons why Caribbean teachers need to master and use questions in their teaching; (b) how these teachers can formulate and ask different types of questions; (c) some of the characteristics of good questions; (d) the guidelines that Caribbean teachers can use to ask good questions of their students and avoid various categories of faulty questions in their teaching; and (e) how teachers can handle their students' answers and questions as well as develop their students' questioning skills so as to improve their students' learning of science and other school subjects.

After reading this article, you should be better able to
(a) state some of the functions of questions in teaching;
(b) formulate and ask different types of questions;
(c) state some of the characteristics of good questions;
(d) use some of the guidelines for asking good questions and avoid faulty questions in your teaching; and
(e) effectively handle students' answers and questions, and develop students' questioning skills in your teaching.

Functions of questions

Effective teaching involves the use of good questioning techniques. Questioning is an art that every teacher needs to learn and master. Among the functions of well-constructed questions are that they (a) arouse students' curiosity, (b) stimulate their imagination, (c) challenge and motive them to search for knowledge, (d) make students think, (e) help students clarify and organize their ideas or concepts on a lesson, and (f) assist teachers to assess the success or failure of their teaching.

Types of questions

Questions can be classified in many ways, for example, (a) according to the processes involved: *low* or *high level,* or according to taxonomic bases - *cognitive, psychomotor* and *affective domains*; and (b) according to the type of answers required: *convergent* or *divergent* (Ornstein, 1990).

LOW AND HIGH-LEVEL QUESTIONS

Low-level Questions focus on memory and the recall of information or facts. They are used to assess students' readiness for complex and abstract thinking, to ascertain whether they can deal with higher cognitive processes and high-level questions involving, say, analysis, synthesis and problem-solving. Examples of low-level questions are: When does respiration occur in plants? What is electrolysis?

High-level Questions deal with complex and abstract thinking. Asking high-level questions from students demands clear reasoning and patience on teachers' part. Even for the experienced teacher, the appropriate timing, sequencing and phrasing, of such questions are not easy tasks. Questions on knowledge are examples of *low-level questions* in the cognitive domain, while those on comprehension to synthesis are *high-level* (or *higher order*) *questions*. Examples of both types are shown in Table 1.

Table 1 Cognitive Questions

Categories		Specimen questions
1.0	Knowledge	
1.1	Knowledge of specifics	What is the symbol of sodium atom?
1.2	Knowledge of ways and means of dealing with specifics	What would you do to test if a food sample contains starch?
1.3	Knowledge of universal and abstraction	What it the method of separating a mixture of ethyl alcohol and water?
2.0	Comprehension	
2.1	Translation	What is meant by "force"?
2.2	Interpretation	How does diffusion differ from osmosis?
2.3	Extrapolation	Based on the global birth rate, what will be the world population by the year 2050?
3.0	Application	What will likely happen if the south poles of two bar magnets are brought near each other?
4.0	Analysis	
4.1	Analysis of elements	How would you distinguish a compound from a mixture?
4.2	Analysis of relationships	What are the similarities and differences in the external features of an adult cockroach and its nymph?
4.3	Analysis of organizational principles	Two objects of the same size were immersed in equal volume of water. One floated, while the other sank. Why?

Table 1 Cognitive Questions (cont ..)

5.0	Synthesis	
5.1	Production of a unique communication	Show how the force of an oscillating body is directed towards a fixed point.
5.2	Production of a plan/proposed set of operations	How would you determine the chemical mass of an unknown substance ?
5.3	Derivation of a set of abstract relations	What is likely to have occurred if a mature, healthy-looking mango tree suddenly starts to shed its leaves during the rainy season ?
6.0	Evaluation	
6.1	Judgement in terms of internal evidence	A boy was diagnosed to have insufficient insulin in his body. What symptoms would you look for to confirm or reject the correctness of the diagnosis ?
6.2	Judgement in terms of external evidence	Two metallic substances - one in a powdered form, the other in a solid form - were exposed to the atmosphere. What will likely happen to them after a long time if they both contain iron ?

Table 2 Specimen psychomotor and affective questions

Psychomotor questions
1. Set up an experiment to demonstrate Archimedes principle.
2. Make a fully labelled diagram of the apparatus you would use for the laboratory preparation of chlorine.
3. Draw and label fully the longitudinal section of an onion bulb.

Affective questions
1. Would you support the call that all nuclear power stations should be closed down ? Why?
2. Do you support the view that AIDS patients should be allowed to mix freely with other uninfected members of the society ? Why do you support or do not support this view ?
3. Do you share the view that condoms should be supplied regularly to high-school students? Why do you share or do not share this view ?

CONVERGENT AND DIVERGENT QUESTIONS

Convergent questions usually have one correct or best answer. Hence, they are often erroneously labelled as low-level and knowledge questions. But convergent questions can deal with logic and complex data, abstract ideas, analogies and multiple relations (Resnick & Klopfer, 1989). Convergent questions usually begin with *what, who, when,* or *where*.

Divergent questions are usually open-ended and often have many different, appropriate, answers. Divergent questions are associated with high-level reasoning processes and can encourage creative thinking and discovery learning in students. Often, convergent questions should be asked first to ascertain what students know before advancing to divergent questions. Ideally, you should ask your students fewer convergent questions (particularly the low-level ones) and more divergent questions.

How or *why* are usually used to start divergent questions. *What* or *who* questions, followed by *why*, are actually divergent questions that are introduced by *what* to arrive at the *why* component of the question. The differences between convergent and divergent questions are shown in the sample questions in Table 3.

In most classrooms, teachers ask convergent questions, which demand **right** answers, resulting in teacher approval and making students become *right-answer-oriented*. Ornstein (1987) is of the view that convergent questions foster authoritarian minds in students. Divergent questions, which foster rational mind in students, demand their ability to cope with not being sure about being right and not always getting approval from teachers. They take a lot of the class time when used, and this is one of the reasons why many teachers shun them.

Table 3 Specimen convergent and divergent questions

Convergent questions	Divergent questions
1. Who discovered the x-rays ?	How are x-rays important in human health care?
2. When was the structure of the DNA molecule discovered ?	Why is the knowledge of the structure of the DNA molecule useful to humans ?
3. What is a mixture ?	How would separate a mixture of sand and table salt?

Gallagher (1965) cited in Ornstein (1990, pp. 282 - 283) classifies teachers' classroom questions into four categories.

Cognitive-memory questions which require learners to reproduce facts or content on the subjects they are taught by rote or selective recall (e.g. What is an enzyme? What is oxidation?)

Convergent questions - as discussed above.

Divergent questions - as discussed above.

Evaluative questions which require learners to make value judgements about the quality, accuracy or adequacy of information using some criteria set by the learners or by some objective standards (e.g. Do your believe that research on the cloning of human beings should be supported? Would you support the view that every human female should be allowed to have an abortion?) Gallagher opines that teacher-student discussions could operate normally if only the first two types of questions outlined above are used in the classroom. Do you agree with his view? Why? If not, why?

CHARACTERISTICS OF GOOD QUESTIONS

Good questions must
(a) be simple and precise, (b) be appropriate to students' ages and abilities,
(c) be grammatically correct, (d) be stimulating and relevant to the lesson,
(e) be varied in length and difficulty level, and (f) not encourage chorus answers.

GUIDELINES FOR ASKING GOOD QUESTIONS

1. Ask questions in a pleasant manner.
2. A suggested procedure for asking effective questions is as follows:
(a) Before you start asking any question , ensure that every student is attentive
(b) Ask a question
(c) Pause for a while to allow your students to think of an answer because increasing the wait time for 1 to 3-4 seconds has other beneficial effects on students' responses.
(d) Name a student to answer.
(e) Listen to the student's response.
(f) Indicate whether or not the answer is correct.
(g) Then, ask another question(s) or go on with your teaching
3. Distribute questions evenly by calling on volunteers and nonvolunteers, low and high-achievers alike to answer so every student can participate in the lesson.
4. Call on disruptive students to answer because it stops them without having to interrupt the lesson.
5. Ask questions sequentially and systematically.
6. Rephrase any vague questions.
7. Ensure that your questions are clearly heard by all your students to avoid repeating them because this encourages some students to be inattentive.
8. The fairly difficult questions should be directed to the high-achievers to keep them on their toes, while the fairly easy ones should be directed to the low-achievers to motivate them to participate in the lesson.
9. Prepare, in advance, *pivotal questions* that relate to the main objectives of your lesson as a part of your daily lesson plan and use them at appropriate stages during the lesson.
10. As the lesson progresses, you need to formulate *impromptu* or *emerging questions* in response to the teacher-student encounters you have generated.

FAULTY QUESTIONS

Good questioning techniques are developed gradually over many years in teachers. The following are examples of categories of defective questions you must **avoid** asking whenever you are teaching (Ornstein, 1990).

1. **Vague or indefinite questions** are confusing and often have to be clearly worded (e.g. What is an equation?" "Why is a root important?")
2. **Yes or no questions** which encourage guessing, impulsive thinking, and right-answer orientation. If you accidentally ask this type of question, you should follow it up immediately with a *why* or *how* question (e.g. Are electrons negatively charged? Did Michael Faraday invent the dynamo and electric transformer?)
3. **Double or multiple questions** Before students can respond to the first question, the second one is asked. Consequently, the students do not know which one the teacher wants them to answer and they respond to the part of the question they feel more knowledgeable about (e.g. What is reproduction and what are the differences between sexual and asexual reproduction?)
4. **Leading or suggestive questions** (e.g. Why is it dangerous to use ganja (marijuana) as a drug?) The question actually demands an opinion but a position or judgement is already stated that is likely to influence the respondent's answer one way or the other.
5. **Whiplash questions** (e.g. A potentiometer is used for what?) The question is not clearly expressed but embedded in the statement. A better wording of the question is, "What is a potentiometer used for?".
6. **Tugging or teeth-pulling questions** (e.g. What else? Can you give me one more term to describe the process?). Here, an answer is required from students when they may not be able to give further answer. In short, the question should be rephrased thus if you are sure that there is another term that can be used to describe the process, *Which other term can be used to describe the process?*
7. **Pumping questions** Some letters of the answer are given by the teacher and the students are required to supply the rest (e.g. The process by which the images of objects are formed on the retina is known as **accommo....**). Such questions are not thought-provoking.
8. **Wordy or overloaded questions** (e.g. With reference to the precarious, increasing depletion of the ozone layer, what predictions can we make about future global climatic changes, and marine water level?). Such questions are indefinite, wordy and confusing to students. Hence, unnecessary words should be deleted and simple vocabulary should be used in phrasing questions.
9. **Echo questions** (Pat, what is the meaning of pressure, I mean pressure?). Here, one or two keys words are repeated. In addition, you should not name a student before you ask a question.

Guidelines for handling student answers

1. Always indicate whether or not your students' answers are correct. Reward correct answers with brief remarks or *social reinforcers* such as, **Correct, Good, That's true, Okay, That's right, Excellent**. But too much or phoney (pretended) praise can have detrimental effects.

Moreover, vary the social reinforcers you use so that one of them does not become your personal mannerism with which your students can re-name you as *Miss or Mister "Correct or Excellent* ! etc.).

2. Politely tell a student if his/her answer is wrong (e.g. *Your answer is wrong. Try again, you can answer it*).

3. Do not repeat students' correct responses when, indeed, you should acknowledge them as correct with complimentary remarks (i.e. social reinforcers). But if you feel that a correct answer should be repeated for emphasis, call on another student to repeat it.

4. If a student's response is partially correct, ask him/her to try again. If he/she cannot answer correctly, then, ask other students to help him/her out. If that fails, supply the answer.

5. Ensure that students answering questions are not interrupted by their mates.

6. Never humiliate any student for giving a wrong answer.

7. Encourage students to talk loud enough for others to hear by occasionally asking those at the back or in front of the class (depending on the location of the student answering the question) whether or not they heard a particular student's answer.

8. Occasionally, ask an inattentive student to repeat the answer just given by his/her mate.

9. Some times, encourage students to comment on their mates' answers.

10. Use a correct answer as a lead to another question to stimulate discussion but do not over-probe.

Guidelines for handling student questions

You should encourage your students to ask you and each other questions in the class and should be glad to welcome such questions.

1. When a student asks you or another student a question, occasionally throw it back to the class. If nobody can answer it, you must answer if you know the answer.

2. If you do not know the answer to your student's question, politely indicate that you cannot remember it at that point in time. Ask the entire class to look for the answer before the next lesson. Assure them that you too will find out the answer and ensure that you do so. Discuss the students' finding and your own during the following lesson.

3. Resist the temptation of giving just any answer (which may be wrong) to your student's question in your attempt to avoid admitting your ignorance (or your forgetfulness?) . Such a conduct is likely to undermine your integrity and academic competence before your students especially if it occurs on a number of occasions!.

4. Politely point out your students' silly questions. For example, *Mike, I won't take that from you. You know better*. Avoid uttering humiliating, contemptuous and embarrassing comments such as, *Nonsense! Hopeless! A ragamuffin!*, if a student asks you a silly question. Such remarks often frighten students from venturing to ask their teachers questions.

5. If a student's question is irrelevant, tell him/her politely that it is not relevant to the topic you are teaching at that moment and that the student should remember to ask you the question again when you are teaching them the topic to which it is relevant.

Guidelines for developing student questioning skills

Usually, students are socialized and conditioned to answer their teachers' questions and are rarely encouraged to ask questions in the classroom. But, actually, young children often ask many questions but older students hardly do. The following guidelines can assist you in developing your students' questioning skills.

1. Increasing the wait-time (interval between asking a question and the student's response) increases students' chance to ask their teachers questions.
2. Do not always give the answer when a student asks you a question. Throw it back to the class for their reaction.
3. Make your lessons interesting so students can ask you questions as a result of their being positively motivated and stimulated.
4. Ensure that the teacher-student relationship is warm and inspiring so students are not afraid to ask you questions.
5. Always encourage students to ask you questions at each stage of the lesson by uttering such comments as, *Please, feel free to ask me any questions on what we have discussed so far, before we continue with the lesson.* If no student asks you any question at that stage, you can comment thus, *Because none of you has any questions to ask me, now, I will ask my own questions on what we have discussed so far.* Then, ask them specific questions on what you have taught them thus far to recapitulate the lesson.
6. Accord appreciation and respect to your students' questions by first of all thanking any student who asks you a question before you either answer it yourself or throw the question back to the class (e.g. *Thank you for that good question, Janet...*)

Study Questions

1. What other purposes can good questions serve in the classroom besides those listed in this Chapter?
2. Construct different types of questions in the cognitive, psychomotor and affective domains on specific topics in your field of specialization (See Tables 1. and 2).
3(a) State some of the likely reasons why divergent questions are not popular among many teachers.
3(b) Write four convergent questions and four corresponding divergent questions on any topics of your choice (See Table 2.3).
4. Are there any other features of good questions you can think of apart from those mentioned in this Chapter? State them.
5. For what reason(s) would you repeat your students' correct answer(s)? How often should this be done?

References

Ornstein, A. C. (1987). Questioning, the essence of good teaching: Part I. *National Association of Secondary School Principals,* 71-79.

Ornstein, A. C. (1990). *Strategies for effective teaching* (pp. 275-295). New York: Harper & Row.

Resnick, L. B. & Klopfer, L. E. (Eds.) (1989). *Towards the thinking curriculum: Current cognitive research.* ASCD Yearbook. (Alexandria, VA: Association for Supervision and Curriculum Development).

Soyibo, K. (1992). *CUS 708/4-6) Biology methods* (pp. 30-36). Lagos: Correspondence and Open Studies Institute, University of Lagos, Nigeria.

SECTION 4
EDUCATIONAL ADMINISTRATION

Chapter 12
Management of Student Discipline and Behaviour in School
*Austin Ezenne and
Oliver Mills* 123

Chapter 13
Teachers and Stress Management in Schools
*Austin Ezenne and
Olga James Reid* 131

Chapter 14
The Role of Educational Foundations in Teacher Education
*Oliver Mills and
Austin Ezenne* 137

Chapter 15
Models of Leadership Behaviour for Educational Organisations
Austin Ezenne 143

Caribbean Perspectives

CHAPTER 12
Management of Student Discipline and Behaviour in School

AUSTIN EZENNE AND OLIVER MILLS

Abstract

Teachers in general have limited training on how to handle students' misbehaviours in the school. This is because the teacher training programmes of many nations do not lay emphasis on how to handle students disruptive behaviours in the classroom and the school. Because of this, teachers often use common sense and personal experiences to handle students disruptive behaviours in schools. It is also a common practice among teachers and educators to use instructional principles to remedy academic problems of students while punitive measures are used to manage disruptive behaviours of students instead of using corrective measures to redirect the students.

Many teachers are now aware that the use of punitive and confrontational methods to solve students disruptive behaviours is counter productive and in many cases ineffective. This is because these confrontational methods tend to cause fears and escalate students' emotions and may make the students more aggressive or withdrawn in the classroom and the school.

Introduction

Students misbehaviour have many negative effects on the students, teachers, the school and the home. Students' misbehaviours disrupt learning by students and teaching by teachers and these lower academic achievement. Teachers waste a lot of teaching time dealing with students' disruptive behaviours. Teachers in general expect students to be orderly, courteous, respectful, quiet and willing to work. They also expect them to be fair in dealing with their classmates and schoolmates as well as showing consideration for school personnel and properties. But many students nowadays do not have these attributes. Many students are unruly, dishonest, uncooperative, aggressive and sometimes violent. At the moment many students have little or no fear and respect for their teachers. The can argue against their teachers and also tell lies against them, because the authority of the teacher has been eroded by many factors in the educational systems of many nations and the society at large. Teachers usually have little backing from school management, parents and the community when dealing with students problems. Parents in particular in many cases, take sides with their children in any dispute with the teacher or the school authority and in some instances parents take legal proceedings against the teacher and the school management, for even the slightest dispute involving their children in the school. Many parents object to giving punishment to their children in the school even when the children have breached school rules. Because of these broad shifts in the position of teacher, teaching, which was a male occupation at the beginning of the 20th century in many countries, has now turned to a female occupation.

A Philosophical Perspective of School Discipline and Punishment

In many developing countries, the schools, which were once the context for positive values and character building, have now become sites for indiscipline, antisocial behaviour, discourtesy and even violence. Many educators are now pondering what has caused this psychological outlook on the part of students, and seek to initiate strategies to deal with these social aberrations. Many ameliorative measures have been suggested, but the traditionalists have taken a very strong stance calling for more discipline and punishment for offences committed in the schools. Are they the same, or is it that one takes a more extreme form than the other?

This question is examined by Hamm (1989). He sees discipline as being confused with punishment and argues that those who reject punishment as a means of control are unwilling to dispense with discipline. He then goes on to describe discipline as submission to rules. These rules relate to subject matter, the conduct of scientific experiments and are also connected to the guidelines which are followed in mathematical reasoning. Discipline here is concerned with complying with the requirements of learning particular skills. It involves application, the following of stipulated procedures and applying principles correctly. *Hamm* then looks at discipline in terms of the learning of rules about concentration, practice and review, as well as taking notes. A third perspective is given on discipline where it involves the following of rules in order that the school may operate efficiently. This concerns rules about attendance, movement throughout the school and emergency measures. Other rules connected to discipline are moral in nature and apply both within and outside the school. These are truth telling, the avoidance of bullying and injury to others and being helpful. These are part of the discipline required for proper social conduct. Discipline then is an integral component of becoming educated.

Discipline can be manifested in a number of ways. It can be self-imposed, imposed by an external authority, or by the recognition that a particular way of behaving brings more benefits than doing otherwise. Self-discipline reflects courage, facilitates learning and helps to develop desirable dispositions of mind. Where discipline is imposed, authority is exercised to produce conformity, irrespective of the desires of the individual involved. Rewards and sanctions are a significant factor here. However, externally imposed discipline produces a psychological feeling of being abused and raises questions about the dignity and integrity of the individual. Self-discipline reflects an understanding of the reason why of things and a commitment to follow rules for the realisation of particular goals.

Punishment for Misbehaviour

Punishment on the other hand produces certain psychological reactions. *Hamm (1989)* states that issues involving punishment refer to its use in justifying particular actions in the context of education. In this context punishment is seen as ameliorative, bringing about a restoration of order and conformity arising from a situation of disorder, whereby the infractions are of such that the mere enforcement of rules cannot adequately deal with a situation which requires more drastic measures to restore credibility to the status quo and to the values adhered to by the organisation. *Hamm* argues that punishment can be regarded as the infliction of pain or unpleasantness by an authority on an offender for a breach of a social rule. He does not regard keeping back children after normal school hours as punishment but insists that the latter is manifested by the infliction of pain or unpleasantness. This is extreme, even sadistic, for any teacher can use psychological methods of bringing behaviour back to acceptable standards. He or she could use reasoning and appeal to the child's understanding and self respect, which creates awareness of wrong doing, and as a result repentance. Educators need to become more humane in the methods they use with children since the aim should be to create good human beings with a reverence and respect for truth, justice, empathy and fairness. Educators therefore need to create a classroom climate where acts of indiscipline are anathema to the kind of environment they would like to prevail in educational settings. After all, education is about producing intelligent, rational beings with a deep sense of morality. Many acts of indiscipline occur precisely because this climate is either lacking, or the will to enforce it is weak.

What is needed therefore, is the development of a philosophical conception of the moral school that would persistently advocate virtues such as deferring to each other, self-respect and respect for others, listening carefully to others to avoid misinterpretation and misunderstanding and being sensitive to the diversity that exists among each other in terms of taste, perception, preferences and choices. Furthermore, when students themselves are involved in a contract with their schools and become active partners in producing the required guidelines, rules and regulations for the effective running of their institutions and when a proper counselling service exists that cares about the interests of students, thoughts of such concepts as discipline and punishment will no longer be necessary, since behaving appropriately will not only be the norm but in a wider sense will be the natural way to operate. Education is therefore central to developing these attributes and dispositions which create humane individuals with an ethic of altruism in their interactions with each other and the society at large. This requires new and positive thinking from educators about the nature of man, his purpose and his role in society, as well as the consideration of the fundamental philosophical questions such as, What is the good life? How can we live amicably with each other? and What kind of society do we want? All these are central to the kind and quality of education needed to produce the kind of individual and social climate necessary which would regard moral and ethical conduct as a normal way of behaving and operating.

The philosopher R. S. Peters (1966) seems to share the views of Hamm (1989) concerning discipline and punishment, the former concept involving submission to rules, or some kind of order and the latter being appropriate where there is a breach of rules and concerns the intentional infliction of pain, or something unpleasant on someone by an authority. I have earlier expressed my objections to this view of the concepts and believe that the position taken by Hamm and Peters is misconceived. They seem to have a preference for authoritarian methods, which in my view exacerbates, rather than effectively transform the situation to be dealt with and leaves the individual feeling demeaned, in a situation where redemption should be the objective. In the context of the school therefore, to view punishment as retribution as Peters did, is to see the school as a penal institution, rather than one that educates. The moral school is therefore the answer to educators with an authoritarian mindset, who are bent on extreme actions which aggravate the situation and convert the individual into someone who becomes vindictive and revengeful. The moral school seeks to impart dispositions such as co-operation, compassion, love, caring non-hostility and reverence for humanity. These values make unnecessary and superfluous any talk about discipline or punishment. The ultimate dilemma that faces Caribbean schools is what strategies can be used to transform the current autocratic climate that pervades the schools, into one that is student friendly and which sees students not as objects to be manipulated but as real human beings with important needs which a quality education has the obligation to deliver, producing citizens who are autonomous, creative and self-disciplined. The moral school therefore seems to be the ultimate antidote for both indiscipline and punishment.

Discipline and Student Control in School

Discipline connotes orderliness and orderliness is essential for teaching and learning in the school. A disciplined person is orderly, responsible, diligent, sympathetic, cooperative, honest, considerate and always tries to do what is right and good according to Jones and Jones (1998). Very often problems of absenteeism, tardiness, vandalism and poor school performance, border on school discipline. Student discipline means that students are provided with an opportunity to exercise self control, to learn and to promote the welfare of the school. Teachers should set examples of self-control and internal discipline for their classes and in the school.

School rules and regulations have to be made to guide students' conduct because where there are no proper rules and regulations, there is always chaos and confusion. School rules are meant to provide a framework of responsibility for the students. School authorities must however note that very rigid school rules and regulations are looked upon as a threat to students' freedom and can easily give rise to student strikes and riots which are typical results of taking away more freedom from students than is justified. Rewards and penalties should be used to support obedience to school rules and regulations. When students behave responsibly, the school should support and encourage this kind of attitude through social recognition and approval. But students who breach school rules and regulations should be subjected to certain penalties including expression of disapproval for that type of behaviour. School authorities should at all times encourage students to cultivate habits of self-discipline rather than use punitive measures to control their behaviours in the school.

There are some general rules about school discipline. The first rule is that both teachers and students should recognise the purposes of school rules and regulations and it is only when they recognise these that they will try to uphold and defend these rules and regulations. School authorities should make rules which put more emphasis on self-discipline. Teachers should then support these rules by setting good examples of disciplined behaviour for the students to follow. Teachers can do this by displaying courtesy, consideration, respect, honesty, punctuality and good speech in their dealings with students and other members of the school community. Students on the other hand, should expect fair punishment for breaching school rules. Punishments for breaching school rules should always be in line with the Ministry of Education and School Board's guidelines.

Teachers and students and the school management, should cooperate in planning, maintaining and revising school rules. This is important because students are more likely to conform to school rules that they have participated in formulating. Effective school communication among students, teachers and school management is very essential for good school discipline. One way of promoting good school discipline, is to keep open at all times, all channels of communication between students and teachers and the school administration.

School management and teachers can do a lot in minimising the problem of indiscipline in the school. The primary purpose of punishment is to create a self-disciplined personality and therefore punishment should be educative in nature and should be based on principles that are considered helpful to the student's overall development. Punishment should be given according to established school guidelines and in fact only when it is right and just to do so. Punishment given for the breach of a school rule should be equal to the offence committed. Administering excessive punishment for any offence is not supported by any school law and therefore teachers should be very careful when administering punishments. It is also important to treat students' problems without delay, in fact as soon as they arise, this is because justice delayed is as good as justice denied.

Some Disadvantages of School Punishment

Punishment for school misbehaviours has many serious problems. One problem is that punishment does not teach the student alternative methods of behaving or what to do to prevent the occurrence of a similar problem in the future. *Jones and Jones* (1998) argued that because schools are educational institutions, it seems contradictory that students who have difficulty in their behaviours should be punished rather than receive instructions on how to behave better in the future. *Englander (1986)* pointed out that punishment appears to inhibit learning. Kounin and Gump (1981) conducted a study involving first grade teachers who differed in their use of punitive behaviour with students. The finding indicated that the students of the more punitive teachers, expressed less value in learning, were more aggressive and were more confused about behavioural problems in school. Other studies carried out by Mortimore and Sammons (1987) suggested that schools in which students learn more effectively are characterised by high rates of positive reinforcement and also by somewhat lower rates of punishment. Nash (1963) in his study of corporal punishment in British schools, noted that the schools where corporal punishment was absent had the best records of behaviour and that behaviour deteriorates and delinquency increases as corporal punishment increases.

The impact of punitive responses to student misbehaviour in school was reported by Becker and Thomas (1975). These researchers found that, when teachers were asked to increase their use of punitive control methods of responding to disruptive student behaviour, misbehaviour in the class actually increased. Punishment makes the student to project blames rather than to accept responsibility for his behaviour. Punishments also make students angry and to blame all persons associated with that punishment rather than accepting responsibility for their mistakes. Glasser (1988) argued that 95 percent of all student discipline problems in schools are caused by students' lack of power and that misbehaviour is an attempt to gain some sense of power. Jones and Jones (1998) pointed out that using such activities as writing sentences, assigning additional home work and lowering of student's grade as punishment may create a negative attitude regarding these activities. Teachers should therefore avoid using these learning activities as punishment.

Methods for Responding to Disruptive Student Behaviour in School

Student's misbehaviour often occurs when students are bored or when they find the learning activities uninteresting, or when teachers use ineffective methods to manage the classrooms. Also, some teachers lack the ability to deal with even minor classroom disruptions. The traditional methods of dealing with students' disruptions such as use of threats, physical punishments such as caining and beating and loss of privileges are being discouraged. Rather, teachers are encouraged to respond to students' disruptive behaviours with dialogue, problem solving techniques and conflict resolution methods. Reverting to the old confrontational methods when resolving students' disruptions may serve to escalate students emotions and this is counter productive. The following are some techniques which can be used to respond to students' disruptions in the school.

Teachers should keep close watch over the classroom and the students activities at all times. They are supposed to walk around the class from time to time in order to identify the problems that arise from students activities and relationships. In this way, the teacher will be able to deal with the disruptive behaviours of students. The seats in the classrooms should be arranged in such a way that the teacher can see and easily move near to all students, without causing disruption. Very often, angry teachers shout on top of their voices even for very minor disruptions and this may create tension among the students. Whenever possible, teachers should ignore minor disruptions such as dropping a maths set or a book on the floor. This can be dealt with by discussing the issue with students either privately or during a class meeting, if many of them are involved in such kind of disturbance.

The tension created by an angry teacher in responding to minor classroom disruptions, can help in increasing students' disobedience to classroom rules and regulations. Brophy and Evertson (1976) studied the negative effects associated with teachers harsh reactions to classroom disruptions and found that rather than improving students' behaviour, students tend to become more anxious and disruptive. They concluded that teacher's firmness in the classroom should be associated with teacher warmth and politeness.

The first step in responding to student's disruptions is to make contact quietly with the student. This can be done with a glance, by moving close to the student, by touching the student on the shoulder or by asking the student to respond to that disruption. Remind students of the classroom rules and procedures from time to time. When one or two students are being extremely disruptive, the teacher should try to focus the other students' attention on their task and later talk privately with the disruptive students. Teachers should try to provide students with choices when they are upset. Instead of using harsh words to talk to them when they are upset, it may be better to talk to them politely about their disruptive behaviours.

Conclusion

Teachers have control over many factors that influence students' achievement and behaviour in the school. Many students' misbehaviours in school are a kind of reaction to school rules and regulations. Clear disciplinary standards that are firm, fair and consistent will have positive influence on students' behaviour. School authorities should use a caring attitude to enhance positive students' behaviour. Both teachers and parents should understand that students' condition of health can affect their learning and behaviour. Students with poor mental health or those with emotional problems will find learning difficult and may not be able to concentrate in school work. Students may have serious problems such as use of drugs, early pregnancy and delinquency and these problems are likely to have negative effects on their learning and behaviour in the school. Teachers very often blame parents for their children's misbehaviour in the school. Some parents on the other hand, sometimes feel that the school is not doing all it is supposed to do, to help the students to learn and behave well. Both teachers and parents must work together in helping students to achieve their goals in the school.

References

Becker, W & Thomas, D. (1975) Teaching: Classroom Management: Illinois: The Research Press Ltd.

Brophy, J. and Evertson, C. (1976) Learning from Teaching: A Developmental Perspective. Boston: Allyn and Bacon.

Englander, M. (1986) Control Theory in the Classroom. New York: Harper and Row.

Good, T. and Brophy, J. (1996) Looking in Classroom. (7th. Edition) New York: Harper and Row.

Hamm, C.M. (1989) Philosophical Issues in Education An Introduction. New Jersey: Falmer Press.

Jones, V.F. and Jones, L.S. (1998) Comprehensive Classroom Management. Boston and London: Allyn and Bacon.

Mortimore, P. and Sammons, P. (1987) New Evidence on Effective Elementary Schools. Journal of Educational Leadership No. 45, pp. 4 - 8.

Kounin, J. and Gump, P. (1961) The Comparative Influence of Punitive and Non Punitive Teachers Upon Children's Concept of School Misconduct. Journal of Educational Psychology No. 50 pp. 44 - 49.

Nash, J. (1963) Corporal Punishment in British Schools. London: The Open University Press Ltd.

Peters, R.S. (1966) Ethics and Education. New York: Allen and Unwin.

CHAPTER 13
Teachers and Stress Management in Schools

AUSTIN EZENNE AND OLGA JAMES REID

Abstract

Caribbean teachers experience a lot of stress in the classroom and the school. Stressful situations can be detrimental to the physical, emotional, and mental health of the individual teacher and this can affect adversely the teacher's performance on the job. The frustration caused by stress and distress make teachers disenchanted with teaching.

Sources of occupational stresses and their harmful effects have been identified. Many techniques have been suggested for monitoring and decreasing levels of stress among teachers in educational organisations.

Introduction

In recent times, educational organisations are paying greater attention to the effects of stress on their staff. Many teachers are not happy with their teaching jobs because students no longer behave well and many of them are not interested in learning and these have negative impact on the teachers' morale in the school. Many teachers maintain that the teaching job is wearing them out, especially now that they can no longer count on the success, respect and dignity that once came with teaching. Teachers argue that the students are increasingly difficult to motivate to learn and to control because students have a lot of other interests outside the school.

Many students in our schools lack a cohesive family structure, and are less responsive to adult authority and can easily become confrontational to the teacher and the school authorities. This confrontational posture of many students in recent times causes stress to teachers and to school administrators. Cruickshank and Callahan (1983) conducted studies to determine what teachers see as their main professional problems in the school. They found that teachers everywhere have five unfulfilled goals such as; the need to establish and maintain positive relationships with students and colleagues, the need to have students to behave properly that is to say, to be quiet, orderly and courteous in the school. Others are, the desire to have mutually supportive relationships with students' parents, student success in school and the time to accomplish necessary personal and professional tasks. Each unfulfilled goal brings stress and distress to teachers and these grow as teachers find themselves unable to deal with those conditions adequately.

The Meaning of Stress

Stress can be described according to Cole (1997) as the adverse psychological and physical reactions that occur in an individual as a result of his being unable to cope with the demands being made on him by his work and the organisation. Stress refers also to the bodily changes that can take place when the external pressures on an individual reach an intolerable dimension causing weakened job performance and ill-health. The level of stress depends on several factors, such as the individual's personality and perceptions of his or her ability to cope with the external pressures. Many teachers cope with a variety of pressure in their working life, and some even seem to thrive on pressure at work, but many other teachers fail to deal with pressure from work or from social life and then symptoms of stress appear.

Symptoms of stress are many and they include; anxiety, frustration, fear, indigestion, nausea, headaches, back pains, loss of appetite, loss of sleep and increased irritability. Other more serious symptoms include; coronary hear disease, stomach ulcers, depressions, and other serious conditions arising from work, domestic, social or political situations. Other life events which can lead to stress include: death of spouse, divorce, death of loved ones or close relative, personal injury or illness, marriage problems, loss of job, retirement, change in financial status or state and so on.

Many researchers believe that stress is a personal reaction to pressure. It depends on the individuals perception and the scale of the problem and the individuals ability to cope with it. If the individual believes that he can handle the situation, the stress symptom may not appear, but where the individual feels that he cannot cope with the problem, then the symptoms of stress occur. Some individuals however bring their problems with them to work, but the effect on individuals whether at work or in social life is that performance is affected adversely. Whatever the cause is, stress leads to reduced employee performance, lack of motivation and increased absenteeism from the work place.

Miller (1979) argued that a moderate stress is essential for the achievement of organisational tasks because if one is totally satisfied and free of stress, one would have little motivation to do anything. Avoidance of stress is not the answer to the problem. Rather a productive life needs appropriate levels of dissatisfaction and stress or tension to make us do the job. The climate in many schools today has created a lot of stress, and excessive stress burdens teachers and school administrators with fatigue, headaches and indigestion. Educators under tension generated by the demands of today's classrooms and schools find it difficult to accomplish tasks in a way that meets their own personal standards.

Factors and Sources of Stress

Many key factors in the work situation according to Cole (1997) can influence the level of stress that may be experienced by the individual. These factors include external environment, the nature of the individual's job, the organisation's structure and culture, the quality of personal relationships in the workplace, the impact of the individual's domestic situation as well as such personal factors as the individual's personality type and the nature of their motivation.

The schools for example are affected by frequent changes in staff and students positions and teachers who are not happy with constant changes are likely to become stressed. The teacher's position in the job hierarchy, individual autonomy on the job, long hours of work, and unsupportive team leaders and sectional heads can be sources of stress to many teachers in the school. Very often too much may be expected from the individual's work in the organisation and this high expectation can be a potential cause of stress for the workers. The quality of work relationships with one's superior, colleagues and subordinates can influence the level of stress at work. If a staff member has good work relationships with the people he is working with, the level of his stress will be normal but if he has poor relationship with his co-workers or management, the level of his stress will be high. Also harassment of staff members is a frequent cause of stress at work in the organisation. The ability of the individual to cope adequately with pressures from everyday life is greatly influenced by personal attributes such as temperament, talents and other factors in the home and work environments.

SOCIETAL SOURCES OF STRESS AND PREVENTION

Stringent funding for education and annual cut backs for educational services reinforce teachers poor image in the society and also add to their stress. A poor public image of teachers and educators is a major source of teacher stress according to (Iwanicki, 1983). Inadequate teacher salaries, lack of promotion prospects and lack of adequate work materials, create social and economic barriers for teachers and can undermine teachers' job effectiveness and job satisfaction and these can easily cause stress among teachers. Many teachers feel compelled to remain in a school system because the employment prospects are slim elsewhere, and therefore they feel compelled to remain in their schools. Many teachers believe that job assignments are used to reward those teachers who support the system and penalize those who do not. Because of this, job assignments can be used to create pressures among teachers in the school.

What teachers can do, to reduce stress arising from societal sources was suggested by Truch (1980), as seeking to improve their teaching skills so that they can withstand teacher burnout. Teachers should also learn to be open minded and should be able to share their feelings with colleagues and students. Teachers should also work towards expanding their professional growth. These practices according to Froyen and Iverson (1999) will contribute to a sense of self assurance and fulfilment. Self-assured and fulfilled teachers will be able to withstand insults in school and will be sufficiently secure to examine the merits of any criticisms and to respond to good suggestions for change.

ORGANISATION SOURCES OF STRESS AND REMEDIES

A number of researchers have investigated organisational based stress by looking at the relationship between personnel and their work environment. Milstein, Golaszweski, and Duquette (1984) identified five environmental categories that exist within any organisations, as Relationships at work, Organisational structure and climate, Factors intrinsic to the job, Roles in the organisation and Career development. These categories are used to describe and examine the stress inducers in the work environment of teachers and the negative effects of these stressful conditions.

Teachers are regarded as very busy workers. Apart from classroom instructions, teachers are always engaged in supervision and monitoring of students and their activities in the classroom and in the school. Teachers carry out low-level management functions such as taking attendance, reading out announcements, collecting fees, attending to visitors who visit their classes and communicating with the school administrator and parents. These responsibilities create tension for teachers and at times cause stress.

STRESS FOR ORGANISATIONAL STRUCTURE AND CLIMATE

Teachers frequently complain about the autocratic and bureaucratic structure of the school system where school administrators very often distrust the motives of teachers even for asking for their rights in the school. Some of these autocratic school administrators do not consult teachers even for important aspects of the teachers work before taking decisions on them.

Many principals devote more of their time in supervision and evaluating school activities, classroom visits and administration of the physical structures of the school. The supervision and evaluation of these activities usually create new tension among teachers about the criteria for judging good teaching, the evidence of effective teaching, and the qualifications of principals to make these judgements. Teachers often feel that they have little to say about the procedural matters associated with the evaluation process and the use of the results, and these become a source of anxiety among teachers any time the evaluation process is taking place.

FACTORS INTRINSIC TO THE JOB

Teacher's daily works in the school are usually accompanied by deadlines and this contributes to pressure and stress for teachers. Raschke, Dedrick, Strathe, and Hawkes (1985) observed that teachers spend most of the day performing instructional and allied duties and may also work in the evenings, at night and on weekends to check the effectiveness of their teaching and how to provide corrective feedback to students. The pressure to disseminate more and more information and to assist students during independent study, eliminate the use of class time to read homework and assignments. Preparations for the next day's lessons must also be done outside of school hours. The quantity of work and lack of the time to do it, create pressures that even a good and efficient teacher find burdensome.

STRESS AND TEACHERS' ROLE IN THE ORGANISATION

Teachers have the problem of developing challenging and creative instructional programmes and materials for their students, devising suitable ways to work with students with special needs, trying to establish positive relationships with co-workers and parents. Without the time and support to engage in these activities, teachers lose their interest in teaching. Froyen and Inverson (1999) pointed out that at times teachers may lose a sense of proportion and can become short-tempered and lash out at students for even minor disturbance in the classroom. Students noting the disproportionate response, attribute the problem to the teacher's personality and then respond to that by being less cooperative. Students' lack of cooperation becomes distressing to the teacher and may lead to tension and distress.

Reducing Organisational and Role-Related Stresses Among Teachers

Many stresses in the school organisation are from internal sources, that is from the school itself. One way of reducing stress is for the teacher to take active part in what is happening in the school. It is necessary to create a healthy work organisation and environment. This type of work environment can exist when individuals or staff members have an opportunity to influence and control their work situations. This gives them a feeling of the sense of belonging to their work groups and also help to satisfy their needs for self-esteem. Teachers must always strive to remove the bureaucratic barriers that usually block responsible expression of teachers' professional interests and talents in the school.

Dealing with role-related stress is crucial to the mental health of teachers and those with whom they work, according to Gold (1988). The choice of techniques will depend on the source of the stress, the specific ways in which the stress is experienced, and the personality of the role incumbent. Teachers and the school administrators will have different impacts if they are told that their instructional materials and supplies budget will be drastically cut. The impact may be more on the teachers who use these instructional materials for teaching in the classroom than for the school administrator whose job is just to allocate the materials to the teachers for their use. Also teachers who have large number of students in their classes will have a lot of strain in selecting suitable methods and materials for instructions.

Teachers should stop being narrow-minded in their areas of authority, but they should begin to respect and encourage diversity in whatever they are doing in the school and in the classroom, and these are likely to encourage a shared responsibility for the educational enterprise as a whole.

At times teachers appear to have little confidence in themselves and their abilities to take up certain responsibilities in the school. What we think of ourselves has a great deal of influence on how we behave and therefore teachers must try to project their self image and drop faulty perceptions that undermine their sense of self confidence and well-being which eventually contribute to distress in their work places. According to Ellis (1973), such maladaptive thinking patterns can be overcome with positive self-talk of themselves. This approach is consistent with the findings of Beck (1970), who concluded that people suffering from severe stress could be characterised by faulty beliefs that they expressed about themselves.

Teachers can reduce the distress associated with negative self-talk by being sensitive to the ways that faulty beliefs distort self-perceptions and should try to replace negative thought patterns with self confidence in their activities in the school. Good communication is another useful means of reducing stress in the organisation. To a great extend, teaching depends on good relationships and strong interpersonal communication skills and this is because individuals who possess supportive communication skills can derive as well as provide, greater satisfaction from human relationships especially in organisational settings.

Conclusion

A lot can be done to make teachers' professional life better than it is now, despite the increasing number of stressful conditions with which teachers must contend with. It is better for the educational systems to make teachers hardworking by providing most of their needs, than have them stressed out by the stressful conditions of the school and the classroom. Teachers should be encouraged to do their work well and their judgement concerning how to teach and how to maintain effective discipline in classroom must be trusted and respected. Teachers should however undertake to improve their lots themselves and should take charge of all matters that affected them. They can relieve most of their stress by prioritizing their activities in the school, employing their time management skills, communicating adequately with parents and taking time off from their routine tasks. Teachers should undertake programmes that prevent the physical consequences of stress. Planned relaxation on a regular basis can be used to control stress and physical exercise programmes can be used to facilitate good health and a sense of well-being. Regular exercises and sound nutrition are the main aspects of a good health plan. Reduced stress among teachers will lead to more enjoyable relationships with colleagues and students and to a greater commitment to the teaching job in the school.

References

Beck, A. (1970) Cognitive Therapy: Nature and Relations to Behaviour Therapy. Behaviour Therapy, 1, 184-200

Charles, C.M. and Senter, G.W. (1995) Elementary Classroom Management. 2nd Edition. New York: Longman

Cole, G.A. (1997) Personnel Management. Fourth Edition. London: Ashford Colour Press

Cruickshank, D. and Callahan, R. (1983) The Other Side of the Desk: Stages and Problems of Teacher Development. Elementary School Journal, No. 83, p. 251-258

Ellis, A. (1973) Humanistic Psychotherapy: The Rational Emotive Approach. New York. Julian Press

Froyen, L.A. and Iverson, A.M. (1999) Schoolwide and Classroom Management. The Reflective Educator-Leader. Third Edition. New Jersey: Prentice Hall and Merrill

Gold, Y. (1988) Recognising and Coping with Academic Burnout. Contemporary Education 59 (3), 142-145

Iwanicki, E.F. (1983) Towards Understanding and Alleviating Teacher Burnout. Theory into Practice, 22 (1), 27-32

Jones, V.F., and Jones, L.S. (1998) Comprehensive Classroom Management. 5th Edition, Boston and London: Allyn and Bacon

Miller, C. (1979) Dealing with Stress: A Challenge for Educators. Bloomington: Phi Delta Kappa Press

Milstein, M.M., Golaszewski, T.J., and Duquette, R.D., (1984) Organisationally Based Stress: What Bothers Teachers. Journal of Educational Research, 77 (5), 293-297

Raschke, D.B., Dedrick, C.V., Strathe, M.I., and Hawkes, R.R. (1985) Teacher Stress: The Elementary Teacher's Perspective. The Elementary School Journal, 85 (4), 559-564

Truch, S. (1980) Teacher Burnout and What to do About it. Novato: Academic Therapy Publications.

CHAPTER 14
The Role of Educational Foundations in Teacher Education

OLIVER MILLS AND AUSTIN EZENNE

Abstract

Educational Foundations as a discipline is a very crucial component of all Teacher Education Programmes. The Teacher Education programme in the Teachers Colleges and the Universities, consists of three main parts, the Teaching subject(s), the Foundation courses and the Teaching Practice. The Foundation discipline is at times neglected by many educators and students. Other problems that face the Foundation discipline include that of conceptual definition of what it is all about, the problem of determining its scope and content as well as the problem of evaluating the contents of the discipline.

We are all witnesses to the unprecedented expansion of the educational systems in Jamaica, and the Caribbean region in the last two decades. There is an increasing demand for places at all levels of the educational systems due to a rapid increase in the number of students at the various levels of education in the region. That being the case, there is dire need for more functional teacher education curricular, which should be used to produce better qualified teachers for the educational systems. No education system can rise above the level of its teachers, therefore there is need to improve the quality of the teachers engaged in the teacher education programmes. Also the value of education to the individual and the society is determined by the teachers. Therefore it is important to secure a sufficient supply of the right kind of people to the teaching profession and ensure to them a status and esteem commensurate with the importance and responsibility of their work.

The Meaning and Scope of Educational Foundations

We can use an analogical method to explain the meaning of Educational Foundations. The word *"foundation"* in architecture is a crucial sub-structure on which a visible and beautiful super structure is erected as argued by Akinpelu (1988). The beautiful super-structure cannot stand without the sub-structure known as the foundation. The super structure is usually beautiful and it stands on the foundation or the sub structure which is below the ground. A damage or crack in the foundation of a building is usually a serious damage because it will sooner or later show in the beautiful super-structure which is above the ground.

This means that if a foundation of a teacher education programme is weak or has a crack, then the teacher education programmes and the teachers produced may be of low quality and may have adverse effect on the teacher quality and performance and this will in turn adversely affect the entire educational system.

The Foundation discipline occupies a similar analogous position in Teacher Education of every nation. The discipline is very often neglected and hardly appreciated and yet it is very important in all teacher education programmes.

THE EDUCATION AND TRAINING OF TEACHERS CONSISTS OF THREE PARTS

1. The teaching subjects such as the traditional academic disciplines for example, Mathematics, Physics, Chemistry, Biology, History, Geography and so on.

2. Then there is the second leg known as the Teaching Practice or Practical Teaching which consists of special methods of teaching the above mentioned subject disciplines in the schools.

3. The third leg is the Educational Foundation discipline which refers to the theoretical and professional study of education as a discipline. Conant (1963) pointed out that Educational Foundations form the third leg of a tripod stand on which education rests in all nations.

It follows that the Foundations occupy an important position in teacher education programmes and therefore we cannot afford to ignore its crucial position in the scheme of training of teachers. One problem facing Educational Foundation is that it is always criticised by teachers and students as being abstract, theoretical, lacking in depth and academic rigor more than the other subject disciplines stated above.

The Components of the Foundation Discipline

The Foundation Discipline consists of the theoretical aspect of education as a professional discipline according to Ezenne (1988) and it includes the following subject areas: History of Education, Philosophy of Education, Sociology of Education, Psychology of Education, Educational Administration, Guidance and Counselling, Curriculum and Instructions, Measurement and Evaluation, Educational Research, Educational Technology, Comparative Education, Economics of Education and Politics of Education. The above subject areas, form the core courses in teacher education programmes. Holders of B.A. (Ed), B.Sc. (Ed), B.Ed and Diploma in Education are regarded as well-trained teachers because they have studied most of these core courses in the Foundation Discipline. The goals and targets of the Foundation Courses in the preparation of well qualified teachers who are the prime-movers of the educational systems are many.

The Goals of Educational Foundation

The main goals and purposes of Educational Foundation in the preparation of well qualified teachers who are the prime movers of the educational systems are as follows:
1. to help the teacher to understand the history, sociology and philosophy of education.
2. to help the teacher to understand the problem of teaching and learning in the school.
3. to give the teacher an insight into the learning processes and teaching methods that can be used for the various subject matters taught in the school.
4. to help the teacher in understanding the academic abilities of his students and in deciding who he should offer extra help in the classroom.
5. to help the teacher in selecting appropriate teaching materials for his lessons.
6. to help the teacher in setting and marking examinations objectively.
7. to help the teacher in handling the problem of indiscipline among students in the school.
8. to help the teacher in grouping his students and in making other important decisions that would help the student, the school and the stakeholders.
9. to help the teacher in curriculum planning and development.
10. to help the teacher in guiding the students in their career choices.
11. to help the teacher in the understanding of research and statistics related to education.

These goals are very crucial in the training of teachers for the various nations. The extent to which public education succeeds in delivering services with an efficient use of scarce resources depends largely upon the quality of teachers engaged in the educational process.

Philosophy of Education as a Critical Area in Teacher Education

One of the foundation areas that is critical to teacher education in the Caribbean, but which has been neglected to a great extent, is philosophy of education. Until quite recently, philosophy of education has been approached not as a critical, analytical area of study but as an aspect of the history of educational ideas. What has compounded the problem of teaching philosophy of education is that those who delivered the subject were not really trained in the techniques, strategies and content of philosophy of education as a discipline. These educators were exposed to pure philosophy in a general way and sought feebly to apply it to educational issues. The result of this was that educational issues and problems were approached in an abstract way, using symbolic logic, rather than the Socratic method which seeks to rigorously interrogate and have students of teacher education justify using rational, logical arguments to justify the various positions taken.

It is only recently that the nature and objectives of the subject have been clarified and understood as an area of study in its own right. White (1999) has taken up this point recently when he said that conferences dealing with philosophy of education should have educational issues and problems at the centre of professional discourse. He added that pure philosophers should not attend these conferences, since they merely try to relate their discipline to educational issues. He suggested that pure philosophers should attend conferences on general philosophy, rather than those dealing with education, because philosophy of education has a concrete reference point which is education, while pure or general philosophy is without any such anchorage. As a matter of fact there is still a debate going on concerning what is the subject matter of philosophy.

It can therefore be said that philosophy of education as a critical element of teacher education has come of age in the Caribbean. At the University of the West Indies, Jamaica, it is now offered as a course at the post-graduate level and its importance to teacher education has been recognised for a number of reasons.

The Value of Philosophy of Education in Teacher Education

Philosophy of education is important to teacher education for the following reasons:

1. It is concerned with the ways in which we can reconceptualise commonly accepted approaches in teaching and educating;
2. It analyses and clarifies ideas, issues and concepts in order to promote understanding and provides a range of alternatives;
3. Philosophy of Education helps in the study of the ways in which teachers can determine the weakness and strengths of their current understanding of educational policies;
4. It encourages the teacher to foster an open mind about educational issues and problems;
5. Philosophy of Education enhances the teacher's ability to influence new directions in education, since by engaging in theoretical discussions of educational issues, they develop the capacity to formulate alternative courses of action;
6. It engenders interpretative and critical perspectives on educational practice and develops an awareness of and sensitivity to ethical issues and dilemmas;
7. It assists in combating dogmatic and conservative views on educational matters and enhances teachers' confidence once they become aware of the theoretical basis of their activities;
8. Philosophy of education generates intellectual curiosity in teachers which better enables them to stimulate the intellectual interests and development of students. The quality of the teacher's effort and role is therefore enhanced;
9. Teachers will also encounter philosophy of education as a disciplined discourse which recognises the problematic, ambiguous, tentative and uncertain nature of human action and understanding in educating, teaching and learning;
10. Philosophy of education fosters an understanding and realisation in teachers that educational conversations continue across the generations and are affected by the presuppositions made about the nature of language, the human person, the organisation of society, views on morality, human values, authority, epistemology, and about being and becoming.

In a wholistic way, therefore, philosophy of education deals with the entire gamut of knowledge and subject areas, including those specifically concerned with the foundations of education. It unearths the latent meanings of sociology, psychology and history and provides critical perspectives on educational administration, curricula issues, research, the economics of education and educational technology. It is also educational politics in action and in essence creates and gives legitimacy to current and emerging epistemologies related to the educational enterprise. A study of the philosophy of education in teacher education, is therefore a study of human beings and the efforts they have made, are making and will continue to make to construct a society that is good and just.

Conclusion

Teachers and their training are crucial factors in the educational development of all nations. This being the case, teachers must understand the philosophy and goals of education. The educational foundation courses aim at giving teachers adequate preparation for their historic mission, that of inculcating in the young people, desirable attitudes for effective living in their societies. The most difficult problem however, lies in the adjustment of the educational systems to suit the changing needs of the Caribbean nations. This can be achieved by training high quality teachers well grounded in philosophy and foundations of education. This will help to strengthen the teacher education programmes at the various levels and the educational systems of the various Caribbean nations.

References

Akinpelu, J.A. (1988) The Problem of the Foundations. A Key Note Address. Proceedings of the Inaugural Conference of Educational Foundations Association of Nigeria. Jos: The University of Jos. Nigeria.

Conant, J.B. (1963) The Education of American Teachers, New York: McGraw Hill Book Company.

Ezenne, A. N. (1988) Improving the Quality and Techniques of Teaching Educational Foundations in Colleges of Education in Nigeria. A Paper presented at the National Conference for Teacher Educators. Kaduna: The Polytechnic, Kaduna, Nigeria.

Hare, W. and Portelli, J. (1988) Philosophy of Education. Introductory Reading, Boston: Detselic Enterprises Ltd.

Hugo, McCann and Yaxley, Bevis (1992) Retaining the Philosophy of Education in Teacher Education. Journal of Educational Philosophy and Theory. Vol. 24, No. 1, 1992.

Kleing, John (1982) Philosophical Issues in Education. London: Groom Helm

Kohli, Wendy (1995) Critical Conversations in Philosophy of Education. New Jersey: Routledge Publishers.

Muir, J.R. (1996) The Evolution of Philosophy Within Educational Studies. Journal of Educational Philosophy and Theory. Vol. 28, No. 2, 1996.

Walker, J.C. (1996) Towards a Contemporary Philosophy of Professional Education. Journal of Educational Philosophy and Theory. Vol. 28, No. 1, 1996.

White, John (1999) Philosophy and Education. Keynote address to the Philosophy of Education Society of Great Britain. London: University of London.

Models of Leadership Behaviour for Educational Organizations

CHAPTER 15

AUSTIN EZENNE

Abstract

This article describes styles of educational leadership that are practised in educational organisations within the Caribbean. After reading this article on leadership you should be able to:
1. Describe the meaning and nature of leadership.
2. Identify the limitations of the traditional leadership model.
3. Understand the dimensions of Getzels and Guba's leadership model.
4. Discuss the initiating structure and consideration dimensions of leadership behaviour.
5. Explain why no one leadership model is ideal in all situations.

The Meaning of a Leader and Leadership

A leader is that person who has the task of directing and coordinating tasks relevant to a group in an organization. A leader is an official office holder or a head of an institution in an organization. The leader is voluntarily granted considerable power and authority by members of the group or the followers, and they accept the leaders influence and direction by shared agreement. Leaders usually establish directions by developing visions for the future in an organization. They communicate these visions to their followers and then inspire them to work to achieve the goals of the organization. Leaders are people who have tasks to perform and also have the ability to get others to cooperate with them in doing the work.

There are many definitions of leadership and these definitions involve an influencing process on the followers. According to Musaazi (1986) leadership is concerned with the implementation of policies and decisions which assist in directing the activities of an organization towards its specified goals. Leadership is a process of influencing the activities and behaviours of an individual or a group towards goal achievement in an organization. Rebore (1988) defined leadership as a process of influencing people to achieve desired objectives and it must take place within the context of a group. Leadership is the ability to influence a group towards the achievement of goals and this influence can be formal, that is, it is provided by the possession of a managerial rank in an organization. A person may assume a leadership role because of his position or rank in the organization. But not all leaders are managers nor are all managers leaders according to Robbins (1998). In other words, leaders can emerge from within a group as well as by formal appointment to lead a group.

The study of leadership behaviour in organizations is important because it deals with the organization and its tasks, the roles the individuals and groups have to take in order to achieve the goals of the organizations. The study of leadership is best done by looking at what makes an effective leader, identifying the personality characteristics which leaders have and by considering the leadership behaviours of leaders in organizations. There are three traditional models of leaderships:

Traditional Leadership Models

There are three types of traditional leadership styles usually associated with educational organizations. These are the Authoritarian or Autocratic leadership style, the Democratic and the Laissez-faire leadership styles. We now look at the various models closely.

THE AUTHORITARIAN OR AUTOCRATIC LEADER STYLE

The authoritarian leadership style refers to situations when a leader issues close instructions to his subordinates and makes most of the decisions by himself. The leader alone determines policies and assigns tasks to subordinates without consulting with them. The leader relies very much on the rules and the regulations of the institution, and over emphasizes goal achievement. This style reduces independence among the staff members because it does not encourage development of initiative. Coercive approach which may be in the form of use of punishment is used to make people to obey the rules and regulations and to work for the organization.

Considerable tension is usually generated with this model between the leader and his subordinates and also among the subordinates. As a result of this, some members of the organization may become passive and uninvolved in many activities of the organization. On the other hand, an autocratic leadership may lead to high productivity especially when used in situations when quick actions are needed to achieve a goal. In educational organizations, some school heads still prefer to dictate to their staff members instead of involving them in discussion and decision making on the activities of the institution.

THE DEMOCRATIC LEADERSHIP STYLE

In the democratic leadership style, decisions are made democratically by the group, encouraged and assisted by the leader. Group participation in the decision making process is encouraged by the head or leader of the organization. Decisions on the various activities in the organization are made after communication, consultation and discussion with the various members of the organization. By doing this, the leader gives his staff the impression that everybody's input is required for the success of the organization. Thus in the democratic leadership style, the leader delegates some of his responsibilities to his subordinates, providing them the opportunity to participate in the organizational decision making, but the final decisions in all matters are made by the leader himself after they have been discussed.

In the democratic leadership style, high cohesion and involvement in the affairs of the institution and staff members show positive attitude towards their leader according to Smith et al (1982). This style uses discussion and bargaining to arrive at decisions, it generates high morale among staff members and promotes greater group productivity. Many successful school administrators practise this participatory style of leadership.

THE LAISSEZ-FAIRE LEADERSHIP STYLE

The Laissez-faire leadership is a passive style characterized by little structure and a lot of freedom for staff members to do what they like. Few restrictions are placed on the staff members concerning choices and procedures for accomplishing job tasks. The leadership gives freedom to groups and individuals to make decisions with the leader himself virtually not participating. In this type of leadership, groups may have low cohesion and involvement and little is usually achieved. Members of staff and students who expect strong leadership may be dissatisfied with management especially teachers and students with high achievement motivation.

The different leadership styles are known to produce certain behaviours among the organizational members. White and Lippitt (1960) examined the responses of children to these various leadership styles, and they concluded that different leadership styles do indeed produce different behaviours, for example, the children supervised in school under the democratic style tended to exhibit high morale, unity, and self-direction. Whereas authoritarian leadership resulted in a higher level of production, but was also associated with a higher level of frustration and lower levels of morale, cooperation and self-direction. The laissez-faire style resulted in inferior work quality, less productivity, and higher degrees of dissatisfaction among organizational members. The findings have far reaching effects on the human relations approach and the general performance of the organization.

GETZELS AND GUBA'S MODEL OF LEADERSHIP BEHAVIOUR

The traditional leadership styles, autocratic, democratic and laissez-faire did not satisfy the needs of management during the first half of the 20th century. In 1957 Getzels and Guba identified three dimensions of leadership behaviour in their study of leadership and followership. These are Nomothetic or Normative, Idiographic or Personal and Transactional styles of leadership.

The Nomothetic leadership style is characterized by centralized authority and it stresses rules and regulations and institutional goals achievement. Much emphasis is placed on the organizational role expectations. Effectiveness is rated in terms of behaviour towards accomplishing the objectives of the organization.

There is little regard for the individuals' needs and expectations. In a school setting you may have a school leader who is always emphasizing rules and regulations and expects his staffs to pay more attention to their school roles and tasks at all times. Such leaders are referred to as Nomothetic leaders. They are production or task oriented and communication in the institution is formal and mainly downwards and interaction with staff members is strictly along authority lines.

The Idiographic or personal dimension emphasizes the requirements of the individual, the personality and the individual's needs and disposition. Idiographic leadership stresses minimal rules but spends much time trying to meet the personal needs of his staff in order to make them happy and contented. The idiographic school leader spends most of his time and energy attending to his personal needs and those of his staff and students. He directs his effort to providing adequate school facilities and good welfare services for his staff and students and he may not show keen interest in enforcing school rules and regulations.

The Transactional leadership, provides a kind of balance between the Nomothetic and the Idiographic dimensions. This dimension is characterized by behaviours which stress both goals accomplishment and individual's need fulfilment. The transactional leader is one who balances people's needs with the organizational needs. This type of leader may be the most successful because he sticks to rules and procedures of the organization and aims at producing as much as possible without upsetting staff members in terms of their individual and group needs. The transactional leader judiciously uses each style as the occasion demands and he always tries to strike a balance between the organizational goals and the needs of the members of the organization. The transactional leadership style therefore represents a compromise between the Nomothetic dimension which stresses organizational needs and goal achievement and the Idiographic dimension which stresses the individual and group needs fulfilment.

The relationship between Nomothetic, Idiographic and the Transactional dimensions of leadership behaviour can be illustrated diagrammatically as shown in the figure below.

Figure 1: Getzels and Guba's Nomothetic - Idiographic - Transactional Model (1975). Adapted from Smith et al (1982).

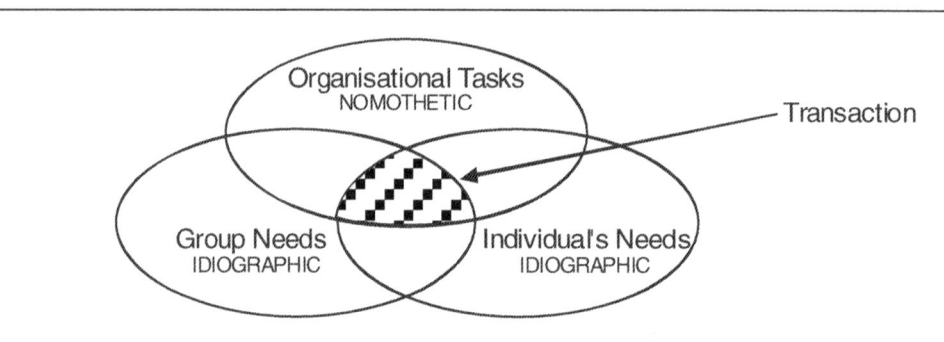

The Nomothetic-idiographic - transactional model of leadership shows three variables at work in a leadership situation. These are: task needs, group needs, and individual needs. Providing adequate leadership means creating the right balance between the three sets of needs. The task functions include setting objectives for the group, planning tasks, allocating responsibilities and setting standards of performance. Group functions include team building, communication, group motivation and disciplinary activities. Individual functions include counselling and motivation of members of the organization.

INITIATING STRUCTURE AND CONSIDERATION MODEL

Research on the Initiating structure and Consideration dimensions of leadership behaviour started at the Ohio State University in the 1950s. The researchers sought to identify independent dimensions of leader behaviour. Halpin and Winer (1957) stated that the basis of this Ohio study was a Leader, Behaviour Description Questionnaire of 150 items, and that when the questionnaires were analyzed, two distinct behaviour patterns emerged. One emphasized organization of the task and was termed "Initiating Structure" and the other emphasized employee relationship and was termed "Consideration".

Initiating structure according to Robbins (1998) refers to the leader's behaviour in delimiting the relationship between himself and members of his work group and in endeavouring to establish well defined channels of communication and methods of procedure. It also refers to the extent to which a leader is able to define and structure his or her role and those of the subordinates in the search for goal attainment. A leader who is characterized as high in initiating structure is someone who assigns tasks to staff members and expects high performance from them within a specified deadline.

Consideration refers to behaviour indicative of friendship, mutual trust, respect and warmth in the relationship between the leader and members of his staff. A leader who is high in consideration is one who is friendly and approachable and treats all subordinates as equals and listens to their personal problems

Many researches have focused on these two dimensions of leadership behaviour. The results of these studies indicated that leaders who are high in both initiating structure and consideration tend to achieve high subordinate performance and satisfaction more frequently than those leaders rated low on either initiating structure or consideration or in both. However leader behaviour characterized as high on initiating structure at times led to greater rates of grievances, absenteeism, turnover and lower levels of job satisfaction especially for workers performing routine tasks. Other studies found that high consideration was negatively related to performance ratings of the leader by his or her supervisors.
The relationship between initiating structure and consideration behaviours of leaders illustrated in Figure 2.

Figure 2: Illustration of Initiating structure and Consideration behaviour relationship. Adapted from Cole (1997)

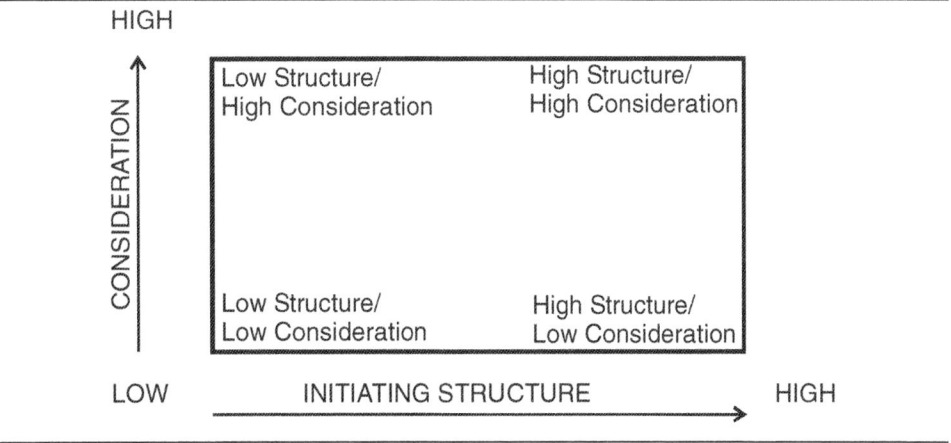

Figure 2 shows that a leader can be scored low or high in any of the two dimensions and low or high on both initiating structure and consideration. Task oriented leaders believe that they get results by keeping their workers constantly busy and urging them to produce while considerate leaders on the other hand are more concerned about the human needs of their workers and usually try to build team work. It has been established that the most successful leaders are those who combine both structure and consideration in their leadership behaviours.

PRODUCTION AND EMPLOYEE ORIENTED MODEL

In the early 1950s Rensis Likert and his colleagues studied the behaviours of supervisors of both high and low producing groups. This study was undertaken at the University of Michigan's Survey Research Center and directed towards the differences which existed in the supervision of high and low producing units. Carefully marched groups of high and low productivity teams were compared from the interviews carried out with both the supervisors and the subordinates. Two dimensions of leadership behaviour which they labelled Production and Employee dimensions emerged.

A production oriented or centered supervisor or leader sees his job in terms of organizing the physical production processes, and he tends to emphasize the technical or task aspect of the job. His main concern is to accomplish the organizational goals and the staff members are the means to that end. The employee oriented or centered supervisor or leader sees his job more in terms of the human relations involved and he tends to talk more about his subordinates and their needs especially when asked what his job involves. Leaders who are employee oriented are described as emphasizing interpersonal relationships and they tend to take personal interest in the needs of their subordinates.

These Michigan Studies indicate that leaders who are employee oriented in their behaviour produce more than leaders who are tasks oriented in their behaviour. In general, employee oriented leaders are associated with higher group productivity and higher job satisfaction while production oriented leaders tend to be associated with low group productivity and lower job satisfaction among the staff.

Leadership and Organization Culture

Leadership positions must exist in organizations, and leadership can only be understood in terms of what the leader does. Some of the duties of the leader in organizations include policy making and implementation and policies form guidelines for directing the affairs of the organization. After decisions have been made, it is the responsibility of the leader to see that these decisions are implemented within reasonable time. Handy (1976) developed the idea of environmental elements in leadership. He viewed leadership as a question of achieving the best between the leader's personal attributes, the expectations and needs of the subordinates, the needs of the task, and the environment in which the events are taking place. He sees the key aspects of environmental culture in any organization as the power position of the leader, the relationship between the leader and the group, the organizational norms or culture, the structure of technology of the organization, the variety of tasks and the variety of subordinates, so in an organization, there should be norms about the way work should be organized, the way authority should be exercised, the way people should be rewarded and controlled.

Leadership is exercised against the background of the above cultures in the organization and this fact has important implications for the amount of power assigned to a leader and the leadership styles he uses to achieve the goals of the organization. The structure of organizations vary very much and each leader should use a leadership styles that suits his organization and by so doing he would be able to achieve the goals of his organization.

Conclusion

Leadership is a dynamic process which is influenced by the changing requirements of the task and the members of the organization. This means that there is no best way of leading but leaders need to be able to exercise a range of behaviour in order to lead effectively. The leader's main role is to influence the group towards the achievement of the organizational goals.

Leadership and followership are vital elements in the social relationships of groups at work. This chapter has outlined some of the major contributions to leadership theories and some practical implications of these theories have also been discussed.

The study of leadership behaviour in organizations is important because it deals with the institution and its tasks, the roles the individuals and groups have to play in order to achieve the goals of an institution. We now know enough about leadership to understand that it is not just straightforward choice between one style or the other, but it is mainly a question of balancing a number of variables such as the nature of the task, the composition of the group, the authority structure and the personal attributes of the leader and this balancing must be done in the context of an organization.

Study Questions

Attempt the following questions after reading this article on leadership and leadership behaviours.
1. Define a leader, leadership and leadership behaviour.
2. Distinguish between Authoritarian, Democratic and Laissez-faire leadership styles.
3. Differentiate between Nomothetic, Idiographic and Transactional forms of leadership.
4. Explain fully the Initiating Structure and Consideration dimensions of leadership behaviour.
5. When do you regard a leader as Production or Employee oriented in the organization.

References

Cole, G. A. (1997) Personnel Management, Theory and Practice. 4th Edition. London: Ashford Press.

Foot, M and Hook, C (1996) Introducing Human Resource Management. London and New York: Longman.

Getzels, J. W. and Guba, E. G. (1957) Social Behaviour and the Administrative Process. Chicago: The University of Chicago Press.

Haplin, A. and Winer, K. (1957) in Cole G. A. (1997). London: Ashford Press.

Handy, C. (1976) Understanding Organizations, New York: Penguin.

Hughes, L. W. (1999) The Principal as Leader. 2nd Edition, New Jersey: Prentice Hall.

Jones, F. V. and Jones, L. S (1998) Comprehensive Classroom Management, 5th Edition, Mass: Allyn and Bacon

Musaazi, J. C. S. (1986) The Theory and Practice of Educational Administration. London and Basingstoke: Macmillan Education Ltd.

Rebore, R. W. (1982) Personnel Administration in Education. A Management Approach. New Jersey: Prentice Hall Inc.

Robbins, S. P. (1998) Organizational Behaviour, Eighth Edition, New Jersey: Prentice Hall Inc.

Smith, M. Beck, J. Cooper, C. L., Cox, C. Ottawa, D. Talbot, R. (1982) Introducing Organizational Behaviour. London and Basingstoke: Macmillan Publishers Ltd.

Webb, L. D. and Norton, M. S. (1999) Human Resources Administration. Personnel Issues and Needs in Education, Third Edition, New Jersey: Prentice Hall Inc.

White, R. and Lippitt, R. (1960) Autocracy and Democracy in Organizations. An Experimental Inquiry. New York: Harper and Row.

SECTION 5
ASSESSMENT AND EVALUATION

Chapter 16
Assessing the Predictive Validity of the ATLP-75
Selection Test for Caribbean Nurses
    Valerie J. Hardware and
    Tony Bastick   153

Chapter 17
Is Validity more Reliable than Reliability is Valid?
    Tony Bastick   167

Caribbean Perspectives

Assessing the Predictive Validity of the ATLP-75 Selection Test for Caribbean Nurses

VALERIE J. HARDWARE AND TONY BASTICK

Abstract

This article reports an assessment of the predictive validity of the Adult Test of Learning Potential (ATLP-75). The test has been used for the past 25 years as part of the selection process for admission to the nursing programme at the University Hospital of the West Indies (UHWI). Applicants who have scored less than 72% on this test have not been admitted to the programme. This means that many applicants have been rejected. However, during this time the predictive validity of the test has never been assessed.

For this study 91 subjects were selected at random from those who had completed the nursing programme and passed the Licensure Examination for Nursing. To assess the predictive validity of the ATLP-75 their scores on this initial selection test were correlated with their scores in the final nursing examination . The results, which showed no significant correlation, offer no support for the predictive validity of this selection test. This finding has considerable implications for the UHWI nursing programme.

Introduction

The first part of this article explains simply what is meant by predictive validity. It simply explains some technical details and highlights some assumptions that may not hold when using predictive validity for course selection. The second part evaluates a very important use of predictive validity in the selection of students for courses leading to qualification as licensed nurses. Critical understanding of these issues is tested in UWI courses on Testing and Evaluation. An example is the following question 3C(iii) from the 1998 Semester I examination of course ED20F Classroom Testing and Assessment (Basic).

'Comment critically on the application of correlation to the predictive validity of placement tests'

Predictive Validity: The basics simply explained

Very simply, when students take a test, and then later the same students take a different test, we can see if the first test puts the students into a similar order as the second test. For example, whether the same group of students who were near the top of the list on the first test were also near the top of the list on the second test. Similarly, whether the students who were near the bottom of the list on the first test were also near the bottom of the list on the second test, and those who were near the middle on the first test, still remained near the middle on the second test. When this happens, you can see that the actual score for a particular student on the first test tends to be linked with the score for that same student on the second test. We then say that the first test has predictive validity for the second test.

The order for all the students on the first test can be compared with the order for all the students on the second test by using a correlation statistic. To calculate a correlation you must have two scores for each student, his or her first test score and his or her second test score. If the orders match fairly well then the correlation will be nearly up to the maximum of $r = 1.000$. If there is hardly any matching between the two orders then the correlation will be hardly anything, that is near $r = 0.000$. *If there is a high correlation between the two tests then, when we know the student's score on one test we can closely predict the student's score on the other test; the higher the correlation then the better will be the prediction. Hence, the correlation is taken as a measure of 'predictive' validity.

Tests that have predictive validity are used to select students for courses. The belief is that, if a test given before a course predicts the test result of a course, then we should select those who do well on the predictive test as these are the ones who are most likely to do well on the course.

Some things to consider about predictive validity

Now to fill in some details for the simple description above. First we fill in some technical points on the meaning and calculation of correlations that are used to measure predictive validity. We also clarify the confusions that sometimes arise between predictive validity and concurrent validity. Then we look more closely at the application of predictive validity to selection for educational courses.

THE MEANING OF NEGATIVE CORRELATION

First we look at what it means to get negative correlations. You may have seen correlations that are negative e.g. $r = -0.234$. This means that the orders tend to be reversed. The student's two scores are as though they were sitting on the two ends of a seesaw. If one score is up then the other score will be correspondingly down. If it happens when we are testing abilities then it means that one test is measuring ability and the other is measuring lack of that ability. It usually indicates that one test is scored by counting correct answers and the other test is scored by counting mistakes.

HOW TO CHOOSE THE CORRECT CORRELATION

A practical point is the choice of which correlation to use. There are many different correlation statistics, e.g. Pearson's product moment correlation coefficient, Spearman's rank order correlation coefficient, the Phi Coefficient, Rank biserial correlation coefficient, Point biserial coefficient, etc. etc. You need to choose the correct one. The most powerful one is Pearson's. This is because it assumes the most information about the distributions of the student's marks. If you only have the rank order of the students, or just pass/fail, then you will need to choose one of the other types of correlation coefficients.

In applications of predictive validity to selection, usually only those who pass the first test go on to take the second test. This selection, as well as course drop-outs, changes the distributions. For example, we do not know how well the students who were not selected would have done. There are corrections that need to be applied because of these range restricted distributions. These corrections add to the calculated correlation, depending on its size.

DISTINGUISHING BETWEEN PREDICTIVE AND CONCURRENT VALIDITY

We also need to separate 'predictive' validity from 'concurrent' validity. The word 'concurrent' means 'at the same time'. However, a student does not usually take two tests exactly at the same time e.g. answering both question ones then both question twos etc. That would be very unusual. One test is usually taken first and then the student takes the second test, maybe at the same sitting. So the problem arises as to how much time must elapse between the two tests in order for their correlation to be measuring 'predictive' validity rather than 'concurrent' validity. Well, it is better to think of 'concurrent' as referring to the same 'mental set' rather than the same 'time'. Mental set is the psychological term corresponding to what we know as 'attitude of mind'.

A student's mental set can be changed if that student's mood, attitudes, values, knowledge or understanding etc. change so that the student approaches the second test differently than the first. If the mental set is different then the correlation can be considered to be a measure of predictive validity. If the mental set is the same then the correlation is considered as a measure of concurrent validity. In the application of predictive validity to selection, the time is at least the length of the course and the content of the second test should be very different from the content of the first test because it assesses a course that the student needed to do.

The validity of predictive validity

As teachers who are responsible for how our decisions affect the future of our students, we need to consider the huge leap of faith between the logic of predictive validity and our educational applications of it. In the following sections, I play 'Devil's advocate' in order to invite you to consider your justifications of your decisions to apply the logic of predictive validity to influence the futures of your students.

The logic is simply stated above in the sentence marked *. The logic is that, if for the same students their order on the first test is correlated with their order on the second test, then when we know one of the test results we can predict the other test result.

PREDICTING THE PAST

You will notice that the word 'predict' in logic has no time value. If the tests are correlated, then we can logically predict a student's first score from his or her second score. Its like an arithmetic question of the form •+•=•. When we know two things, the correlation and one score, we can 'predict' the third. We know the third number because its value already exists. We only have to calculate it. Our future and past are not involved in the logic. However, when the logic is applied for selection then the word 'predict' refers to a number whose value does not yet exist. Hence, when we calculate the predictive validity by correlating two tests, we are not looking into the future. We are looking back into the past, and saying in hindsight, as though we were back in the time when the students took the first test that "this test will predict their scores on the second test". However, 'we cannot step into the same river twice'. It can never happen again for these students and these tests.

STULTIFYING EDUCATION

What is worse, is that the real 'predictive validity', as it is defined, does not exist either. Remember, in the logic it was the same students who took the second test. In the selection application, we have different students to whom we are trying to apply the results from the first students. We have to believe that the next batch of students will be the same as the last, and damningly for our education system, we must assume that there will also be no contrary up-dating to the course.

When we look at the extreme length of time required for this belief system to work we can see the stultifying effect that maintaining predictive selection has on our education system. In the example we give in this article, the time between students taking the first 'predictive' assessment (ATLP-75) and taking the second criterion assessment (RENR) is about three years and two months. 3.2 years is the time required to find if the first test has predictive validity. If it has, then this same test is used to select the next batch of students who will be taking the same second assessment a further 3.2 years later. Hence, for just one application, this belief requires the system to stay unchanged for 6.4 years. It is possible to then check whether your belief in the predictive validity of the first test was justified by calculating the correlation for the second batch of students.

The problem is that, whether the results correlate or not, either way you lose. If the results from the second cohort do not correlate then you have used an inappropriate selection test and likely rejected many good students. If the results do correlate, then you may not have been up-grading your course. If the predictive validity improves with successive batches of students, then you may be digging yourself into a rut by changing your course to fit the pre-course abilities of the students as tested by the pre-course test.

THREE QUESTIONABLE BELIEFS

What is even worse than the two difficulties above, is that often the predictive validity of a test has not been assessed even though the test is used to reject applicants who are otherwise qualified. Tests are simply designated as 'predictive'. This designation is based on one or two further beliefs. The use of predictive validity for educational selection depends on three questionable beliefs - should prerequisite content be predictive of success or is learning ability more important. Do you believe that we should select students of high intelligence because they are more likely to do better?

New content in old bottles

The first is where the selection test is a content test. From the recognition that the content is a prerequisite for the later course, the belief is that a high score on that prerequisite content predicts a high score at the end of the later course. This ignores any difference in the abilities needed to display the prerequisite content and those needed for the course and any differences in the learning environments. For example, how well would a good CXC result, obtained by rote learning under strict teacher supervision, predict a degree classification obtained under self-directed study?

The motivation of interest

The second belief is in testing general pre-course learning ability and assuming that this will continue during the coming course. In this case the selection test(s) tend to be types of intelligence tests. ATLP-75 is a type of intelligence test. This belief assumes that the motivations to learn will remain the same even though the content will be different. In particular courses that are selected, as later courses tend to be, are usually selected because of particular interest and this is expected to improve learning. However, intelligence tests do not allow for this increased learning motivation.

Ethics of selection by intelligence

There is an interesting ethical dilemma in using intelligence for course selection. Intelligence is determined by heredity and environment, just like social class and physical impairments. If you believe that a student should not be discriminated against because of their heredity and environment, then, should you be rejecting students because of their low intelligence?

For 25 years the University Hospital of the West Indies has been using the ATLP-75 as a selection test for the course leading to the Regional Examination for Nurse Registration (RENR). During this time the predictive validity of the test has never been calculated. This is now evaluated as an important practical application of predictive validity.

The association is calculated between performance in the Adult Test of Learning Potential – T75 and academic performance in the Regional Examination for Nurse Registration 1994-1997 at the University Hospital of the West Indies School of Nursing.

BACKGROUND

As a privileged observer in the Department of Nursing Education University Hospital of the West Indies (UHWI), I, Valerie Hardware, have been aware of the use of pre-entrance tests as part of the selection process for candidates for the nursing program. These tests are used to choose from among the academically qualified applicants. One of the tests is the Adult test of Learning Potential -T75 (ATLP-T75). The test developer stated that candidates who gained a particular score has the ability to successfully complete the nursing program and, by implication, be successful in the Regional Examination for Nurse Registration (RENR).

This assumption generates certain questions. Do all who gain the required score on the ATLP-75 and are selected to do the nursing program pass the final RENR? This use of the ATLP-75 as a criterion for admission assumes that the desirability of candidates is proportional to their ATLP-75 scores and that such scores are associated with, or predict success in the RENR at the end of the nursing program. This is the question to be investigated.

PURPOSE OF STUDY

The purpose of this study is to evaluate the use of the ATLP-T75 in the selection process and to determine if student's performance on the ATLP-T75 relates in any way to performance in the regional or final nursing examination.

THE PROBLEM - STUDENT SELECTION AND PERFORMANCE IN THE RENR

The demand for entry into the Registered Nurse programme at the Department of Nursing Education U.H.W.I. has usually exceeded the available capacity. In 1997, 55 students were selected from a pool of 248 academically qualified applicants.

Failure rates among UHWI students have varied over the period 1994 –1997, showing a high of 58% in 1994 to a low of 12% in 1996. These failures have brought into focus questions of educational accountability and students' ability. To achieve quality in nursing, and nurses who perform well, the school of nursing must aim to select candidates in whom they perceive ability, and then endeavour to nurture that ability towards the final academic success.

This test has been used in the recruitment process of nursing students for over 25 years and no study has been done to evaluate Reid's claim that performance on this test relates positively to performance in the final nursing examination. It is therefore the aim of this study to determine if the test used for this purpose is valid.

REGIONAL EXAMINATION FOR NURSE REGISTRATION (RENR) OF CARICOM COUNTRIES

In April 1994, the University Hospital of the West Indies School of Nursing wrote this examination for the first time. It consists of four papers, Papers 1 and 2 are Clinical Nursing, with 4 essay items and 100 MCQ items respectively. Functional Nursing has 4 essay items and 50 MCQ items making up Papers 3 and 4.

Selection and Training

Subject requirements for entry into the Registered Nurse programme are English Language, a Science, Mathematics and one other subject from an approved list. The Department of Nursing Education UHWI, Mona, uses pre-entrance tests to select candidates for the nursing programme from among the qualified applicants. Failure in any one of these tests brings the application to a close.

Table 1: Qualified applicants performance in the pre-entrance test and numbers selected for training

Year	Total Pre-qualified	Total sat Pre-entrance tests	Total passed Pre-entrance tests (%)	Selected (%)
1997	248	180	78	55
1998	184	178	92	56

Source: Admission Section, School of Nursing Records

The Adult Test of learning Potential –T75

Part of the pre-entrance test battery is The Adult Test of Learning Potential – T75 (ATLP-T75) developed locally by Laurie Reid, a former Professor in the Department of Education, University of the West Indies (circa 1970). On request from the Director of Nursing Education UHWI for a test to use to discriminate among students who would most likely be successful in the nursing programme, Professor Reid provided this test. It is an intelligence test, which was primarily designed to infer ability in a future learning activity.

It is a standardised test. Reliability was developed based on teachers entering the School of Education UWI (Reid L.– interview). Using Guilford's Structure of Intellect model as the basis for describing the ATLP-T75 Items 1 to 70 would fit in the cognition-semantic relations cell as they require recognition of the relations between word meanings. The numerical items require numerical reasoning and would be classified as cognition-symbolic-relations. Items 71 to 100 have diagrams would fit in the cognition-figural-relations cell. This test results in a single score or a single index of abilities combining verbal and non-verbal scores. It is not a pass/fail test.

Reid L. has posited a claim that applicants for nursing who obtain a score of 72% and above are more likely to master the nursing content. Implicit in this claim is the inference that they would be more likely to pass the RENR. Based on this claim the school uses the score of 72% or higher in its decision to select applicants for further processing.

SIGNIFICANCE OF THE STUDY

The methods of recruitment and selection of student nurses are important indicators of performance in both the process and the product of nurse education (Land, 1994 p.1030). This emphasises the relationship between the input, the ability of the student at the start of the training, and the output, the licensed practitioner, at the end of training.

This study is a pioneer research in Jamaica into the association of a Learning potential test to academic performance in Nursing. The ultimate importance of this study lies in the effort to validate actions to select students who will best utilise the opportunity for training and to perform at high standards to improve the quality of nursing care given to Jamaicans.

Review of Literature

Admission criteria for tertiary and professional educational programs are varied. Many professions still use fixed subject matter prerequisites. Increasingly, however, other procedures and instruments have been used, as more students are seeking tertiary education. There have been increasingly more investigations into which tests used as pre-admission criteria, best predict success at tertiary level.

TYPES OF TESTS

There are two broad categories for the basis of the nature on measurement: Measures of maximum performance and measures of typical performance (Cronbach, 1984). Achievement tests indicate degree of success in some past activity while aptitude tests are primarily designed to predict success in some future learning activity (Gronlund, 1990). Both types of test measures maximum performance from which we can infer ability. High scores are equated, reasonably with successful learning and good instruction, and low scores or failing scores call into question the teacher's and the students' accountability (Pophan, 1990). Tests can be used properly or improperly and need to be used to match the purpose for which they were developed.

The use of standardised college aptitude and intelligence tests began after World War II and today there is more general acceptance of their value in predicting the chances of success at tertiary level (Gonzalez, 1964). Aptitude tests or Tests of Learning Potential make a special contribution to selection processes as they are designed to predict some future performances in some activity. (Gronlund, 1990; Pophan, 1990). Although both achievement tests and aptitude tests measure what a student has learned and are used to predict future success, the types of learning measured by each test and the types of prediction for which each is used are different (Gronlund 1990).

A spectrum of ability tests according to the type of learning measured, adapted from Cronbach (1984), shows a continuum, with aptitude tests being within levels C, D and E and achievement tests being within levels A and B. Aptitude tests are therefore seen to be less dependent on any particular set of learning experiences. Moving away from content oriented tests and tests of general educational development, they tend to focus on verbal, numerical and problems solving abilities, some of which were learnt in school and some derived form the general culture. The use of aptitude tests between C and E are primarily aimed at identifying students with the latent or undeveloped learning potential and can be used before the student has training in a particular area (Gronlund, 1990).

Both tests can predict future achievement, however the content-oriented achievement test can predict how well students may handle that particular content in the future. It does not have great value in predicting future learning in another content area unless there is some relationship or similarity between the content being measured and the content for future learning. On the other hand, the aptitude tests can be used before the student has had any training in a particular area (Gronlund, 1990). Based on cognitive activities being measured in the aptitude test, we infer inherent ability in the student that can be applied to master the area of study.

The majority of the nursing literature relating to prediction of student nurses' academic performance is American in origin. The American College Test (ACT) has been used as criteria for admission to colleges in the United States of America. The criteria for admission involves cut-off scores in ACT English and Maths. The ACT sub-test and composite scores have been shown to have reliabilities ranging from .83 to .96 (American College Testing Programme Inc., 1986).

McClelland, Yang, and Glick (1992), used 80% (n=1069) of the graduates from nine baccalaureate programmes between 1985-1988 and findings suggested that students ACT scores predicted future performance on National Council Licensure Examinations for Registered Nurses. The highest predictor was the ACT Composite score ($r = .48$). (McClelland et al, 1992, p. 345). Lengacher (1990), investigated 146 graduates of one college in Florida from July 1987 to July 1988, and found that the ACT composite score was the best predictor for performance on the NCLEX-RN ($r = .75$) (Lengacher, 1990, p. 163). Felts (1986), and Fowles (1992), had similar findings. Stein (1978), examined the usefulness and validity of the GRE in predicting success in a graduate-nursing programme. Pearson's product moment Correlation was used to test the relationship with the graduate Grade Point Average (GPA). Results showed a moderate positive correlation with graduate GPA ($r=.413$), thus having a moderate predicting value for considering graduate nursing performance (Stein, 1978, p. 17).

One of the non-cognitive criteria examined in many studies is the age of the student. Interestingly age was found to have no predictive value to nursing success by Lengacher (1990), Allen (1988), McKinney (1988) or Clemence and Brink (1978). In contrast, Stein (1978), Safian-Rush and Belock (1988) and Houltran (1996) found students age to be a significant predictor – the older the student the better the result. Statistical analysis has shown highly significant differences between the 17-21 age group and those over 22 ($p<0.001$) (Houltran, 1996, p. 1094). The older students fare as well, if not better than the younger students. Limitations identified are the use of one college only, the non-random sampling procedure and small numbers in the 17-21 age group.

No study has been done locally to examine how pre-admission procedures relate to success in nursing. Other than past academic achievement, there are no clearly identified criteria that consistently predict a student's success in nursing and the licensure Examination that can be measured before admission (McClelland et al, 1992).

Design

This was a retrospective ex-post facto study. Retrospective analysis of data recorded for the randomly selected ninety-one (91) students from four (4) classes who completed nursing training 1994 – 1997 was done. Scores from the pre-entrance ATLP-T75 will be compared to scores on the RENR.

HYPOTHESIS

U.H.W.I. Nursing Students with high performance scores in the Adult Test of Learning Potential –T75 tend to obtain higher scores in the final Regional Examination for Nurse Registration than students with low performance scores in the ATLP-T75.

RESEARCH QUESTIONS

1. What association exists between
(a) overall ATLP-T75 performance scores and means performance scores for the RENR ?
(b) overall ATLP-T75 performance scores and means performance scores for the Clinical Nursing Papers and the Functional Nursing Papers for the RENR ?
(c) overall ATLP-T75 performance scores and discrete age grouping in the sample ?
(d) mean performance scores for the RENR and discrete age grouping in the sample ?
2. What level of significant differences exists in the association between performance in the ATLP-T75 and the RENR?

INDEPENDENT VARIABLE: The Adult test of Learning Potential –T75 scores
DEPENDENT VARIABLE (CRITERION OF ACADEMIC PERFORMANCE) The Regional Examination for Nurse Registration (RENR) scores. In any prediction study, the most important measure is the criterion used for success. In educational settings, considerable emphasis is placed on measures, such as examination results. Successful performance is widely used as evidence that a student has benefited from a course of instruction.

STATISTICAL MEASURES AND ANALYSIS

Data were analysed by computer using the SPSS program. Pearson's product Moment Correlation was used to examine the relationship between performance on the ATLP-75 and performance on the RENR, and also to examine if age of candidates influenced performance on the RENR. A t-test for independent samples of pass-fail was also done

LIMITATIONS

The main limitations include the sample number being under 100. No local studies have been done and the tests abroad are not similar in structure to the ATLP or the RENR. The use of only one school limits generalisation. Inability to control the numerous complex intervening variables that affect test taking and learning is also a limitation.

INTERPRETATION AND DISCUSSION OF FINDINGS

The sample is a young sample, 67% under 20 years. This is likely to be because for many candidates, Nursing is their first choice of a career after leaving school. The absence of records, especially some of the ATLP-75 scores reduced the sample size to 91. There was no evidence of intent to defraud and it was apparent that delayed charting was never completed. As there is a cut-off score for the ATLP-75, there is no score available below 72% and corrections were made for this. The majority 81% got above 80%, 7 of whom got above 90%, which suggests a sample with excellent potential.

Computing the average of all four papers of the RENR is not done, as students must pass Clinical Nursing with the adjustment and Functional Nursing with its adjustment. There is therefore a discrepancy in that some students who got above 60% have failed. Using 60% as the pass mark would identify that only 14 (15%) students failed. However 43 students in the sample failed the examination. This means that 29 of those who failed the RENR had an average over 60%. They would have had 54% and lower on one of the papers. All four papers are criterion- referenced tests and have small ranges. The Functional Nursing Essay paper has the largest range (43) which suggest low discrimination. No corrections are made in the examination process at the Nursing Council to correct for guessing in the MCQ tests and marks are not deducted for incorrect answers. Students appear to perform better on functional Nursing than on Clinical Nursing. This could probably be due to the fact that from the inception of the examination, students and tutors seemed to fear the Functional Nursing. The students requested more revision in that area and they seemed to work harder at it. It is probable that they do worse at Clinical Nursing because they assume they know it, or they do not write the needed basic content. The clinical practice on the Wards and in the Clinics is limited as students are given routine repetitive assignments especially in the absence of a tutor.

There appears to be no apparent association between the ATLP-75 and the RENR ($r = .1$). The ATLP-75 bears no resemblance to the subject content of Nursing. The level of test, according to Cronbach (1984), that may better show aptitude for nursing would be level C with some related content that are congruent to activities for needed nursing. Stein (1978) concluded that achievement in nursing courses might better be predicted by aptitude tests in supportive sciences. Fowles (1992) supported the finding that NCLEX-RN success could be predicted by the ACT composite score and the Social Science sub-scale score.

Table 2: Correlation Coefficients for the ATLP-75 and First Sitting of RENR

		ATLP-T75	RENR	Average Clinical Nursing Essay & MCQ	Average Functional Nursing Essay & MCQ	Clinical Nursing MCQ
ATP-T75	r	1.0000	0.1068	0.1588	0.0333	0.2231
	sig p	-	0.313	0.133	0.756	0.034
AGE	r	0.1331	0.0079	0.1151	0.1250	0.1928
	sig p	0.209	0.941	0.277	0.238	0.067

Having used the test for 25 years and believing that it was actually identifying candidates with better potential to accomplish the nursing course would fit into an expectancy model or be a self-fulfilling prophecy. The tutors believed they were working with students who have great potential. Students accepted for training were internally motivated by the knowledge that they had achieved the required score.

Of interest is the low correlation or low relationship between the ATLP-75 and Clinical Nursing MCQ ($r = .2$). The possible similarity, here, could be the structure as both tests are multiple choice tests.

Age had a slight almost negligible negative correlation ($r = -.1$) with the ATLP-75 and an extremely low negative correlation ($r = -.008$) with the RENR. This suggests that age does not predict performance scores of the students in the sample. It appears however that the younger students performed better than the older students did. (See Table 7). This was not supported by the literature. It should be noted that the older students in the studies abroad (Houltran, 1996) were 22 years and over, and were working at jobs while doing their training.

Conclusion

The ATLP-T75 is an intelligence test, which measures aspects of cognition on which we infer inherent ability. Such tests are used to distinguish low achievers from those with higher potential. The ATLP-T75 which has been used for the past 25 years to select nursing students who have the potential to be successful in the final RENR does not have any relationship or does not predict success in the RENR. The ATLP-T75 should not be used for this purpose as it denies other possible suitable candidates a chance in their career choice. Students enter UHWI Nursing School at a young age, soon after leaving school, and tend to perform better than the older students.

There is a need to find an instrument that could be utilised to discriminate among applicants and identify those best suited for nursing education.

RECOMMENDATIONS

1. Immediate search for, and adaptation of, an instrument or instruments to aid selection of applicants with an aptitude for nursing. This aptitude will have a stronger association with success in the nursing course.
2. Do a comparative blind longitudinal study of two classes of students where some students are admitted with low scores on the ATLP-75. The performance of both groups could then be compared.
3. The ATLP-75 be used after commencement of training to determine where remedial assistance may be needed.
4. Improve record-keeping in the Department of Nursing Education to facilitate efficient functioning and to provide data for future research. (This is already in progress).

References

Allen, C.B., Higgs, Z., & Holloway, J. (1988) Identifying Students at Risk for Academic Difficulty. Journal of Professional Nursing 4 (2), 113-118. Cited in Houltram (1996)

American College Testing Programme Inc. (1986). Content of the Tests in the ACT Assessment, Iowa City: Cited in McClelland (1992)

Clemence, B. & Brink, P. (1978). How Predictive are Admissions Criteria? Journal Of Nursing Education 17 (4), 5-10 Cited in Houltram, (1996).

Cronbach, L.J. (1984). Essential of Psychological Testing. (4th Ed.) .New York: Harper & Row. Cited in Gronlund (1990).

Entwistle, N., & Wilson, J. (1997) Degrees of Excellence: The Academic Achievement Game. London: Hodder & Stoughton.

Felts, J. (1986). Performance Predictors for Nursing Courses and NCLEX-RN. Journal Of Nursing Education 25 (9), 372-377

Fowles, E. (1992, February). Predictors of success on NCLEX-RN and within the Nursing Curriculum: Implications for early intervention. Journal of Nursing Education, 31 (2), 53-57.

Gay, L-R., & Diehl, P.L. (1992). Research Methods for Business and Management. New York: Macmillian Publishing Co.

Gonzalez, Edgar (1964), Prediction of Academic Success in the University of Costa Rica (Doctorial Thesis) University of Wisconsin.

Gronlund, N. & Linn R. (1990) Measurement and Evaluation in Teaching. New Jersey: Prentice Hall.

Guilford, J.P. (1956. Fundamental Statistics in Psychology and Education. New York: McGraw Hill Book Co. Cited in the perception of the relationship between the Administration involvement in fund raising activities and effective management of school operations. Thelora U. Reynolds 1993 MA Theses.

Houltram, B. (1996). Entry Age, Entry Mode, and Academic Performance on a Project 2000 Common Foundation Programme. Journal of Advanced Nursing, 23, 1089-1097.

Land, L. (1994). The Student Nurse Selection Experience: A Qualitative Study. Journal of Advanced Nursing, 20, 1030-1037.

Lengacher, C., & Keller, R. (1990 April). Academic Predictors of Success on the NCLEX-RN Examination for Associate Degree Nursing Students. Journal of Nursing Education 29 (4), 163-169.

McClelland, E., Yang, J. & Glick, O. (1992, Nov-Dec). A Statewide Study of Academic Variables Affecting Performance of Baccalaureate Nursing Graduates on Licensure Examination. Journal of Professional Nursing, 8 (6), 342-350.

McKinney, J., Small, S., O'Dell, N., & Coonrod, B. (1988). Identification of Predictors of Success for the NCLEX-RN and Students at Risk for NCLEX- RN Failure. Journal of Professional Nursing 4, 55-59.

Polit, D., & Hungler, B. (1983). Nursing Research Principles and Methods JP Lippincott.

Pophan, W. (1990). Modern Educational Measurement: A Practitioner's Prospective. Boston: Allyn & Bacon. Boston : 2nd Ed.

Pophan, W.J. (1993). Educational Evaluation. Boston: Allyn and Bacon. 3rd Ed.

Quinn, F. (1995). The Principles and Practice of Nurse Education. London: Chapman And Hall: 3rd Ed.

Reid, U. (1994). A Comprehensive review of Nursing Education, Jamaica February-April 1994. Human Resource Development Pan American Health Organisation, Barbados: April 1994.

Richardson, M. (1988). Classroom Testing and Evaluation Units 1-111 UWI Distance Teaching Enterprise. Faculty of Education University of the West Indies.

Sadler, J. (1986). The Prediction of Tertiary Success: A Cautionary Note. Journal of Tertiary Educational Administration, 8(2), 151-58.

Stein, R. (1978, July-August). The Graduate Record Examination: Does it predict Performance in Nursing Programmes? Nurse Educator 3 (4), 16-19.

Tuckman, B. (1978). Conducting Educational Research, (2nd Ed.). New York: Harcourt Brace Jovanovich.

Is Validity More Reliable than Reliability is Valid?

CHAPTER 17

TONY BASTICK

Abstract

This article uses the question in its title to acknowledge the difficulty that even experts have in reconciling the concepts of reliability and validity. It goes on to give standard definitions of both concepts and to explain them. Using the explanations of these definitions, this chapter illustrates an original supposition; namely, that confusion arises because the definitions of validity are based on constructivist beliefs whereas definitions of reliability are based on positivist beliefs. Hence, the concepts of reliability and validity are as incompatible as the two sets of beliefs upon which they are based. However, by replacing these terms with their explicit positivist and constructivist counterparts, it is possible to bring a new clarity to the issues and to answer the question in the title of this article.

The arguments are illustrated by references to Caribbean examinations.

Confusing the concepts of reliability and validity

This title illustrates the confusion people find between the concepts of reliability and validity. If you can correctly answer the question in the title then you are not one of those confused people and have no need to read on. However, even experts in testing get confused. Here is a heavyweight example:

> A test that is valid must be reliable. "Reliability refers to the degree to which test scores are free from measurement error" (AERA, APA & NCME, 1985, p. 19). As a basic textbook on testing points out, "The ceiling for possible validity of a test is set by its reliability" (Thorndike & Hagen, 1977, p. 87).

This quotation is from a recent report on the validity and reliability of well accepted tests given in Massachusetts to teachers - the Massachusetts Teacher Tests (Haney, Fowler, Wheelock, Bebell, & Malec, 1999). What these experts are saying is that validity must be less than, or equal to the reliability. So, for example, if reliability is 0.9 then validity has to be 0.9 or less. We will now see that what they say is wrong. Consider as an example a lesson where you only learn one thing - say the telephone number of the University. Then a test that asks the single question "What is the telephone number of the university?" will have 100% content validity - because it covers all the content that was taught. As the test has not yet been given it has no reliability - so how can its reliability be more than its validity. This is true of all tests before they are taken. However, it the test is taken now and then again next week so that the test-retest reliability can be calculated, it is unlikely to be 100% because some test takers who got it right on the first test will have forgotten the phone number during the week. Hence, the test-retest reliability is going to be less than 100%, which is the value of the content validity. This simple example of the reliability being less than the validity contradicts what the experts said.

The above example illustrates the confusion even experts feel about validity and reliability. A question was posed to the testing experts in February 1999 on the Measurement and Research Methodology discussion list AERA-D@ASUVM.INRE.ASU.EDU asking experts what they thought was the major issue in testing today and the consensus was that the hottest current issue in testing was the concept of 'validity'. This also illustrates that the concept of validity is a current problem even among the experts. However, experts seem more satisfied with the concept of reliability. To resolve these issues we need to look more closely at the definitions of validity and reliability.

Analysing definitions of validity

A glance through the textbooks will show you that there is a bewildering list of different types of validity - face validity, content validity, concurrent validity, consequential validity, predictive validity, ecological validity, construct validity, etc. How can we make sense of all these validities. People have tried to categorise validities as one of three main types, either as a content validity or a criterion validity or as a construct validity (Guion, 1980). This "trinitarian view is clearly the prevailing one in the field of psychology today and has been at least since the 1950s." (Cohen, Swerdlik, & Phillips, 1998, p. 175). However, this trinitarian categorisation scheme does not work very well because these three categories overlap and some validities, like consequential validity, do not seem to fit very well into any category. There are other ways of trying to categorise validities. For example, Murphy and Davidshofer (1998) use two categories; the validity of measurement and the validity for decisions (p. 146). We get similar problems when we try to use these other categories that experts have devised.

Most textbooks use definitions like these 'A test is valid if it measures what it is supposed to measure, or 'A test is valid if it measures what you think it is measuring', or 'A test is valid if it is appropriate', etc. You will notice in these definitions that validity depends on something outside of the test, something else that you are supposed to know about - what the test is supposed to measure, or what you think it is measuring, or if you think it is appropriate. If you do not know what you are measuring, or do not have some other way of knowing if the test is appropriate, then you will not know if your test result is valid. On the other hand, if you know what you are measuring, and have some other way of knowing that your measure is appropriate, then you do not need the test result. You can calculate reliability from the test results alone but just the test results alone will not tell you the validity. Validity depends on what you know about things that are outside of the test. However, test users typically think that their test results are a more valid indicator of what they are measuring than what they already know, especially if it confirms their belief, even though they have no way of justifying this. It is like guessing someone's weight to the nearest pound (120 lbs. say) and then guessing their weight in pounds to three decimal places (120.147 lbs. say) and believing that the extra calculation added accuracy to what you know. To summarise, a problem with these definitions of validity is that they only confirm what you think you know. If the test result disagrees with what you believe from the outside source, then you can say that the test result is not valid - see the validity exercise at the end of this chapter.

VALIDITY IS A CONSTRUCTIVIST CONCEPT

Dictionaries define 'validity' as 'truth'. A problem with this definition is that what is true varies from person to person and from place to place. Even the truth of rules like 'Thou shalt not kill' might be considered false by some people in some places - in war or self-defence for example. The same action that is valid to a Feminist may not be valid to a Moslem. To give examples from classroom testing in the Caribbean: calculus questions are valid for GCE maths but not valid for the CXC maths that replaced it; thinking IQ type questions are valid for the Common Entrance but not for the NAP that replaced it.

The idea that truth is relative to a particular group or culture is called Social Constructivism. This means that what is true is determined by the group. Cultural relativity is a form of Social Constructivism, as in the CXC v GCE example above where GCE is valid in England, CXC is not; CXC is valid in Jamaica, GCE is not. Validity is also a form of Social Constructivism. When the test is appropriate for the people using it, when it confirms what they believe is the truth, then for them it is a valid test. So the validity of a test is not inherent in the test but depends on those who use it. This means that we can construct different types of validities that are meaningful for our own purposes.

An examination question in the 1998/9 Semester I ED20F examination, Question 3C, was relevant to this:

> "Invent a new type of validity, (i) define it, and (ii) describe a situation in which a test user or a test constructor might find your new type of validity to be useful. (10 marks)".

One answer was: Time Validity, (i) the percentage of examinees who finish before the end of the exam. (ii) This new type of validity would be useful to a tester who wanted every child to have enough time to attempt all the questions.

Analysing definitions of reliability

A glance through the textbooks will show you that there is also a bewildering list of different types of reliability: test-retest reliability, split-half reliability, inter-scorer reliability, internal consistency reliability, parallel-forms and alternate-forms of reliability, etc. There is also a bewildering range of methods for measuring these reliabilities: Pearson r, the Spearman-Brown formula, the Kuder-Richardson formulae KR-20 and KR-21, the Kappa statistic, different variance ratios, Guttman lower bounds, Cronbach alpha, etc. How can we make sense of all this? Sometimes, because reliability is considered as a lack of error, textbooks classify the sources of error in order to simplify the types of reliability; error in administering the test, or error in designing the test, or error in marking the test, or error in taking the test, etc. I find it simpler to consider reliability as consistency, that is lack of variation. Variation in an individual's repeated responses can be measured using standard deviation (or variance) and variation within a whole test, taken by many individuals, can be measured using appropriate types of correlation. If the items are consistent in measuring the same thing then we have internal consistency. This can be assessed by item-total correlations (C-alpha) or by comparing scores on different halves of the test (split-half). If the test is consistent over time, we have stability. This can be measured by comparing a list of test and retest scores (Pearson r). The consistency and stability of the scorers can be measured in the same way.

Reliability theory works well for quality control of machine parts, where we measure the variability of the parts produced by a machine to make sure that the parts are not likely to be too big or too small. However, machined parts do not interact with the measuring process to make themselves bigger or smaller, but the learning process does interact with how it is measured. We actually hope to improve our test results by practising test questions. That is, unlike machine parts, we expect practice measurements to increase what is being measured. This is just one of many such assumptions in reliability theory that do not hold when it is applied to measuring learning.

RELIABILITY IS A POSITIVIST CONCEPT

The idea that 'there is an absolute truth and that our observations vary because they are imperfect versions of that truth' is called Positivism. The Greek philosopher Plato (c. 428-347 B.C.) likened our observations to the flickering shadows that a fire casts on the wall of a cave. We can see only the shadows and from these we must deduce the form of the object that casts the shadows. Similarly, we assume that a student has a mathematical ability that we cannot see. We must deduce the student's ability from his/her test results, which can change with each test. These changing test results are the flickering shadows of his/her ability. The more the shadows flicker and change, then the less reliable they are. Similarly, the more the test results change the less reliable they are. It is this Positivist belief that results in teachers disregarding an unexpected test score with excuses such as 'This is not a true picture of the student's ability', 'S/he must have had a bad day', or 'S/he is not so good at taking exams', etc. In contrast, a Constructivist would say 'This is the ability of the student under these conditions. Under other conditions his/her ability may be different."

Question 4C from 1998/9 Semester I ED2OF exam is relevant to this:

> Q4C. Children who consistently attain a high standard in coursework assessments can consistently produce lower standards in examinations. This can be interpreted in three ways, as (a) the examinations did not show the child's true standard (b) the coursework assignments did not show the child's true standard or (c) because both forms of assessment are reliable then the child's standard is unreliable i.e. it is high when he/she was doing coursework and low when doing examinations. Despite the extra cost, lower accountability and lower reliability, the swing towards coursework and away from exams indicates that the preferred interpretation is (a). What justifications are there for preferring this interpretation? (18 marks)

The 'validity of reliability' and the 'reliability of validity'

The science of testing cannot take both a Positivist view of reliability and a Constructivist view of validity without contradictions and confusions arising. In this chapter I am suggesting that perhaps it is because the science of testing uses these conflicting views together that validity is currently the hottest issue in test theory.

We can see this if we return again to the article with which we started, concerning the validity and reliability of the Massachusetts Teacher Tests (Haney, Fowler, Wheelock, Bebell, & Malec, 1999). From the following quotations taken from the report we can see these Positivist/Constructivist confusions by contrasting how the stakeholders defined the validity of the test with how the authors of the report defined the validity of the test:

> ".. in the New York Times, John Silber wrote that the exams had been 'validated by teachers and scholars who prepared it . . . [and] again by the panels of distinguished teachers, administrators and college professors who reviewed the questions for fairness and agreed on minimal passing scores.' What this defense does not take into account is that a test cannot be validated simply by having people review test questions.
>
> Test validation refers to the meaning of test scores and that meaning depends not just on test content, but also on a host of other factors, such as the conditions under which tests are administered and how they are scored."

From this extract we can see that the authors of the report differ from the stakeholders of the MTT in what they consider constitutes validity. The report authors implicit consensus is to look for Positivist type numerical evidence of reliability which they call validity. Whereas, the stakeholders implicit consensus of validity is the agreement of experts on a passing score and on the fairness of the test. In fact the report authors could find nothing that they might accept as evidence of validity and so they concluded that the tests had not been shown to be valid. They were then only left with what they considered was valid reliability evidence.

> "In the absence of sufficient data to assess the concurrent validity of the MTT, we decided to inquire into their reliability." (Haney, Fowler, Wheelock, Bebell, & Malec, 1999).

Now, using the positivist/constructivist distinction above, we can answer the title question. The following is a trial answer to illustrate one process we can use to answer the question, vis. by replacing the terms 'validity' and 'reliability' by their appropriate positivist and constructivist equivalents. For example, we can answer by replacing 'reliability' with 'variability' and replacing 'validity' with 'consensus', which is itself assessed by the lack of variability of opinion.

The following is a test answer that contains a major error. Can you spot the major error in this answer?

1. 'validity of reliability' means 'is reliability valid?' This becomes 'is there a consensus that lack of variability is important'. The answer to this is 'Yes'. This is because the process of consensus is being used and so it must be important or it would not be used. The process of consensus is the assessment of 'lack of variability' in opinion. Hence, 'lack of variability' is important. So reliability is valid to anyone who asks the question 'is reliability valid?'

2. 'reliability of validity' means 'is validity reliable?' This becomes 'is there a lack of variability in consensus'. The answer to this is also 'Yes'. This is because consensus is reached when there is a lack of variability in opinion.

Hence, the logical value of both statements is 'Yes' and so validity is just as reliable as reliability is valid.

What is the error in this answer?

The correct answer is now left as an exercise for the reader.

EXERCISE - HOW USEFUL ARE DEFINITIONS OF VALIDITY?

Collect at least five definitions of validity from different sources. Remember to give the references of your sources. Look at your list and make a statement about how useful any of your definitions is for deciding if a particular test result is valid or not - given that you have no other information but your test results.

References

American Educational Research Association (AERA), the American Psychological Association (APA) and the National Council on Measurement in Education (NCME) (1985). *Standards for Educational and Psychological Testing*. Washington, DC: APA.

Cohen, R.J., Swerdlik, M.E., and Phillips, S.M. (1998). *Psychological Testing and Assessment* (3rd Ed). Mountain View, CA: Mayfield Publishing Company.

Guion, R.M. (1980). On trintarian doctrines of validity. *Professional Psychology, 11*, 385-398.

Haney, W., Fowler, C., Wheelock, A., Bebell, D., & Malec, N. (1999). Less Truth Than Error? An independent study of the Massachusetts Teacher Tests. *Education Policy Analysis Archives, 7*(4).

Murphy, K.R. & Davidshofer, C.O. (1998). *Psychological Testing*. (4th Ed.). Upper Saddle River, NJ: Prentice-Hall, Inc.

Thorndike, Robert and Hagen, Elizabeth (1977). *Measurement and Evaluation in Psychology and Education* (4th Edition). New York: Wiley.

SECTION 6

PHILOSOPHY OF EDUCATION

Chapter 18
Education and Choice: The Family or the State?

Oliver Mills 175

Chapter 19
Spirituality and Education: Epistemology as Ethic
Oliver Mills 187

Caribbean Perspectives

CHAPTER 18

Education and Choice: The Family or the State?

OLIVER MILLS

Abstract

Education is a contested concept which is frequently used in dialogue concerning choice in the academic market place. Although many writers have tried to define it, they usually end by prescribing what it should do, rather than specifically stating what it actually is. The idea of what education is, has been associated with who should educate. Many views have been advanced, some claiming that it is a family responsibility, others impute this responsibility to the state, which it is claimed represents a wide constituency which is the country as a whole, and is therefore responsible for its well being. A further view acknowledges the responsibility of the individual child, since it is only he who has the right to know what is in his interest.

This chapter discusses the competing claims regarding who should educate in relation to the parties involved. The chapter defines what education is, and then examines the issue of parental or family choice. It will then view the state as a contestant to the family position because of the responsibilities it holds for educating its citizens, and examines the rights of the individual child as opposed to the obligations of the state. The chapter concludes by discussing some philosophical issues regarding the wider issue of education and choice, and who should educate.

According to John Locke, education should aim at fostering virtue, wisdom, breeding, and learning(1). The issue here is that Locke seeks to educate the gentleman of the privileged strata. Education therefore becomes an elitist enterprise, confined to a selected and narrow sector of society. Who will choose the tutor to educate the gentleman? Is it the family? Obviously, in this case, the gentry would be able to afford it, so that it can be presumed that family, or parental choice would be exercised. Should the state, however permit one section of the society to receive this kind of education, which by comparison with the other sectors would be unequal? Conversely, should there be some intervention by bringing the entire educational enterprise under its responsibility in the interest of democracy and fairness?

John Dewey sees education as 'a process of development and growth. (2) For him, development and growth involves change and modification. Education is therefore concerned with the reconstruction of experience based on problem solving, since development is a continuous process. But Dewey feels that the individuality of the child should be respected, and the sharing of experience fostered. This represents a democratic ethic. Since the interests and individuality of the child are respected, the imposition of a system is not the purpose, rather, it is the facilitation of an environment, where exploration and discovery are encouraged. The child then has some responsibility for his own development, and the idea of respect for persons is being manifested here. The central concern of Dewey is to develop critical intelligence, which provides the child with the autonomy to consider and arrive at conclusions uninfluenced by others. The individual can then be said to exercise ownership of the educational process.

Richard Peters says of education that:

It implies that something worthwhile is being or has been intentionally transmitted in a morally acceptable manner. (3)

He sees education as related to what is valuable, but does not say who will decide what is worthwhile or valuable. Is it the family, the child, or the state? If the state guarantees the interests of the individual, shouldn't the interests of each be the sum total of the interest of society in general? Wouldn't this mean that the interests of each individual would be best realised when they are incorporated within the framework of the whole? Where would this place the special responsibility that the family has for the child? Would the family be necessarily involved in selecting and advocating the interests of the child as part of the whole, or does the responsibility of the state take precedence over even the rights of the family in relationship to the child? What about the child? How old would he have to be before it can be determined that he is sufficiently mature to realise what is in his interest and so be able to exercise rational choice, or would the family have to do this, pending the development of mature judgment on the child's part? Since families are choosers of state policies, what level of choice would the latter allow, and at what point would it invoke its greater responsibilities to its citizens as a totality? How would this affect the family, as persons entitled to respect, and having authority over the child? What are the limits or claims of democracy, given this episode?

In Pedagogy of the Oppressed, the Brazilian educator Paulo Friere describes education as 'an act of depositing, in which the students are the depositories and the teacher is the depositor.(4)

He feels that because of this, students are not empowered, and goes on to propose what he refers to as 'a problem- posing education, ' which he calls the practice of freedom. Through dialogue and interaction, the dominant role of the teacher as an authority changes, and both teacher and students become responsible agents for 'a process in which all grow. '(5) But who decides that problem posing by itself is the most appropriate means of educating? Is it the family, the state, or the child? Who will chose the problems to be posed? Is it the state through the educational process? At what point would parents become involved, or would they? These issues are intertwined in the most complex of topics. The following section will therefore examine the controversial idea of family choice in education.

The Idea of Family Choice

What should be the relationship of the family to the educational process? Should certain elements of education be distributed between the family and the state, or should the former be unimpeded in its choice of the kind of education it desires for its siblings?

Initially the family has the first opportunity to socialise the child into the preferred culture. This initiation can shape early perceptions and preferences. The family also provides for the social, economic and security needs of the child, has its own educational philosophy, and seeks to educate the child in a particular way through the institutions it feels would best realise its aspirations. Having this initial responsibility, the family takes the position that it knows best what is good for the child, and seeks to have him exposed to those values that are regarded as most desirable.

But a contrary view is advanced which alleges that the family lacks the attributes for its own development, and that it is neither a good nor effective educator of the child. This view further claims that the family also does not have either the time, or the broader perspective of the role education should play, and would choose from individualistic rather than altruistic positions, and so segment society further. The opposing argument takes the view that the state brings a national perspective, and a greater sense of cohesion to the educational process through its institutions. It is therefore more likely to be impartial in its activities. Brubacher states that 'capacity for parenthood is not by any means highly correlated with capacity for educating.'(6) However at the later years of a child's life, the family chooses a number of schools at particular levels, for example high schools, or secondary schools to send their child. Should the family have this choice, or should the state decide who should be educated, and where, in order to foster a democratic citizenry with a common, although not identical outlook?

If the family chooses a private education for its child, should the state seek to influence this choice by funding teachers' salaries, or through establishing a national curriculum, or legislate that all schools, whether public or private must have a designated number of places to accommodate those who are not endowed with the necessary resources to attend those institutions whose costs are prohibitive? How should the family respond? Is this tantamount to an infringement of free choice in a democracy, or is it a case of the state promoting equity and equality of opportunity? Is the family obliged to support the initiatives of the state in education even if it feels that the latter has become too intrusive, or should the family seek to decentralise the educational process facilitating more local control of education. Would not this restrict the hegemony of an expansive state? Since the family is an integral element in the political system, is it not morally accountable to the state, and therefore should support those policies which were arrived at through majority decision, irrespective of what its minority position is?

Family accountability is a factor, in that the family is obliged to ensure that the child receives the quality of education that would guarantee his all round development, and enable him to become a productive citizen. Any negligence in performing these responsibilities to the child which might result in moral harm could incur the intervention of the state. (7)   But what should be the position of the family when tensions arise between it and the state concerning the direction of education, including the implementation of controversial policies? What is the effect on policy of public opinion which is articulated through the mechanism of the family? Is public opinion an important element in public policy formulation, or should the view be seriously taken that 'even if we should carry out a hundred per-cent referendum, so that every member of the public was recorded as 'Yes', or 'No', or 'Don't know', we should still have only a very crude indication of what people really thought.(8)

The assumption is, that each person has his individual opinion, none of which is identical. In this case, should the state over-ride parental opinion, and seek to implement its educational policies, based on what it sees as its mandate, and its moral obligation to its constituents as a whole? In all matters of educational transformation and change, is not the responsibility of the state to use education as a means of re-engineering society, precisely because of the resources it possesses? Is it not the case that the family's view of education often lacks coherence, and is based on emotionalism and bias, rather than a considered position of how it could promote the common interest? When the state acts, is it not therefore promoting the common good, which is the well being and flourishing of its constituent members? Is it not also the case that part of this well being involves individual autonomy, or the freedom to determine one's own actions and way of life?(9) Should the family then not seek to advocate for an education which aims at realising a community, where the distinction between one's own, and others' private interests, is unknown, in a situation where all contribute to the well being of the family-community as an wholistic entity?

The crucial questions however are, what kinds of decisions are the family entitled to make about education for its children? And, what specific decisions can the state make? (10) When can the state over-rule the family, and when can the school act independently of the family's wishes? The family, being the initial authority, reserves the right of 'first responsibility,' where decision making on the child's behalf is concerned, since it nurtures helpless humans in the initial states. The right to make decisions on behalf of the child is also based on ownership in the sense that having begotten the individual, it belongs to the family in a custodial sense. The state merely is a mediator, or regulator, and not a paternalistic intervener. The rights of the family therefore take precedence over those of the state, as a result of the former being the 'first cause.' This is further reflected in the initial historical decision made by the family to create the state to perform the role of enabler, and not controller. This reflects consent through democratic choice which brought the state into being as an instrument of the populace, not its patriarch.

The family further possesses the right to change the nature and purpose of the state when that entity abrogates the responsibilities entrusted to it. The state therefore cannot over-rule the body that brought it into existence, except by the consent of that body. This body, the national family, through the democratic process, can both over-rule and direct the state to realise the interests of the general will. In the same way, the school cannot operate independently of the wishes of the family, since through the existence of boards on which parents are represented, any untoward actions by the school can be thwarted through the invoking of parental power. Parental power and choice are therefore effective instruments that can ensure a just and fair system.

The Responsibility Of The State

What is the position and responsibility of the state in the educational enterprise in a wider sense? It is the view of Gordon and White that:

> The state is nothing but a community of individuals; its well-being, the common good, is merely the wellbeing of its constituent members. Part of that wellbeing is individual autonomy, the freedom to determine one's own actions and way of life.(11)

The implication here is that the state is an wholistic entity which seeks what is common among individuals, and that this commonality reflects the interests of its members. There appears to be a contradiction however between a sense of community, and what is common to that community. What is common refers to a statistical representation and not an integrated whole. It suggests that many individual interests that may be opposed to what is common will be subsumed in the interest of commonality. What is common therefore, is not representative of the totality. Where education is concerned, such a situation would favour one group over the other. The interests of some would take precedence over those of others, and individual interests would be de-emphasised to promote the common good. Democracy would cease to exist in the strong sense of giving others their due. What could result from this is that some families would either have to acquiesce with the state's policy, which would be imposed with possible sanctions, or seek to establish independent institutions, since the interest of all would not be dealt with in a just manner. To equate the common good with individual autonomy is therefore a contradiction, resembling a dichotomy of interests. This means different educational provisions for different interests, since many would exercise autonomy and establish their own system. Those without the resources would be deprived. The state then, instead of reconciling opposing agendas would promote division through advocating an elusive common good along with the myth of individual choice. The two are logically incompatible.

What the state should therefore do to promote equality is to intervene in those cases where the child has a moral right to be educated in order to become a fully functioning and responsible citizen. However in the circumstances mentioned, this right would be infringed on by the family. The state then has an obligation to enforce this moral requirement, despite any objections and concerns parents might have. Where the rights of the child are concerned, the state needs to become more assertive, since education is such an area of importance, that it should not be left to chance, or the private preferences of others.

But the state comprises and represents multiple interests. The concern is, that in deciding and establishing what it feels to be most important, it might unconsciously promote a provincial perspective of what education is about, seeing it as an expense rather than as being fundamental to the growth and development of the individual and the society. Indeed, in recent times, through downsizing and re-engineering, education has been the first area to be cut, in terms of the resources available to it. The philosophy of value for money has been advocated. Education is now being regarded as a business, subjected to the instability and unpredictability of market forces. In such a context, should education be left to the state which requires educational institutions to do more with less?

Is this not where family responsibility and authority should become more pronounced so as to prevent education from being just another market driven enterprise? If the state is not to be perceived as totalitarian, then it should recoil from full responsibility for education and allow the family to make direct decisions and choices about fundamental educational initiatives. The real interests of the populace could then be catered for. Independent schools should therefore exist alongside those administered by the state, if the pluralistic nature of the society is to be respected and preserved. State run schools should also be privatised. A monopoly on education held by the state presents a serious challenge to a democratic and civil society.

In a democratic society, it is not usual for the state to accrue unto itself the right to act in a paternalistic way towards its citizens.(12) This is why it should subscribe to radical plurality in education, since if it assumes overall responsibility for this important sector, it could be seen as having political motives, rather than being rationally committed to

the educational process. If the state claims it is acting in, and defending the interests of its citizens, what this does, is to reduce the latter to entities incapable of reasoning for themselves, and deciding what their real needs are. Circumscribing the role of the state in education, and devolving the responsibility to the family, is an indication of respect and trust, and a recognition of the right of the family to be engaged in a fundamental way in the education process.

If the society is integrated, though diverse, and the state regards itself as a referee bringing balance to each sector, should it have the right to intervene in family decisions about education? How and when should this be determined? What could the family do to curtail the activities of an ideologically driven state that imposes on itself the obligation to make decisions on behalf of its constituents, and interpret what is good for them'? Strike notes in this case that:

the state may over-ride parental claims under two kinds of conditions: either when the assumptions that establish the prima facie case in favour of parental authority are rebutted, or when the public interest is at stake.(13)

This, however raises serious considerations. Who decides when the assumptions referred to have been rebutted? Why is an absence of consensus replaced by an outright decision that the position of the state carries, or that a rebuttal by the state represents a final judgment? Is a rebuttal the ultimate test of what should be? Who determines the effectiveness of the rebuttal, and how does the state arrive at what constitutes the public's interest? Suppose the public disregards the position taken by the state, that what the latter has decided on is in the former's interest? Would this not represent an abuse of state power?

What credentials do the state possess, apart from coercive might, which confer on it the right to make decisions for, or on behalf of the family? Many state entities, particularly those responsible for the care of children, homes for senior citizens, and even psychiatric institutions have been shown to be abusive to their clients. Even many educational institutions that are owned and administered by the state are in a condition that cannot be described as desirable. Where then, is the nurturing, caring hand of the state? Where is the neutrality, responsibility and competent management? If in normal circumstances the state cannot manage these wards effectively, how can it assume such a mammoth task as education in order to ensure justice and fairness? This demonstrates the urgent necessity for having the family in control of its children's education and of the educational enterprise generally. If, on the other hand the family abrogates its responsibilities to its offspring, it should then be the obligation of the state to intervene and rectify the situation amicably. Since education is a public service, the state, which embodies the public's aspirations should act to restore integrity to the educational process when the activities of the family are likely to cause harm to the child. This could be in the form of arresting the child's educational development, and by extension, that of the public at large.

The issues to be considered involve instances where family choice results in an inferior quality of education being delivered, which does not meet the standards established by the state. This is particularly the case where the necessary materials and technology used in fostering an effective educational process are lacking, where the training of teachers is suspect, or where for religious or ideological reasons, the type of education chosen will severely hamper the intellectual and social development of the child. The state is then obligated to restore proficiency to the process, despite its own constraints.

In cases of censorship in education, what should the position of the state be? If the family feels that certain types of literature should not be used in the curriculum because of its morally offensive nature, or there is the feeling that creationism should be taught alongside evolutionism, should parents have the authority to take the actions they deem appropriate, over the objections of the state? Suppose the state should put forward the proposition that education in its widest sense is subjected to the market place of ideas, and that freedom of choice should not be restricted, since unfavourable ideas will not be accommodated. What is the proper action that should be taken here? Is not the teaching of controversial issues an integral part of the idea of open-mindedness in education? And is not open-mindedness a pre-requisite in the quest for truth? If a close-minded approach is taken, would others not be denied the opportunity and right to decide their own preferences? What is it that makes particular ideas desirable? Do parents or the state have special insights into what the interests of the child really are which justify actions on his behalf? When decisions are made about what is presumed to be in the child's interest, are not the family and the state unconsciously inhibiting the healthy exposure of the child, which would later generate preferred tastes for selected things, and abhorrence of others? Is it sufficient to expose the child to only those things we think are appropriate, in order to shape preferences in a particular direction?

The state refers not only to the existence of a governmental machinery, but also to the functioning of that machinery in the interest of all. (14) The state projects evidence of the need to manage situations which cannot normally be resolved through goodwill or consensus. Does this make its actions both right and moral? Since the state comprises individuals with competing perceptions of what is desirable, how can it as an institution be relied on to make fair and just decisions? Even if decisions are arrived at through compromise, this does not mean that they are right, but rather that they are convenient. Who then can claim that the state will represent the views of everyone, when each has his own perspective? Who decides, and with what validity what constitutes the predominant, and therefore acceptable view? What about the position that the state should enhance the autonomy of the child to make choices through rational analysis? Suppose after rationally analysing a situation, the child reaches an opposing conclusion that was not anticipated? What happens here? Does the state or the family seek to indoctrinate by imposing a preferred view on the child? What are the limits of autonomy that can be exercised by the child in relation to parental or state control and supervision?

Rights Of The Individual Versus State Responsibility

Any serious discussion of parental rights and state responsibility must consider the rights of the child. What rights do students have in relation to the educational sector? Should their rights be identical to those of adults, or should rights only be extended to students when they have reached the age of intellectual maturity. This period refers to the point where they are conscious of their responsibilities, and can then be morally accountable for their actions. But who is to decide the advent of this period, and with what authority? John Harris, in commenting on this issue states that:

> the traditional distinction between adults and children, which incapacitates children because of their supposed incapacities, does not in fact distinguish adults and children. It may distinguish the competent from the incompetent, but if full political status is to be granted only to the competent, then a large and significant proportion of children must be granted full political status and a very great number of adults must be disenfranchised. (15)

This argument supports the view, that many children can indeed make competent choices that are in their interest. There is a further view which states that until students have absorbed, or been acquainted with a particular body of knowledge, and a certain breath of experience they need assistance in making prudent choices. The possibility is, that they may possess this capacity even at the preparatory stages of their education, but because of the perception that adults have of the age factor and the assumed competence associated with it, they are reluctant to allow children to exercise this franchise. It is further argued that many parents, particularly those from deprived social and economic backgrounds, are incapable of making informed decisions on behalf of their children. What is to be done in cases such as these?

In some countries, many children are kept from school and sent to work for economic reasons. Although many governments have legislated against such practices, enforcement often presents great difficulty, particularly for governments with limited resources. The situation is therefore one of the delinquent parent and the delinquent state. The question to be asked is, what kind of educational choice can the child make? If an adolescent selects a particular school because his friends attend it, does this constitute choice in the strict sense, or is it merely peer pressure? Is it not the case that in this technological era, that a child at any level of the educational process is capable of being knowledgeable concerning what he/she wants to pursue? If this is the case, should not students then be active agents in determining not only their own interests, but also the kind of educational system society needs in order to function effectively? This position can be disturbed with another observation that what students possess is not knowledge that can be drawn on to make informed decisions, but mere fragments of information which lack coherence and an wholistic view of education. They are seen therefore as being ill-equipped to make appropriate decisions concerning their educational welfare. The arguments advanced by John Harris, however, effectively disposes of this position.

Despite the various arguments, the central question re-emerges. Who should make the decisions concerning education? Is it the child, the family, or the state? We have seen the deficiencies involved in this trio in terms of 'choice competence, ' and the morality of choice. But there is another variable which is external in origin. In many instances, choice is not determined by interest, feelings, family preference, or based on the area one is most competent in. It is governed by what various entities in society such as industry, commerce, technology, or the professions prefer. Choice then becomes a matter of ministering to the needs of these external actors, and is made for purposes of survival, rather than on considerations of what we want as autonomous moral agents. But if choice is made on the basis of externally driven considerations, can it really be characterised as such? Does it therefore mean, that educational choice has been superseded by the requirements of a technologically driven, entrepreneurial society?

To revisit the concept of the right of the individual to choose, and the obligations of the state, important questions can be posed. Should the school, as an agent of the state possess the authority to decide on the course of studies the child should pursue? Who should determine the curriculum to be followed? Should the child not be involved in decisions in this vital area? What about the extra-institutional forces with powerful influence of a cultural and political nature which impact on curricula thinking? In this wider societal framework, the child's education could be affected by hidden agendas, the hidden curriculum, and other subtle, covert ideological influences and preferences. The implications are that the apparent choices which are made by the child will be unsuspectingly directed along those avenues supported by those who uphold the preferred culture. Instead of having students who are educated to think reflectively, the reality would be that this education was cleverly shaped along the desired paths by the protectors of society's 'real' culture. Is educational choice then, a myth?

Some Philosophical Observations

The question of who should be responsible for educational choice, the child, the family or the state, seems to elude consensual resolution. This is because of its complex nature and the fact that it crisscrosses varied interests. Those who take a pluralist, and therefore a democratic position, believe that the state should exert minimal interference in the affairs of its citizens, leaving them with the maximum freedom to exercise choice unhindered by the rigid requirements of the state in the form of rules, regulations, or altruistic moral pronouncements. A further view is taken by the defenders of the rights of the child who advance the case that children, like adults, also have rights that should be respected and protected, and that one of these is the right to choose the kind of education they feel suits their interests. Other arguments have been put forward contesting this, and alleging that the child is incapable of making such educational choices because of limited experience and knowledge. But how much experience and knowledge are required, and what is needed to foster this maturity?

If we should assume that it comes from the ability to think critically, then a further controversy develops. William Hare recently looked at debates on this issue. He says that Russell did not think it possible to train the intelligence without imparting information.(16) This implies that to think critically, children require an information base, which is officially regarded as being provided by the school, which is a state institution. If this is the case, then the problem arises that the trained intelligence referred to by Russell will also be passed on in the form of methodologies regarded as appropriate by the state, which again implies subtle control and direction by this institution. But what about spontaneity where the children are concerned? Where do the spontaneous answers to issues and problems come from? Will the information provided to the children have all the requirements to enable rational choice to be made? Would not choice be limited to the particular framework in which that information was structured, and could it not be limiting, rather than liberating, bringing about the kind of critical thinking that education seeks to foster? How can we determine the precise age and amount of knowledge a child requires in order to affirm with authority that he has reached the age where rational, critical thought is now possible?

What about those choices children make in their everyday interactions? They certainly know what harms or hurts, what to avoid, what is regarded as a prudent decision, as opposed to one that they disagree with, and are quite capable of discerning consequences, where their actions are concerned. This is why misunderstanding results with their peers, which are often over the most important strategies to employ in particular circumstances as opposed to others, and involves what actions would bring the most desirable as opposed to the most undesirable consequences. Children often complain, even at the lower levels of the school system, about conditions at school, the behaviour of their peers, and the attitudes of some teachers. They are able to weigh, assess, and arrive at conclusions about these teachers and their own preferences, and devise survival or coping strategies. This would seem to indicate that they have intuitive notions of what is good for them. And if it is, as Plato states, that knowledge is innate and the teacher's job is to help the child to remember, then there are implications for the system of education in terms of its relevance and purpose. If we all possess knowledge, what happens to our theories of child development, including when children are supposed to reach the age of maturity, which is presumed to facilitate rational choice?

The issue of innate knowledge as opposed to empiricism, or the acquisition of knowledge by experience has been taken up recently by Peter Simpson. He compares the position of Descartes and Locke. Descartes argues for innate knowledge, while Locke defends knowledge by experience. Simpson states that what tends to impress Descartes, and causes him to argue for the position of innate ideas, is that 'the content of our knowledge is such, that it cannot be accounted for in purely empirical terms. (17) This is where considerations have to be given to non-rational, non-empirical factors such as intuition and spontaneity. If in our attempts to find the truth through knowledge we make choices based on our preferences and hidden biases, and delete competing theories, rather than see knowledge as holistic and integrative, then we will deny ourselves of very valuable experiences and insights. We would also not be too quick to attach unfavourable labels such as 'immaturity,' and 'inexperience' to others, which are often employed to deny or restrict, rather than expand and enrich.

Whose choice is it then to educate? Is it the child's, the family's, or the state's? If an holistic perspective is taken of the educational process, all three, are to some extent involved at particular levels, in partnership with the other. Although there may be quibblings about who specifically should be responsible for what, the point is, that responsibility is collective, despite the fact that each entity seeks to assert its rights as pertinent issues emerge. What is at stake, is the entire society, and a consensus on what is required. What is also really of significance to note, is, as Jeffreys eloquently asserts:

We cannot think of the 'State' without also thinking about 'public opinion.' While the State exerts formal control through the various instruments of government, a great deal of informal control is exercised by public opinion. In a sense public opinion is more powerful than government. For no government can for any length of time run counter to the prevailing climate of opinion, or exceed what public opinion will support.(18)

If this line of argument is accepted, is it not the family, which includes the child, that constitutes, and is responsible for the existence of a government, which runs the state? And conversely, is not the state the people, who comprise the national family, and therefore public opinion? Does this not therefore mean that educational choice in a strict sense is collective, and as a result is not the preserve of any single entity? Furthermore, is not collective decision making involving multiple parties one of the basic tenets of democracy and reflects an important value which education as an agent of change seeks to promote?

References

1. Nathan Tarcov, Locke's Education for Liberty: University of Chicago Press, 1984.
2. M. Gillett, Readings in the History of Education: McGraw-Hill, 1969:195.
3. Richard Peters, Ethics & Education: George Allen & Unwin Ltd., 1966:195.
4. Paulo Friere, Pedagogy of the Oppressed: Penguin Books, 1972.
5. Op.cit. : 67.
6. J. Brubacher, Modern Philosophies of Education: McGraw-Hill, 1962.
7. R.B.Wagner, Accountability in Education: A Philosophical Inquiry: Routledge, 1989.
8. M.V.C.Jeffreys, Education: Its Nature and Purpose: Unwin Educational Books, 1971.
9. Peter Gordon & John White, Philosophers as Educational Reformers: Routledge & Kegan Paul, 1979.
10. K. Strike, Liberty and Learning: St. Martin's Press, 1982.
11. Peter Gordon & John White, op. cit. :36.
12. K.Strike, op.cit.: 157.
13. op.cit. : 158.
14. M.V.C.Jeffreys, op.cit.:10.
15. John Harris, The Political Status of Children.
16. William Hare, Context and Criticism: The Aims of Schooling: Journal of Philosophy of Education, 29.1.1995 :49.
17. Peter Simson, International Philosophical Quarterly: 25.1.97. March 1995 :18.
18. M.V.C.Jeffreys, op.cit.: 10.

Spirituality and Education: Epistemology as Ethic

CHAPTER  19

OLIVER MILLS

Abstract

Parker Palmer in his book "To know As We Are Known," states that our way of knowing becomes our way of being, and that our epistemology becomes our ethic. This implies that our theory of knowledge, or the way knowledge is acquired and utilised, will impact on and determine the kind of behaviour that is exhibited. This presupposes that care and rationality should be exercised when we are presented with various epistemologies since these could shape perceptions and orientations either enhancing or enriching human well being and experience, or distorting and misrepresenting it. Philosophers of education should therefore become the purveyors of knowledge strategies that contribute to individual and societal flourishing in an altruistic way, rather than advocate ideologies that foster divisiveness and political and social mistrust.

The Cultural Context

Education as a discipline has come under increasing analysis in recent times because of extraordinary occurrences in many of our educational institutions globally. Many schools have experienced vandalism, violence, challenges to authority in a way that seeks to undermine rather than assert democratic rights, extensive fraud, and in some cases fatalities have occurred. One Caribbean official has spoken of students being exposed to organised dishonesty, and a minister of education and culture has stated that an important outcome of these developments is the realisation of just how important education is for individuals and the nation as a whole. The role of education seems to be contradictory. In one instance it is regarded as an instrument of transformation, but in others, a contradiction presents itself, since the very institutions in which it is being promoted, are the ones that are plagued with problems. The response has been to enforce discipline further by invoking the rules, and in addition, there are calls for more extra-curricula activities which it is hoped would channel the energies of students into more positive ventures. The expansion of civic activities has also been recommended, where students will learn the virtues of responsibility, pride, accountability, and the importance of having shared values.

But these measures have not been rationally thought through, and represent spontaneous reactions of a superficial nature to issues and challenges that transcend, or go deeper than mere mechanical responses. These ad hoc attempts at solutions do not take into account the wider metaphysical issues of who we are, the nature of the self, what our purpose is, and the issue of values, or even more profoundly, concerns about the need for a new epistemology that redirects and transforms human actions and behaviour. In the corporate environment, a similar situation of alienation is present, particularly in cases where downsizing, corporate mergers, authoritarian structures and minimal participation in organisational decision-making are factors that govern everyday relationships. There are feelings of emptiness, of a lack of self-control and mastery, and a sense that a wider purpose is lacking. But some corporate officials are beginning to recognise this deficit in the lives of employees and these organisations have become more sensitive to the inner feeling and emotional and spiritual needs of individuals. They have therefore encouraged meditation, praying, engaging in introspection, and the practice of silence, which employees say enables them to empty the self of negatives and acquire fresh perspectives about who they are, and their purpose and mission beyond the status of mere employees.

These values that are practised are spiritual in essence, and in a wider sense are concerned with trust, harmony co-operation, honesty, and achieving balance and perspective. These are also the corporate values that employers seek to foster, so it can be said that the reason why spirituality is encouraged is because it contributes to making the individual more moral and productive, and ensures healthy profits for the corporations. But a wider dimension is at work here. Spiritually conscious corporate officials recognise that there is a basic humanity that is involved. They are aware that efficiency, effectiveness and productivity are not the only goals of individuals and corporations, but that the individual who achieves inner peace, a sense of balance, and who through a unique experience can relate to others in the work place through values such as respect, caring and commitment, will be more fulfilled, with repository benefits to the organisation. It means a more humane organisation, where people can transcend everyday challenges, where work is fun and not a drudgery, and where people are valued over technology. A spiritual ethic is therefore being fostered in both the corporate enterprise, and in education generally.

Spirituality as an Ethic

But what in a more expansive sense is spirituality and the spiritual ethic? King (1993) says that spirituality is not something that is added on to life as a separate pursuit, but grows out of the tensions and the fibres of our experience. For her, it is the human quest to seek fulfilment, liberation, and points towards transcendence within the dynamics of human experience. She speaks of the many who seek a sense of direction and identity and question the meaning of life, asking what are its fundamental goals and values. Spirituality therefore involves a search for direction in times of crises. It is a process of transformation and growth, an exploration into what is involved in becoming human, and an attempt to enhance one's sensitivity to the self and others. Spirituality as presented here is intertwined with life itself and involves an active search for values that transcend individuality, reflecting an altruistic morality. It provides meaning whereby people are able to make sense of their experiences and relates to the quest for a more responsive and compassionate humanity. Spirituality is not about religion, or seeking to convert people to a particular religious orientation. It is about recognising that every person possesses his or her own truth, integrity and dignity, since people are not just biological organisms, but also have embodied in their pysche positive emotions such as being helpful to others, being courageous, showing concern and reciprocity in their relationships, and valuing others and themselves.

Spirituality also involves mutual trust, well wishing, keeping promises, fostering self-esteem, showing self-respect and self-confidence, and the capacity to hope. It further means deferring to others when in doing so, a greater good would be achieved. Fox (1991) states that spirituality takes a path that leads away from the privatised and individualistic into the deeply communitarian. Spirituality here is therefore represented as involving community, where the interests of all take precedence over the personal, but where the personal and individual are more fully refined to become the authentic self in its interactions with the wider community. Price (1996), when asked to enunciate the common characteristics of spiritual beings listed these as having a spiritual priority in life, a sense of unconditional love, peace, right judgment, and the practice of the presence of God. He describes 'unconditional love 'as being filled with the love and joy of living repelling all negatives, and peace' as the art of peaceful relaxation whereby serenity is experienced. 'Right judgement involves common sense being transformed into spiritual wisdom, and discernment. He sees spirituality as the quality of oneness with spirit. This is a vague expression which needs further explanation and elaboration. It does not provide additional information and fails to enrich the concept with new ideas. He describes the spiritual life as taking control of our thoughts, words and emotions, and working through negativity and depression, and regards being on the spiritual path as being joyful, cheerful, gleeful, buoyant, jubilant, glad and light-hearted. For Price, the spiritual life also encompasses doing the best you can, helping others, and radiating love and peace. What he does not provide, is a strategy for accomplishing these virtues. He also does not say whether these represent a consensus, or are his personal views after carefully reflecting on the issue. However, the virtues mentioned could form the basis of an educational programme in schools dealing with mutual respect, conflict resolution, and interpersonal relationships.

On commenting on spirituality, Moore (1992) states that:

> Spirituality doesn't arrive fully formed without effort. Religions around the world demonstrate that spiritual life requires constant attention and a subtle, often beautiful technology by which spiritual principles and understandings are kept alive.. Sacred technology is largely aimed at helping us remain conscious of spiritual ideas and values (p.204).

Moore seems to be saying that spirituality requires a context which is provided by religion and can be regarded as its technology. Here he differs from other writers, including some of those mentioned here, who see spirituality and religion as separate entities with particular functions, although these might cohere in some respects. Moore further states that a degree of asceticism is a necessary part of spirituality. However, there are others who feel that spirituality involves abundance, the enjoyment of life, self-fulfilment and self-flourishing. Denial in any way is seen as not using one's capacities and gifts to maximise and enhance the quality of life and existence.

Moore seems to be unable to erase the traditional asceticism practised by the early church. This is re-enforced by the fact that he is a monk by training. His spirituality in many instances appears to be more rooted specifically in religion, rather than in experience, a rational reflection of the meaning of life, and the quest to find meaning and serenity in the dynamics of everyday existence. However, he sees spirituality as being reflected in sensitivity, being emotionally connected, nourishing and transforming our sense of ourselves, and having a depth of feeling and imagination. These qualities could form important ingredients of a curriculum which seeks to foster education for spirituality. It means that students will become more caring, mindful of others, develop an aesthetic appreciation, and become more tolerant, respectful and humane towards each other. The concern here is how can a spirituality of education be taught without the fear of being accused of indoctrination. What methodology could be used to present the information in such a way that students come to their own conclusions about the issues, without being psychologically shaped to accept a particular way of thinking and being.

In a further section of his discourse, Moore states that:

> spirituality does demand attention, mindfulness ,regularity, and devotion. It asks for some small measure of withdrawal from a world set up to ignore the soul.

It is true that an education for spirituality must be continuous and be attended to in order to further enrich its values. It also involves mindfulness and devotion. This is necessary to maintain a commitment to a new set of values, defend them where challenges arise, but be mindful of the radical changes and new and different interpretations which inevitably arise. Open-mindedness is therefore central to a spirituality of education. But Moore's view that spirituality demands a measure of withdrawal from the world is ambiguous. In a positive sense, this could mean withdrawal to assess and move further on, but it could be interpreted in the strong sense as forsaking the world. If the latter is meant, it would imply that the individual would be seeking to protect his or her spiritual values from the invasion of a society from which he or she is an integral part. It is this very society that provides the dynamics and fertile ground for the expansion and enrichment of both education and spirituality. Moore appears unable to escape the influence of his previous training as a religious figure. This is again seen when he says that the loss of formal religious practice is a threat to spirituality, and observes that a potential source of spiritual renewal is the religious tradition we were brought up in. This could cause some controversy among educators who see spirituality as an epistemology and practice that exists independently of any doctrine.

The inclusion of religion would suggest attempts at doctrinal advocacy , or a subtle move to proselytise and orient the individual in a particular direction. Spirituality, however involves the practice of freedom, of free individuals interacting with their environment and garnering positive experiences which enable them to embrace each other as humans, honour the individuality of each other, empathise, and promote the interests and aspirations of society through the transformed consciousness of each individual. It advocates harmony, a sense of identity and purpose, individual dignity, inner peace and tranquillity, and societal cohesion through the recognition of a common identity and goals. It seeks to liberate and not indoctrinate, and aims at realising freedom of choice, freedom to question, and an acceptance of the importance of the individual and what he or she engages in. Spirituality is therefore self-realisation and self-discovery and aims at self-renewal through self-transformation. It is not something that is imposed, but emerges from the experiences and developing consciousness of the individual that the values and knowledge embedded in this epistemology make sense, and therefore bring about the greatest happiness for the greatest number, since acceptance presupposes certain levels of awareness have been attained.

In her discussion of spirituality, Myss (1996) says that it is more than a psychological and emotional need, but an inherently biological one. For her, our spiritual task is to learn to balance the energies of the body and soul, of thought and action, and physical and mental power. She feels that all of these constitute the same force. It is her view that this balancing brings about healing, since when there is inner harmony and peace, other forces are released to perform psychological healing and the recreation of lives. This is another dimension of what spirituality is, and can accomplish. Of course, when our disparate thoughts are given rational direction, we are able to think more clearly and logically, and rash or irrational action is avoided. We then choose prudently, and this could form the basis of psyche tranquillity. This is probably what Myss means by 'spirituality bringing about healing,' and is re-enforced by her statement later that all human stress corresponds to a spiritual crisis, the resolving of which is brought about through a serenity of the mind which generates meaning and purpose. She states further that a spiritual crisis is reflected in such symptoms as an awareness of an absence of meaning and purpose, experiencing strange, new fears, and the feeling of a need to experience devotion to something greater than the self. Can a spirituality of education help the individual to resolve these psychological challenges by designing educational technologies that equip him or her with the knowledge to recognise these symptoms, and impart the skills and appropriate dispositions to successfully confront the disorders mentioned? Would this not mean a new and radical function for education, resulting in a different type of training for educators, and the formulation of a new curriculum?

An important contribution to this concept of spirituality is given by management thinker Charles Handy (1998), when he states:

> we all need a taste of the sublime, to lift our hearts, to give us a hint of something bigger than ourselves and of the infinite possibilities of life.

This echoes the meaning, spirit and emotion of the previous statements made by the other writers mentioned. Such phrases as a taste of the sublime,' 'something bigger than ourselves,' and 'the infinite possibilities of life,' all speak to a kind of transcendence associated with spirituality, which encompasses the aesthetic, and a sense of the metaphysical and mystical. Handy then presents the official definition of spirituality given by the Department of Education in the U.K., which is 'The valuing of the non-material aspects of life, and intimations of an enduring reality.' This definition incorporates the meaning and intent of the others given earlier, and presents a non-religious perspective. A spirituality of education, with non-religious components or emphasis has the capacity to attract a vast number of persons who are uncomfortable with dogma, and want to adopt a value system that is free of the influence of official religion. They respect and love nature, feel a sense of awe when contemplating the universe, and have a consciousness of an essence which is greater than themselves. But they also want to feel in control, and be the agents of their own hopes and direction. They also feel connected to others in an inexplicable bond, and want to be more human. However, they do not want to feel overwhelmed by a force they cannot manage, or one that reminds them of their frailty and helplessness. They want a value system that makes them feel empowered, autonomous, and which provides a sense of self-mastery. Spirituality becomes the ethic comprising these values. It shapes their understanding and interpretation of life, and directs their being.

This quest for a deeper meaning of life, and the desire to make sense of the dynamics of existence and transcend the routine and predictable, leads to the search for inner peace, self-fulfilment, positive valuing, and creative imagining. Together these reflect the ingredients of spirituality, and the content of an educational philosophy with spirituality as its cornerstone. Such an education leads to transformation through the fostering of a higher consciousness. These values generate an ethic of service, commitment, tolerance, and the search for a greater truth. The individual sees a noble purpose in life, and seeks to nourish and enrich his or her humanity, and that of others. A positive mental shift occurs, where individuals become more socially responsible, and perform acts of goodwill towards others. Dyer (1996) expresses similar sentiments when he says:

> When I talk about spirituality and being spiritual, I am describing an attitude towards God and the inner Journey of enlightenment. I am speaking of expanding the godlike qualities of love, forgiveness, kindness and bliss within ourselves. In my interpretation, spirituality is not dogma or rules. It is light and joy and focuses on the experiences of love and inner bliss, radiating those qualities outward.

These thoughts to the critic might be described as mystical and bordering on new age philosophy. They represent however, an honest attempt to capture a new perception of what a new quality of human relationships and values should entail, and fit appropriately into the kind of transformed curriculum that would reflect a spirituality of education. With the many problems in our global institutions and societies such as a lack of trust, violence in schools, white collar crimes, corruption and deception, these spiritual values present an alternative way of thinking and being. They challenge our humaneness, sense of honour and integrity, which enable us to realise that we are not merely commercial and economic units, but beings with a higher, noble purpose which involves fashioning a society based on civility, deference and harmonious living.

There are others who see spirituality as encompassing broader social and societal aims. Templeton (1998) states that:

> Spiritual progress has both inner and outer dimensions that promote personal and social improvement. Spiritual progress involves something that is new. And spiritual progress often includes, or is combined with, progress in other fields of endeavour. For example, new ways of helping the poor and underprivileged in our world may be to help donees to become donors.

This position presents spirituality as socially responsible, and as a practical mechanism for changing the status of the underprivileged. It seeks to radically change the status of those who are marginalised, and presents a rallying call for those with social deficits, to claim their humanity and dignity, and by so doing, become equal members and co-participants in the wider development process. This means that previous receivers become givers, thereby bringing about equality and equity in human intercourse. The writer further goes on to mention spiritual subjects, which he describes as love, prayer, meditation, thanks-giving, giving, forgiving, and surrender to the divine will (p.68). This list repeats in some ways the elements of spirituality mentioned by other writers, but is more expansive. It also includes a reference to a higher entity which is recognised as the ultimate source. These perceptions are typical of those that often describe the ingredients of a philosophy of spirituality, although in some instances religious overtones are revealed, such as those referring to prayer, thanksgiving, and the divine will. This however reflects the inclusiveness of the concept of spirituality, which is not tied, or limited to one set of rigid categories. In addition, when a spirituality of education can include other dimensions that widen its brief, it means the promulgation of a kind of education that is wholistic. Is this not what education should be about, involving the widening, deepening, and open-ended pursuit of truth?

Education: A Philosophical Perspective

Education is a contested concept in the sense that any attempt to define it is immediately followed by an assessment, critical evaluation, and the advancement of new perspectives of meaning. This is as it should be, since the discourse seeks to uncover deficiencies and inaccuracies in the pursuit of truth. Peters (1970) states that education implies the transmission of what is worthwhile, involves knowledge and understanding, and rules out some procedural methods which lack wittingness and voluntariness. Of course, there have been several debates around Peters' conceptualisation. Arguments have been advanced questioning what is worthwhile, and who decides. Critics have also stated that knowledge and understanding are not the attributes of the educated exclusively, since many who have not been exposed to education in the formal sense to any significant degree possess these qualities as well. Peters' view has therefore often been described as representing an elitist concept of education, something which a spirituality of education would find repulsive. Again, the procedures involved in delivering the educational product have attracted much discussion, and indoctrination has been ruled out, with the learner coming to conclusions based on a rational and critical analysis of the issues presented. However, Peters' perspective provides a foundation and guide for considerations and discussions about education and its role. Peters' position that knowledge and understanding must be an integral part of education and that choice is involved by the learner reflects the perspective embedded in an education with a spiritual orientation. A spirituality of education facilitates an environment where the individual ,without coercion, comes through reasoning to accept particular views, through his or her own contribution to the discourse. Here, knowledge and understanding provide the data base for individual choice. The ethics of the process is also reflected in the non-authoritarian nature of the way the search for truth is pursued.

An interesting approach concerning what education is all about is taken by Carr (1995) . He uses the philosopher Plato to state that:

education in the true sense of the term is the process through which people acquire that kind of philosophical enlightenment that will emancipate them from the dictates of ignorance, dogma and superstition.

He goes on to say that as portrayed in the Republic, philosophy is the ultimate end of education as well as the means to its critical understanding and transformation. Here, education and philosophy are intertwined resulting in an enhanced understanding and the transformation of perspectives. The ethic of a spirituality of education is also the refashioning of our way of knowing, which alters our way of being. Spirituality and philosophy, with education as an end, seek emancipation through the use of reason and dialogue, instead of adherence to received wisdom and ideological dictates. The result of this is enlightenment through wisdom. In connection with this view of education as enlightenment or transformation, White (1989) in writing on democratic education states that:

a democratic education will help people to determine in a thoughtful way what they should do in a certain situation to promote or defend democratic values, rather than falling back on stereotypes.

Here, decisions are arrived at autonomously by individuals from the exercise of critical thinking about the issues. A spirituality of education has the same purpose, with the individual and his or her experiences being at the centre of the educational process. No standard ethic is proposed to which conformity is required, rather a plurality of experiences and positions are assumed and encouraged. Martin (1996), gives a critical and different perspective to the definition of education. She argues that:

Education is also gender-related. Our definition of its function makes it so. For if education is viewed as preparation for carrying on processes historically associated with males, it will inculcate traits the culture considers masculine. If the concept of education is tied by definition to the productive processes of society, our ideal of the educated person will coincide with the cultural stereotype of a male human being, and our definitions of excellence in education will embody masculine traits.

Education is portrayed here as non-neutral, presenting the picture of a male activity, discriminating against the other sex. Martin seems to be alleging that education re-enforces gender stereotypes. If this is the case, then bias would be attributed to a concept and practice that should be non-prejudicial. This is where an education with spirituality as its cornerstone differs. A spirituality of education is not gender-centred, but is all inclusive. It represents equality and fairness, and honours and respects diversity, while seeking harmony over divisiveness. Education aims at building, enhancing and enriching, rather than at excluding and separating. In a wider philosophical sense, education provides the perspective whereby the individual comes to see the interconnection of various phenomena. He or she develops an holistic view of the issues and is able to rigorously critique them and arrive at the most prudent position. Education further enables the individual to discriminate between and among options, or even refuse to make a decision if it cannot be rationally defended. It shapes and enriches our taste, helps us to select those situations which empower us, and broadens our horizons, enabling us to see the changing nature of events and circumstances. Education can therefore be said to provide the kind of environment from which spirituality is spawned. Both are therefore interconnected and mutually enriching aspects of the same phenomenon.

Spirituality as an Educational Ethic

Spirituality is concerned with providing the qualities and values that make the individual more humane, responsible, caring and compassionate. Education provides the theoretical framework and practical programmes and strategies that operationalise the ethic of spirituality. Education therefore becomes a spiritual journey in search of what is true, good, right and just. In a globalised world faced with the threats of environmental devastation, terrorism, military conflicts, and the development and production of weapons of mass destruction, an education in spirituality provides the content, strategy and perspective that points to an alternative way to manage the complex affairs of our world. Spirituality as an educational ethic shows a new way of knowing which informs our being. It reflects the integratedness of humanity, exposes the common nature of our problems and concerns, and provides a perspective that calls for unity, harmony and consensus in bringing about potential solutions. It portrays wholeness, and describes a way of knowing and educating that might heal rather than wound us and our world' (Palmer, 1993). As an educational ethic, spirituality registers a new morality, whereby we come to treasure the world community as the common property of humanity in general, to be explored and utilised for the benefit of every inhabitant irrespective of country of origin, ethnic or racial extraction, or socioeconomic position. Using power and resources to dominate are replaced with the ethic of employing these assets to discover new sources of knowledge that cure threatening diseases, and formulate new strategies that resolve conflicts amicably, because of a shared commitment to the process of human advancement through knowledge.

Spirituality as an educational ethic further seeks to create a greater reverence for nature and for life itself; foster an awareness of the individual as a noble being, with a contribution to make to the perfection of a new and different society; and advances the view of society as a community engaged in the pursuit of the good for everyone. The vision of society is one where sensitivity to suffering, social ills and political extremes, and the pursuit of solutions to these becomes the norm. In essence, a spirituality of education seeks to transform the cause of these traditional crises, and creates a situation where neither the climate nor the environment can exist that breeds these ills. Through education, a new individual with a developed consciousness emerges who is altruistic and communitarian in outlook, and ethically disposed to want to engage in those acts that advance society's aspirations. In a further sense, it enhances our knowledge of ourselves, is concerned with empowering behaviour and not manipulating others, and fosters authentic, spontaneous relationships between individuals. It connects the knower to the known, and it is from this interdependence that truth emerges (Palmer, 1993).

In a critique of spirituality and education, Carr (1996) states that the most striking feature of the idea of a spiritual education is the urgent need for a rigorous philosophical analysis in a realm where the bulk of the talk is notoriously fast and loose. He argues that the recent celebrations of the educational significance of a spiritual education could hardly be meaningful in the absence of identifying what the curricula claims of the spiritual, as distinct from the moral or religious might be. He notes further, that a common conception of spirituality refers not to any particular category of human experience, activity or endeavour which are otherwise unremarkable. He describes this as the reductionist concept, and feels that this idea of spirituality for spiritual education does little to identify specific practical goals which it might be the business of a distinctly spiritual education to set out to achieve.

Carr's position provokes an immediate response. In describing talk about a spiritual education as being fast and loose, he misses the central point that this 'talk' is a result of a philosophical analysis of the concept, and emerging from this is a body of ideas, thought and knowledge concerning what is integral to it. The case is therefore advanced for its inclusion in the curriculum, because of specific features that serve to shape dispositions, intentions and thinking about the meaning of life, education and society, presenting an alternative value model of how these challenges can be approached. Carr is again mistaken in thinking that conceptions of spirituality are inexplicable or mysterious, even unremarkable. As has been pointed out throughout discussions on this issue, spirituality is about none of the descriptions that Carr provides of it. It is clearly explained and is not mysterious, but represents a remarkable change in philosophy and direction of a different view of the kind of knowledge and values that could transform our lives and world. A spirituality of education suggests a new ethic of interpersonal relations, which connects with the governance of the self and society. Carr also misinterprets the intentions of a spirituality of education when he states that the idea of spirituality for spiritual education does little to identify specific practical goals it should set out to achieve. The fact is that a spiritual education is itself goal-oriented. Many of these have been discussed in this chapter. However, Parker Palmer expands on these when he states with reference to spirituality in education, that it is concerned with:

— non-exploitation and manipulation, but reconciliation
— a re-unification and reconstruction of broken selves and worlds
— becoming members of one community
— using minds not to divide and conquer, but to raise consciousness and awareness of the communal nature of reality
— overcoming separateness and alienation
— acquiring a knowledge which allows love and compassion to inform our relations with ourselves and others
— seeing beyond self-interest to showing compassion
— regarding ourselves and the world with trust and hope
— realising that a compassionate education creates a counter current to cynicism and violence
— practising disciplines that empower us to engage in the kind of teaching that will reform students and the world

These values represent clear goals and objectives of an education for spirituality. They are integrated and all encompassing and together form a coherent body of thought for current practice and analysis in order to further expand and enrich our understanding. Another weakness in Carr's arguments is that he uses spirituality and religion to mean the same thing, when one is really an aspect of the other in one sense, and in another have separate and distinct references and meanings. Carr's position however provides another perspective on an emerging and philosophically contested area, although others will contend that the core philosophical principles of a spirituality of education are clear and unambiguous.

Some Critical Perspectives and Conclutions

A spirituality of education is an emerging concept, and will therefore be initially be approached with caution, suspicion, and in some instances with humour. However there will be others who will view it as an alternative epistemology which deals with human beings as fully functioning individuals with the capacity to re-engineer their circumstances, and transform their way of being to become empathetic, resilient in the face of challenges, and exercise emotional intelligence when dealing with issues and each other. In this process, a spirituality of education does not involve dogmas, doctrines or rules, but a new way of understanding the world and our place in it. If a spirituality of education is to be considered as a viable philosophy, catering to the unmet and unrealised needs of clients in education, then it would require that teachers be educated differently to reflect this new ethic. Currently education is seen as a conservative enterprise. The teachers of a spiritual education would have to be trained to be open-minded, assertive, caring individuals with a love for humanity. This requires a psychic shift in their perceptions and in how they process knowledge and information. It would mean the development of new kinds of educational technologies, making the educational process more student friendly, and new methods and strategies of classroom management which see individuals as important elements in the educational endeavour, to be encouraged and praised, and not belittled and devalued.

A spirituality of education would also require a change in curricula content, methods, objectives and aims, which would reflect the advent of the new kind of person and society with the qualities and values mentioned throughout this discourse. The curriculum of schools is often very conservative, and takes a long period to change and reflect new developments. However the new spirituality curriculum will require commitment, tolerance and understanding in the face of initially hostile reactions. This will happen because some will see it as a subtle manoeuvre to introduce religion, while others will see it as creating passive, praying individuals who turn the other cheek, and fail to honour their responsibilities to society. It might even be thought in some instances that a new kind of cult is being foisted on the schools, duping innocent children into acceptance of a new value system which challenges traditional values.

There are still many other individuals who will see spirituality as a threat to fostering courageous and critical citizens, and as possessing authoritarian attributes in a disguised form which will impact negatively on democratic ideals. Some conservative educators will view it as being too idealistic, and against their philosophy of individualism and incrementalism. The pragmatists would argue about its practical application to the serious problems that are faced by educational institutions, and call for more experimentation, and an objective, scientific approach. The idealist educators would welcome it as a further contribution to the development of ideas about education and its capabilities as a discipline, since the belief is that everything has its origins in ideas. Cynics and sceptics would perceive the new spirituality of education as unrealisable, and manifesting the tendencies and principles of the new age movement. They would therefore regard it as mystical and extra-dimensional, and even inappropriate to be associated with a serious area such as education.

The philosophical point is, that the idea of a spirituality of education emerged from the dissatisfaction of many with current philosophical ideas and strategies about the aims and objectives of education. It includes broad and varied perspectives concerning how education and spiritual principles interact and mutually influence each other. It seeks to create a new and caring personality who is ethically disposed to undertaking virtuous acts, and who sees the world as an integrated place, where all meet to share its resources. It appeals to what is good, just and fair in individuals, and aims at creating wholesome relationships among civilised persons, who receive and share each other's gifts. On the question of sharing, Leonard (1995) in "Handbook for the Soul" states that 'When you share your own personal story, you find it isn't just your story; it is so many other people's stories ... In sharing each other's stories, we feel the common human bonds that unite us (p.8[1]). Globalization, by making the world a smaller place can bring about the oneness of countries. An education rooted in spirituality can result in a united humanity.

References

Carlson, R.,& Shield, B.(Eds.) Handbook for the Soul: Little Brown & Company, 1995.

Carr, D., Journal of Philosophy of Education: Vol.30, Issue 2, July 1996.

Carr, W., For Education: OUP, 1995.

Dyer, W.W., Your Sacred Self: Harper, 1995.

Fox, M., Creation Spirituality: Harper, 1991.

Handy, C., The Hungry Spirit: Broadway Books, 1998.

Hare, W. & Portelli, J., Philosophy of Education: Introductory Readings: Detselig Enterprises Ltd., 1996.

King, U., Women and Spirituality: Macmillan, 1993.

Maday, M. A., New Thought for a New Millennium: Unity Books,1998.

Moore, T., Care of the Soul: Harper Collins, 1992.

Myss, C., Anatomy of the Spirit: Harmony Books, 1996.

Palmer, P., To Know as we are Known: Education as a Spiritual Journey: Harper, 1993.

Peters, R. S., Ethics and Education: Allen & Unwin, 1970.

Price, J., Practical Spirituality, Hay House, 1996.

White, P.(Ed.), Personal and Social Education: Philosophical Perspectives, Kogan Page, 1989.

SECTION 7

PSYCHOLOGY OF EDUCATION

Chapter 20
Facilitating gifted learners in Jamaican primary schools:
Challenges and explorations
*W. Madge Hall and
Marguerite Narinesingh   201*

Chapter 21
Subjectivist Psychology and its Applications to Teaching
Tony Bastick   209

Chapter 22
Learning Styles as a Foundation of Instructional Activities
Susan Anderson   219

Caribbean Perspectives

CHAPTER 20

Facilitating gifted learners in Jamaican primary schools: Challenges and explorations

W. MADGE HALL AND MARGUERITE NARINESINGH

Abstract

The chapter presents one facet of an on-going approach to provide support for gifted learners in the Jamaican primary school system. Within the frame of theories relating to task commitment, contextual factors and achievement, the major focus is on an emerging model to facilitate academic diversity in the classroom.

General Context

It is acknowledged that among the 313,591 children currently enrolled in the Jamaican primary school system (PIOJ, 1997), there are gifted children. It is also an established fact that the needs of these children are not being met, due to several factors. Prominent among the contributing factors are the absence of appropriate identification measures and approaches, inadequate support from policy markers, misconceptions about learners with diverse abilities, and the inability of many educators to use strategies that take into account the differing needs of children.

With regard to identification, the use of standardized testing is still dominant although increasingly, there is interest displayed in other approaches and combinations of approaches. It is anticipated that this interest will at least in part, facilitate the involvement of classroom teachers in the identification process. The support provided by policymakers is primarily tacit. For example, the Ministry of Education and Culture (MOE&C) articulates equity for all children, but most of the recommendations made by a National Task Force for the Education of the Exceptionally Gifted (TFEEG) in 1991 are yet to be implemented. Among the findings of the TFEEG was an emphasis on school achievement as the main criterion for being gifted. In the absence of a national definition of giftedness, the Task Force proposed that gifted individuals be defined as ,'those with the potential to perform or create at a level that is superior too that of their age peers' (p.61).

Narinesingh (1994) examined the conceptions of giftedness held by Jamaican teachers, and noted that the emphasis was also on achievement in school. Teachers participating in her study consistently cited behaviours demonstrated by high achievers as being indicative of giftedness, with little or no value given to motivational factors. For example, when a Teachers' Rating Scale was used which contained clusters of items which positively and strongly correlated with a traditional intelligence measure, in the domains critical thinking, creativity, psycho-social, leadership characteristics and motivation, the latter was assigned the least importance. The study showed that an understanding of motivation, and its influence on both identifying and facilitating the abilities of gifted children were not evident in the practice and expressions of the teachers. It is plausible that the narrow perspective of the construct of giftedness is fuelled by the emphasis on performance goals as defined for example, by McInerney, Roche, Valentina, McInerney and Marsh (1997).

In this chapter, the construct of giftedness is conceptualized as multi-faceted, and relates to the theories of Renzulli (1986) who points to three areas, task commitment, above average ability and creativity. Further, it is believed that task commitment/ motivation or the energy brought to bear on a specific task can be nurtured in children. In addition, there is an awareness that motivation is unstable, varying with specific tasks.

As mentioned previously, there are several factors that must be addressed in facilitating support for Jamaican gifted learners at the elementary level, but this chapter addresses one factor, namely the need for teachers to provide inclusive classrooms. The position taken by us is that gifted education should be an integral part of the service provided for all children. Further, at the primary level we stand by the premise that programmes developed for gifted students are usually appropriate for children in general education. Therefore, given the contextual realities of limited resources, a continuum of services can become available in the primary schools, and these can support gifted learners.

The chapter is primarily conceptual and is influenced by the views of several researchers for example, Renzulli (1986), McInerney et al (1997) and Pintrich, Marx and Boyle (1993). The research question is 'What is required to help teachers to use sound pedagogical principles that will cater to diverse abilities in the classroom?

The Challenge

A focus on teachers in the classroom is essential, because if they do not participate actively in the process all other efforts will be futile. For example, teachers need to recognize the reasons for adopting an inclusive approach in their classrooms. They need also to develop expertise in differentiating curriculum and instruction in ways that extend the potentials of all learners. Many teachers are not only aware of the need to deviate from the traditional approach of teaching with a focus on children perceived as average, but also they want to change. This realization is evidenced in the teachers frustrations with their inability to facilitate the many children who are labelled slow or functioning below grade level. The main issue is the necessity to provide a feasible path to foster change. Pintrich et al (1993) among others present compelling arguments on the influence of classroom context on students motivation and cognition, and the importance of building links between the motivational and cognitive components of students' learning.

An emerging model highlighting the areas of emphasis in this quest to find a suitable path is illustrated in Figure 1. There are four interrelated classroom factors influencing school motivation and achievement, according to Pintrich et al (1993) among others, and each is highlight below. Regarding school motivation and achievement, the premise is that achievement goals guide students' cognitive behaviour as they perform academic tasks. Two of these goals are mastery or task oriented goals and performance or extrinsic goals (e.g. McInerney et al. 1997). The belief is that persons pursuing mastery goals develop new skills and improve levels of competence, and these are self-referenced. Essentially, performance goals are focused on personal ability and manifest themselves in social comparisons, for example, performance above or below the norm. Within the Jamaican context, the implication is that the relevance of an appropriate equilibrium between the two sets of goals have to be stressed.

Figure 1: Four classroom factors influencing school motivation and achievement

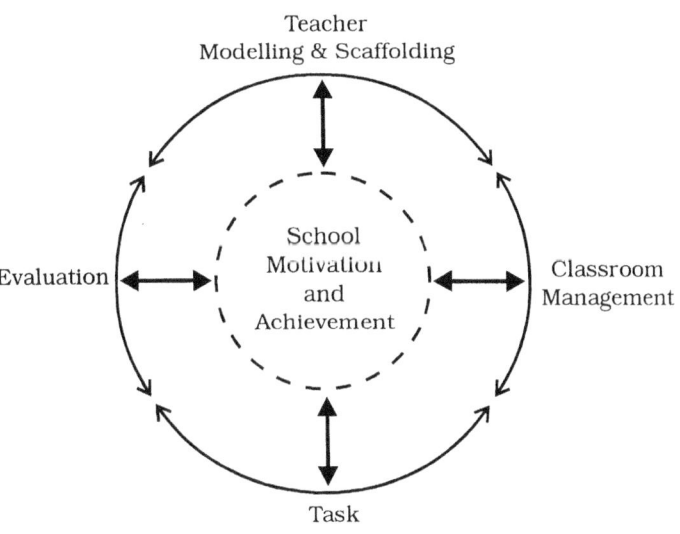

Teacher modelling and scaffolding

This relates to teachers' cognitive interpretation of pedagogy and manifests itself in part, in the individual's philosophy of teaching and learning. For example, does the teacher conceptualize at least in part, teaching as an experiment? What thinking styles are being displayed by the teacher in interacting with the students?

Classroom management

Included here is the overall classroom structure and organization. For example, what methods and pedagogic principles are in place to decrease the role of 'teacher authority' and facilitate the development of mental self- management in learners? Issues relating to use of time and the avoidance of premature closure of learners cognitive engagements during tasks are also part of this cluster. It is unfortunate that usually, time for each task in traditional classroom is standardized, with equal time given to all students to complete tasks. What has to be stressed is the development of flexible models of time usage as well as skills to develop student-centered classes.

Classroom Tasks

Here the emphasis is on value components that are personalized. Issues of interest, goal orientation, activities relevant to life skills and beliefs relating to ability to perform come to the fore. There is also recognition that students may differ from the teachers in their perception of the cognitive demands of tasks, for example, those that are structured versus the ones without specific structure. In reality, there is an emphasis on coverage of the syllabus, and difficulty is displayed when attempts are made to deviate in classrooms not oriented to the practice of multi-tasks. Tasks are usually standardized, and if these are not done in a specific way, the perception is that time is lost. The agenda, using this model has to include work on developing skills to identify key characteristics of concepts and designing strategies that foster differential approaches

Evaluation

The stress is on ensuring the understanding of concepts. As Grigorenko and Sternberg (1997) note, there is diversity in the learning styles of students and this implies the need for variety in assessment. The overall aim is to highlight the strengths of students, so evaluation is improvement based, hence, weakness displayed must be viewed as a way to foster development. Usually, student assessment is standard and summative. The way forward must stress instructional assessment, ongoing assessment with a formative focus and instructional adjustment based on new information. Fortunately, the Ministry of Education and Culture has begun the implementation of some forms of non-summative evaluations in primary schools. Grading is another facet which is characterized by a standard format, based on comparison among students, hence the need for alternatives such as contract grading, portfolio and checklists to show individual growth.

Generally, classrooms are characterized by uniformity, but models desired are those focusing on communities of learning for all as a fundamental principle. Each should reflect a variety of learning and thinking styles from which sometimes children can engage in their preferred style.

Essentially, the content of this emerging model is best shared in an in-service format during teachers professional development workshops. Tomlinson, Callahan, Tomchin, Eiss, Imbeau and Landrum (1997) attest to the efficacy of an in-service approach stating that teachers are likely to keep and use new strategies if they are coached in a relevant locational context. The teacher in this context is likely to have the opportunity to teach for understanding rather than coverage, the assessment would be a tool, directly concerned with growth, and the tasks relevant, varied and specifically designed to ensure growth.

Some Explorations

The activities explored within the local school context, relate to the emerging model. Workshops were held with teacher educators, teachers and children. In the workshops for adults, the content extended beyond the confines of the emerging model, because content was guided in part, by specific requests. However, in trying to resolve the matter of multi-level teaching, a practical path was to link the emerging model with ideas from Renzulli (1986) and Schlichter, Larkin, Casareno, Ellis, Gregg, Mayfield and Rountree (1997). These researchers highlight approaches that are based on constructivist principles..

In one approach, ideas from the Talents Unlimited format were utilized. In this structure, content listed as talents help to draw teachers' attention to concepts and strategies that must be highlighted in the teaching /learning act. Further, each 'talent' area requires a definition so, both teachers and students have an opportunity to determine suitable definitions and commensurate activities from within or outside the boundaries of the syllabus. In essence, this approach fosters the utilization of the classroom factors emphasized in Figure 1- classroom management, teacher modelling and scaffolding, tasks and evaluation procedures. Figure 2, on the next page, illustrates areas of 'talents, definitions and activities.

Since 1996, a series of workshops and an annual summer camp have been planned and implemented by one the authors for children. These activities are held outside of school time thereby allowing the children to operate in a social context other than the schoolhouse situation. The activities also serve as 'models' for classroom teachers.

In most cases participants for the workshops and camps are selected on the basis of a profile built around information received from teacher and parent nominations, a Teachers' Rating Scale (TRS) used for screening, an intelligence test, and work samples. The profile consists of both qualitative and quantitative data, and provide a means whereby the selection can be oriented towards demonstrated interest and talents. The intelligence test used to screen for potential giftedness is the Raven Standard Progressive Matrices. The attraction of this measure is that it requires minimal verbal content to understand the instruction and is therefore accepted as being less biased linguistically and culturally. This is an important consideration given that the Jamaican Creole is the mother tongue of most Jamaicans.

Figure 2 – Talents Unlimited Applications (Applying the Talents Unlimited Approach)

TALENT AREAS	DEFINITION	SAMPLE ACTIVITY
Academic	To develop a base of knowledge and skills about a topic or issue through acquisition of information and concepts	Participants are taught to take notes on famous pirates of Jamaica from a variety of sources
Productive Thinking	To generate many varied and unusual ideas or solutions, and to add detail to the ideas to improve or make them more interesting	During a brainstorming exercise, participants who are investigating the "rise and fall" of Spanish Town as the capital of Jamaica, are asked to develop "webs" of interesting and related topics
Decision Making	To outline, weigh, make final judgments and defend a decision on the many alternatives to a "problem"	Participants select a particular National Hero as the subject for a video by listing, critiquing, evaluating and prioritizing ideas according to the interest of the group, the availability of resources and equipment, time constraints, feasibility, etc.
Planning	To design a means for implementing an idea by describing what is to be done, identifying the resources needed, outlining a sequence of steps to take, pinpointing possible problems in the plan	Participants who are going to produce a video based on the story of The White Witch of Rose Hall outline the sequence of filming by creating a storyboard
Forecasting	To make a variety of predictions about the possible causes and/or effects of various phenomena	Before going on a field trip to Port Royal, participants are encouraged to make predictions about the possible effects of the major Earthquake in that town
Communication	To use and interpret both verbal and non-verbal forms of communication to express ideas, feelings and needs to others	A group of participants who have learned about the history and lifestyle of the original inhabitants of Jamaica, share their knowledge and express their feelings in a dance-drama based on the Taino legend of "Mountain Pride"

The TRS developed by Narinesingh (1994), rates the learner on behaviours which indicate high levels of initiative and self-direction, sustained interest and enthusiasm, persistence and involvement over time as well as goal directedness and success-orientation. Items on the scale were generated from ideas supplied by Jamaican primary school teachers as well as what is know from the literature.

The programme for the workshops and camps comprise carefully structured learning experiences which include stimulating activity based tasks intended and organized to motivate the participants. Some of the specific aims reflect the focus of the activities and these include participants:

-developing research skills (all programmes)
-using paper as a medium for creative productions (Paper mates)
-using different media such as computer and video camera as a creative tool (Media Micks)
-acquiring knowledge regarding the nations' heritage (summer camps).

Within the organized structures participants are allowed to select and concentrate on an area of interest, to choose a topic for further investigation and decide among possibilities for production according to personal interest. Consequently, paper bag puppets may represent a variety of characters while participants tell a folklore or may design a T-shirt to depict a beauty spot in Jamaica such as Dunns River Falls.

Future Directions

Given the needs and the realities, the plan is to continue workshops with both teachers and children and in the process continue to build the emerging model. We think that a crucial aspect of the development process is to compile a package with the content relevant to the model, to facilitate self-instruction within the classroom context. This would require mentoring from an expert teacher, who would also conduct workshops. This approach is feasible because, the MOE&C is committed to employing 'master teachers' in each primary school. Further, the revised primary school curriculum highlights integration and provides opportunities for teachers to pay attention to the factors that can enrich all learners.

References

Grigorenko, E. L. & Sternberg, R. J. (1997) Styles of thinking, abilities and academic performance. *Exceptional Children*, 63 (3) 295-312.

McInerney, D.M., Roche, L.A., McInerney, V., & Marsh, H. W.(1997). Cultural perspectives on school motivation: the relevance and application of goal theory. *American Educational Research Journal*. 34 (1) 207-236.

Planning Institute of Jamaica (1997). *Economic and Social Development of Jamaica* Jamaica: Author

Narinesingh, M. (1994). *Teacher ratings as a means of screening for gifted learners in* Jamaican primary schools. Unpublished MA thesis. University of the West Indies, Mona Jamaica.

National Task Force on the Education of the Exceptionally Gifted. (1991) *Working Document*. Ministry of Education Youth & Culture, Jamaica

Pintrich, P. R., Marx, R. W. & Boyle, R. A. (1993). Beyond cold conceptual change: the role of motivational beliefs and classroom contextual factors in the process of conceptual change. *Review of Educational Research*. 63 (2)167-200.

Renzulli, J. S. (1986) The three-ring conception of giftedness: a developmental model for creative productivity. In R.J. Sternberg & J. E. Davidson (eds.,). pp 52-92. *Conceptions of giftedness*. Cambridge University Press: Cambridge

Schlichter, C. L., Larkin, M. J., Casareno, A. B., Ellis, E.S., Gregg, M., Mayfield P. & Rountree, B. S. (1997) . Partners in enrichment: preparing teachers for multiple ability classrooms. *Teaching Exceptional Children*. 29 (4) 4-9.

Tomlinson, C.A., Callahan, C. M., Tomchin, E. M., Eiss, N., Imbeau, M. & Landrum, M. (1997). Becoming architects of communities of learning: addressing academic diversity in contemporary classrooms. *Exceptional Children*. 63 (2) 269-282.

CHAPTER 21

Subjectivist Psychology and its Applications to Teaching

TONY BASTICK

Abstract

This article describes Subjectivist psychology as an extension of Constructivism (Ernest, 1994; Glasersfeld, 1989, 1994; Saxe, 1991; Weinberg & Gavelek, 1987) and illustrates its use for guiding teaching and learning in the Caribbean.

Social Constructivism is currently a popular philosophy guiding thinking in school science and mathematics. Also, teachers tacitly accept that the affective components of learning can act as powerful multiplying factors in the constructivist classroom and so they endeavour to manage learning to promote interest, motivation, excitement and student's personal involvement. However, there is not as yet an accepted constructivist pedagogy to guide practising teachers of mathematics and science in this utilisation of affect. It is suggested that one of the factors contributing to this state of affairs is that Constructivism is a cognitivist philosophy which lacks consideration of the affective concomitants of social learning. Subjectivist psychology, however, is an affective-constructivist paradigm that focuses on both the cognitive and the affective experiences of learning. It focuses on the subjective experience of learning.

Subjectivist psychology describes the natural affective-cognitive enculturation processes that children experience in learning the skills, understandings and values of their society. These affect-laden processes of enculturation are transplanted to the constructivist classroom where they become the teaching techniques of the subjectivist teacher. The aims of subjectivist teaching are to empower students and enculturate them into the skills, understandings and values of their subjects. Enculturation techniques centre on needs-driven social communication activities. These value-laden activities are designed to accentuate the students' needs to communicate at the limits of their abilities. This successful communication validates attainment of socially agreed skill levels and confirms acceptance of the values implicit in the activities. Empowerment techniques teach students self-cuing coping strategies and ensure that students take credit for their own success.

The main principles of subjectivism are illustrated by examples of subjectivist teaching in a Grade 7 mathematics class. See also applications to foreign language teaching on pages 85-88 of this book.

Constructivism cognitivist theory of knowledge

Constructivism is a popular paradigm for teachers across subjects as diverse as university pharmacy courses to elementary science (Beeth, 1996; Damon, 1997; John & Bancroft, 1989; Lin, 1998; Oliver, 1997). The constructivist approach is widely valued because it can formalise understanding, pose problems of emerging relevance to learners, structure learning around "big ideas" or primary concepts, seek and value students' points of view, adapt curriculum to address students' suppositions, and assess student learning in the context of teaching. It promotes current positive pedagogic values such as active engagement, authenticity, collaboration, community, complexity, generativity, multiple perspectives, subject ownership, personal autonomy, personal relevance, pluralism, reflectivity, self-regulation, and transformation (Brooks & Brooks, 1993; Lebow, 1995; Pirie & Kieren, 1994).

Although constructivism is a popular and valued teaching paradigm, from Piaget through Bruner to von Glasersfeld it is an overwhelmingly cognitivist theory of knowledge (Bruner, 1960, 1966; Cooper, 1993; Drescher, 1991; Garrison, 1993; Glasersfeld, 1996; Greenberg, 1988; London, 1988; Lyddon, 1990; Mareschal & Shultz, 1996; Niaz, 1995; Quartz & Sejnowski, 1996; Reynolds, 1995; Sigel & Cocking, 1977; Spiro, 1991; Stahl, 1995; Steffe, 1990; Wadsworth, 1971). Constructivism emphasises cognitive aspects of learning at the expense of the affective concomitants of social constructivism (Daniels, 1994; Niaz, 1994).

Affective multipliers of learning

This cognitive emphasis ignores the efforts teachers make to build affective multiplying factors into their lessons to enhance students' learning. Good teachers know that affective factors, such as building motivation, interest, curiosity and social recognition have the power to transform routine lessons into exhilarating experiences that drive life long learning and a love of the subject (Arnone & Small, 1995; Beebe & Ivy, 1994; Boekaerts, 1988; Bomia, et al, 1997; Brigham, 1991; Simpson, 1987; Sylwester, 1994). For this quality of teaching it is necessary to consider how to use both emotion and cognition together (Carter & Yackel, 1989; Fielding, 1989; London, 1997; Oldfather & Dahl, 1995). As yet there is no rigorous psychological paradigm to show these teachers how to combine affect with constructivism and explain to them why it works. Unfortunately, constructivism has had no pedagogy to guide teachers in using affective adjuncts to cognitive learning in their classrooms (Huinker & Madison, 1995; Hwang, 1996; Roblyer, 1996; Savery & Duffy, 1995; Willis, 1995).

Subjectivism

Recently, Subjectivism has been proposed (Bastick, 1999) as a paradigm that integrates constructivism and affect. Subjectivism explains how teachers can use affect to enhance constructivist learning and to design authentic affective/cognitive learning experiences. It is a psychology of the subjective experience of learning. It adds affective experiences to constructive theory and explains how this acts to enhance learning. The theory also suggests techniques that teachers can use to design Subjective learning experiences for their students in their own classrooms. Subjectivism recognises two overarching aims that teachers have when they use affect multipliers to enhance learning: (i) enculturation into the skills, understanding and values of their subject and (ii) empowerment of their students to become self-directed life-long learners. Empowerment and Enculturation go hand-in-hand and are the aims of Subjectivism. Empowerment by Enculturation, and Enculturation by Empowerment, are the twin humanistic intents of the Subjectivist teacher.

These two aims of Subjectivism are achieved through classroom activities called 'surface purposes'. These can be simple rote-learning games or complex need driven social communication assignments. What they all have in common is that surface purpose activities encourage students to dissociate from the 'pedagogic purpose' of the teacher by focusing their awareness on the surface purpose of the activity. What the teacher's pedagogic purposes all have in common is that students should gain some skills, understandings or subject values that are designated by the subject syllabus. Each surface purpose is designed to be such an engrossing experience that the students learn these aspects of the syllabus at the limit of their abilities. The quality of content learning is assessed traditionally by appropriate criterion standards using tests, exams or various performance assignments. The quality of the Subjectivist learning/teaching experience is assessed by asking what students liked or disliked about the activities. Subjectivist teaching and learning are a success when the students only report liking or disliking the surface purposes. The activities should have enabled the students to dissociate from the teacher's pedagogic purposes so that classroom management, content structuring and all the traditional lesson design features are not mentioned because they were so peripheral to the students' activity focus.

Enculturation and empowerment: the two aims of Subjectivism

The enculturation methods that are used in the design of surface purposes are the same naturalistic enculturation processes by which the students gain the skills, understandings, and values of their out-of-school socio-subcultures. Examples of enculturation processes used are peer pressure, social recognition, compliance with authority, shared experience, establishing role identity, in-group bonding, and out-group competition. Students experience content learning through the same enculturation processes by which they experience Enculturation into their families, peer groups, religious sects, community fellowships and institutional associations. The common subjective experience of these processes ensures that, for each student, content learning is an 'authentic' learning experience.

Empowerment aims for students to come to know what content and process talents they have in the subject area. Empowerment is realised by students being increasingly able to identify areas that will interest them and ways in which they personally can most effectively learn in those areas; that is, students increasingly become self-directed learners. To develop empowerment the subjectivist teacher must induct students into many perspectives of a content area, and ways of understanding it, so that the students have sufficient experiences on which to soundly base their growing empowerment.

Design of surface purpose activities

In practice, the subjectivist teacher empowers students by designing activities that will result in success. However, the hand of the teacher is so well hidden, that the students take complete credit for their success and so feel empowered. Three techniques that are used to accomplish empowerment are: (i) affect-structuring (ii) covert directives and (iii) self-cuing coping strategies. These are techniques that have been adapted from Brief Therapy change processes. Affective structuring techniques utilise strong affect for directed motivation towards surface purposes. Covert directives are techniques that deal with the problem that extensive direction is necessary in teaching yet extensive direction undermines empowerment. The subjectivist solution is to use covert directives so that students have the subjective experience of choosing their actions. Self-cuing coping strategies empower by putting the initiation of meta-cognitive-affective processes under the conscious control of the student. For example, the student can initiate the mental set required for 'critical evaluation' or for 'on-task concentration'. The learner is empowered because the initiation of these states of awareness, that are necessary for different aspects of learning, become under the learner's conscious direction.

There is only space in this chapter to briefly illustrate how three affective-structuring techniques are used to design surface-purposes. These three affect-structuring methods are:
(i) The emotional anchor - this ensures the relevance of all learning states
(ii) The motivator - this implies success, recognises ownership, and gives an entrance to the activity
(iii) The cognitive direction - this guides students in organising their tasks and guides them as to what information is relevant to the tasks.

A Subjectivist teaching application

Two surface purpose activities are now described to illustrate classroom applications of subjectivism. They were designed and taught according to subjectivist principles. They both teach aspects of circles; namely, revision of parts of a circle by rote learning and, in pedagogic contrast, concepts of curvature.

First activity: to revise the names of parts of a circle

The pedagogic purpose of the first activity was to revise the names of parts of a circle - tangent, circumference, chord etc. The lesson is generic so could have taken place in almost any lower secondary mathematics class. It actually took place in a rural secondary school. There were 31 boys and girls sitting in rows of double desks to the front of the class on a concrete floor. The concrete floor was one contextual factor utilised by the male teacher. The other was his knack of drawing on the blackboard, in an instant, an almost perfect circle; which he knew from previous experience much awed the children. For this revision lesson, on the parts of the circle, he asked the children to turn to the children in the next double desk so that they could conveniently work in teams of four.

He gave each team of four children a broken piece of chalk. While the children watched him, waiting to know what to do with their chalk, he 'instantly' drew, as if by magic, a near perfect circle on the blackboard, to the astonished surprise of the children. "I wonder which team can draw an exact copy of this circle on the floor at the back of the class". The children were very keen to try but he delayed them by saying. "How will we all know which circle belongs to your team. Your team needs a name to write on their circle. Choose the name of part of a circle for your team". He then gave the easiest examples "such as centre or tangent". After giving the teams a few moments to choose their name, he pointed at each group in turn to ask them what name they would write on their circle. After the third group the names started to be repeated so he pointed much slower with a puzzled look on his face. The children quickly realised that each team must have a different name to write on their circle and so some children asked the first repeaters to choose a different name. As the teacher continued pointing to successive groups you could see the children hoping their name would not be chosen first by another team, and you could see those teams whose name was chosen first quickly trying to find a part of the circle that had not been chosen by an earlier team. Towards the end, when it was more difficult because there were few choices left, other children called out 'helpful' suggestions, which the current team had to evaluate because some of the names suggested had already been chosen.

ANALYSIS OF THE FIRST TEACHING ACTIVITY

First we analyse the execution of the pedagogic purpose, which was to rote learn the names to the limit of their ability. The teacher gave the easiest examples knowing these would be chosen first. As is appropriate for rote learning, the names were rehearsed many times; first during the teams' first selection of a name. As each team announced its name all children needed to remember what names had been chosen and to mentally compare these against the other possible choices. This was all done mentally as none of this was written down. When there was any doubt the earlier groups quickly confirmed if their name was being re-chosen. The children then had to remember their own team name throughout the next activity.

Secondly we analyse the subjectivist design and its execution.
The emotional anchor: The teacher used his knack of drawing a near perfect circle that he knew the children would like to emulate.
The motivator: Children realized that their team must have a unique name.
The cognitive direction: The teacher indicated for each group in turn to let others know the name they had chosen.
Empowerment: The teacher had the 'slowest' children in the front desks, and he asked them first, so that they would be sure to succeed. He initiated an obvious pattern of choosing the teams (down each row of double desks from the front) so that the 'next' team were 'self-chosen'. He allowed names to be called out so that at the end everyone could contribute to everyone's success. He also gave recognition to the children's abilities by allowing other teams the authority of confirming if a name was being re-chosen.
Enculturation: The names that a team chose acted symbolically like a logo. Each team

was socially bonded by the name upon which they have agreed. "We are the tangents". This was reinforced by publicly claiming ownership of the name when it was mistakenly re-chosen "That's our name!". Individual students sought and got social recognition by calling out a name that was needed by the later groups to choose.

SECOND ACTIVITY: TO APPRECIATE THE CURVATURES OF CIRCLES

The second activity was for the teams to draw an exact copy of the blackboard circle on the concrete floor at the back of the class and to name their circle. Teams learnt surreptitiously from one another. For example, when one team member went to measure the circle on the board, members from other teams later followed suit. They also followed the lead of some teams in rubbing out parts of their circle and redrawing these parts of the circumference. Most interestingly, some teams who wrote their name anywhere on the their circle, saw that others had drawn the part of the circle corresponding to their name and had written their name on the appropriate part and copied this idea. Teams that finished first went around comparing the work of others' to their own.

When all were finished the teacher asked everyone to stand back against the walls "so we can see how well you have done". After the circles and names had been perused for a few moments he asked the students to decide which circle was the best, other than their own. After a few more moments he said "go and stand in the circle you think is the best - not your own". Students were given time to change between circles for their own reasons (social or judgmental). There was some laughter as many students tried to stand in one of the better circles. That was the end of that activity.

ANALYSIS OF THE SECOND TEACHING ACTIVITY

We now analyse the design and execution of the pedagogic purposes which were to (i) again revise the parts of a circle (ii) appreciate the constant curvature of a circle of fixed size, and (iii) appreciate how the curvature 'flattens' as the size of the circle increases. The following observations indicate how each of these pedagogic purposes was achieved:

(i) To enhance rote learning of the names the activity encouraged rehearsal of the names in two ways. First, most teams realised that it was 'better' to write their team name on the appropriate part of their circle. Secondly, when comparing circles from the side of the classroom, students found it necessary to name the circles as well as point to the ones to which they were referring. (ii) Some students started drawing 'instant' circles as the teacher had done. These needed a lot of redrawing and repairing. In order to do this students needed to appreciate the constant curvature of their circle. Similarly, students worked within their teams to criticise irregular curvatures, agree on which parts should be rubbed out, and changed and recharged the circumferences to their own standards. (iii) Students copied the idea of taking measurements from the board to be more exact. These students had to 'flatten' or 'bend' the curvature of their circles when they realised that they had drawn them either too large or too small.

We now analyse the subjectivist design and its execution.

The emotional anchor: This continued from part one. The children wanted to emulate the teacher's fast, perfect drawing of a circle.

The motivator: Children saw how 'easily' the teacher did it and wanted to show they could be as good at it as their teacher.

The cognitive direction: The teacher indicated that the children could go and draw their circles on the concrete floor of the classroom.

Empowerment: Children were not subservient to the teacher's commands. Only one 'instruction' was given: an indication to start. Children choose their own areas in which to draw, how/what to draw, what/when to change their drawing, the standard required and when to stop. Most importantly, the children were given the social constructivist power to define the 'right' answer. The teacher did not use his authority to decide which was the best result. The children each made their own choice. The 'correct answer' was not even ratified by the teacher's authority, but by the children's choices. In addition, all the drawing decisions were negotiated within the teams. Hence, students who made these decisions were empowered by their team's endorsement. At the close of the activity, by moving away from team action toward individual decision, and preventing self-choice by a team member, the individual was not felt to have 'lost' as the bonding within 'losing' teams was broken. On the contrary, individuals could 'win' by standing in a circle with their peers.

Enculturation: There was no teacher interference with the working of the teams. Students negotiated roles, decisions and standards within their teams as they do out of school. There was some inter-team competition in the team mode, when groups copied what they thought were good ideas from other teams (positioning the name, measuring the circle size, trying to copy the 'movement' used by the teacher). For the final judgement, it was evident from the changing and rechanging of positions, that peer pressure, leadership expectations, and other enculturation processes came into play to influence the final choice of where to stand. Finally, the activity ended with children laughing and hugging each other to help stay inside the circles they had chosen. 'Right' or 'wrong', they experienced enjoyment in the process of learning mathematics. These two activities lasted from 11:10am to 11:30am.

References

Arnone, M. P., & Small, R. V. (1995). Arousing and Sustaining Curiosity: Lessons from the ARCS Model. *Proceedings of the 1995 Annual National Convention of the Association for Educational Communications and Technology (AECT), 17*, Anaheim, CA.

Bastick, T. (1999, January). *'Subjectivism - A learning paradigm for the 21st Century*. Paper presented at the Third North American Conference on The Learning Paradigm. San Diego, CA.

Beebe, S. A., & Ivy, D. K. (1994, November). *Explaining Student Learning: An Emotion Model*. Paper presented at the Annual Meeting of the Speech Communication Association, New Orleans, LA.

Beeth, M. E. (1996, April). *Teaching from a Constructivist Paradigm: A Way of Knowing and Learning or a Case of "Pedagogical Tricks?"* Paper presented at the Annual Meeting of the National Association for Research in Science Teaching, St. Louis, MO.

Boekaerts, M. E. (1988). Emotion, Motivation, and Learning. *International Journal of Educational Research, 12* (3), 227-345.

Bomia, L., Beluzo, L., Demeester, D., Elander, K., Johnson, M., & Sheldon, B. (1997). The *Impact of Teaching Strategies on Intrinsic Motivation.* (ERIC Document Reproduction Service No. ED 418 925).

Brigham, F. J. (1991, October). *Generating Excitement: Teacher Enthusiasm and Students with Learning Disabilities.* Paper presented at the Annual Meeting of the Council for Learning Disabilities, Minneapolis, MN.

Brooks, J. G., & Brooks, M. G. (1993). *In Search of Understanding: The Case for Constructivist Classrooms.* (No. 611-93148). Association for Supervision and Curriculum Development, 1250 North Pitt Street, Alexandria, VA.

Bruner, J. (1960). *The Process of Education.* Cambridge, MA: Harvard University Press.

Bruner, J. (1966). *Toward a Theory of Instruction.* Cambridge, MA: Harvard University Press.

Carter, C. S., & Yackel, E. (1989, March). *A Constructivist Perspective on the Relationship between Mathematical Beliefs and Emotional Acts.* Paper presented at the Annual Meeting of the American Educational Research Association, San Francisco, CA.

Cooper, P. A. (1993). Paradigm Shifts in Designed Instruction: From Behaviorism to Cognitivism to Constructivism. *Educational Technology, 33*(5), 12-19

Damon, L. (1997, February). *Preparing Teachers for Tomorrow: A Constructivist Approach.* Paper presented at the Annual Meeting of the American Association of Colleges for Teacher Education, Phoenix, AZ.

Daniels, T. G. (1994). Developmental Counselling and Therapy: Integrating Constructivism and Cognitive Development in Counselling Settings. *Canadian Journal of Counselling, 28*(2), 142-53.

Drescher, G.L. (1991). *Made-Up Minds : A Constructivist Approach to Artificial Intelligence.* MA: MIT Press.

Ernest, P. (1994). (Ed) *Constructing Mathematical Knowledge: Epistemology and Mathematics Education.* London: Falmer Press.

Fielding, R. (1989). Socio-Cultural Theories of Cognitive Development: Implications for Teaching Theory in the Visual Arts. *Art Education, 42*(4), 44-47.

Garrison, D.R. (1993). A cognitive constructivist view of distance education: An analysis of teaching-learning assumptions. *Distance Education - An International Journal 14*(2).

Glasersfeld, E. v. (1989). Constructivism In Education, In T. Husen, and T. N. Postlethwaite, Eds, *The International Encyclopaedia of Education, Supplementary Volume.* Oxford: Pergamon Press, 162-163.

Glasersfeld, E. v. (1994). *Radical Constructivism: A Way of Knowing and Learning.* London: Falmer.

Glasersfeld, E. v. (1996, September). *The Conceptual Construction of Time.* Presented at Mind and Time, Neuchtel, 8-10.

Greenberg, L. S. (1988). Constructive Cognition: Cognitive Therapy Coming of Age. *Counseling Psychologist, 16*(2), 235-38.

Huinker, D., & Madison, S. K. (April, 1995). *The Struggles of Kay and Aaron: Mathematics Minors in a Constructivist Paradigm of Elementary Mathematics Instruction.* Paper presented at the Annual Meeting of the American Educational Research Association, San Francisco, CA.

Hwang, A. (1996). Positivist and Constructivist Persuasions in Instructional Development. *Instructional Science, 24*(5), 343-56.

John, A. & Bancroft, J. (1998, April). *Students' Perceptions and Supervisors' Rating as Assessments of Interactive-Constructivist Science Teaching in Elementary School.* Paper presented at the Annual Meeting of the National Association for Research in Science Teaching, San Diego, CA.

Lebow, D. G. (1995). *Constructivist Values and Emerging Technologies: Transforming Classrooms into Learning Environments.* Proceedings of the 1995 Annual National Convention of the Association for Educational Communications and Technology (AECT), 17, Anaheim, CA.

Lin, W. (1998, April). *The Effects of Restructuring Biology Teaching by a Constructivist Teaching Approach: An Action Research.* Paper presented at the Annual Meeting of the National Association for Research in Science Teaching, San Diego, CA.

London, C. (1988). A Piagetian constructivist perspective on curriculum development. *Reading Improvement 27*, 82-95.

London, M. (1997). Overcoming Career Barriers: A Model of Cognitive and Emotional Processes for Realistic Appraisal and Constructive Coping. *Journal of Career Development, 24*(1), 25-39.

Lyddon, W. J. (1990). First- and Second-Order Change: Implications for Rationalist and Constructivist Cognitive Therapies. *Journal of Counseling and Development, 69*(2), 122-27.

Mareschal, D., & Shultz, T. R. (1996). Generative Connectionist Networks and Constructivist Cognitive Development. *Cognitive Development, 11*(4), 571-603.

Niaz, M. (1994). Pascual-Leone's Theory of Constructive Operators as an Explanatory Construct in Cognitive Development and Science Achievement. *Educational Psychology: An International Journal of Experimental Educational Psychology, 14*(1), 23-43.

Niaz, M. (1995). Cognitive Conflict as a Teaching Strategy in Solving Chemistry Problems: A Dialectic-Constructivist Perspective. *Journal of Research in Science Teaching, 32*(9), 959-70.

Oldfather, P., & Dahl, K. (1995). *Toward a Social Constructivist Reconceptualization of Intrinsic Motivation for Literacy Learning.* Perspectives in Reading Research No. 6. National Reading Research Center, College Park, MD.

Oliver, K. M. (1997). *A Case-Based Pharmacy Environment: Cognitive Flexibility + Social Constructivism.* Paper presented at ED-MEDIA/ED-TELECOM, Calgary, Alberta, Canada.

Pirie, S. E. B., & Kieren, T. E. (1994). Beyond Metaphor: Formalising in Mathematical Understanding within Constructivist Environments. *For the Learning of Mathematics, 14*(1), 39-43.

Quartz, S. R., & Sejnowski, T. J. (1996). The Neural Basis Of Cognitive Development: A Constructivist Manifesto. *Behavioral & Brain Sciences.*

Reynolds, T. H. (1995). *Addressing Gender and Cognitive Issues in the Mathematics Classroom: A Constructivist Approach.* (ERIC Document Reproduction Service ED 404 183).

Roblyer, M. D. (1996). The Constructivist/Objectivist Debate: Implications for Instructional Technology Research. *Learning and Leading with Technology, 24*(2), 12-16.

Savery, J. R., & Duffy, T. M. (1995). Problem Based Learning: An Instructional Model and Its Constructivist Framework. *Educational Technology, 35*(5), 31-38.

Saxe, G. B. (1991). *Culture and Cognitive Development: Studies in Mathematical Understanding.* Hillsdale, New Jersey: Erlbaum

Sigel, I. & Cocking, R. (1977). *Cognitive Development from Childhood to Adolescence: A Constructivist Perspective*. New York: Holt, Rinehart and Winston.

Simpson, R. D. (1987). Keeping Excitement in Teaching. *Innovative Higher Education, 12*(1), 16-21.

Spiro, R. J. (1991). Knowledge Representation, Content Specification, and the Development of Skill in Situation-Specific Knowledge Assembly; Some Constructivist Issues as They Relate to Cognitive Flexibility Theory and Hypertext. *Educational Technology, 31*(9), 22-25.

Stahl, R. J. (1995, November). *Cognitive Psychology and Constructivism: Concepts, Principles, and Implications within the Social Science Disciplines and Applications for Social Studies Education*. Paper presented at the Annual Meeting of the National Council for the Social Studies, Chicago, IL.

Steffe, L. P. (1990). Inconsistencies and Cognitive Conflict: A Constructivist View. *Focus on Learning Problems in Mathematics 12* (3-4), 99-109.

Sylwester, R. (1994). How Emotions Affect Learning. *Educational Leadership, 52*(2), 60-65.

Wadsworth, B. J. (1971). *Piaget's Theory of Cognitive Development*. New York: David McKay Company, Inc.

Weinberg, D., & Gavelek, J. (1987). A Social Constructivist Theory of Instruction and the Development of Mathematical Cognition. In Bergeron, J C , Herscovics, N and Kieran, C (Eds.). *Proceedings of PME 11 Conference*. Montreal: University of Montreal Vol. 3, 346-352.

Willis, J. E. (1995). A Recursive, Reflective Instructional Design Model Based on Constructivist-Interpretivist Theory. *Educational Technology, 35*(6), 5-23.

CHAPTER 22
Learning Styles as a Foundation of Instructional Activities

SUSAN ANDERSON

Abstract

Everyone has strengths, but different people have different strengths. Students can be encouraged to capitalize on their learning style strengths. Teachers can definitely benefit from the use of learning styles as a foundation of their instructional activities. No published work has reported the teachers' perspectives on administering learning style inventory to their students and the purpose of the resultant findings on the local scene. The voices of those who must carry out the dictates of the system should be listened to. The study reported here aimed to determine the level of acceptance for Learning Styles as an assistive device in aiding teachers' instructions and in fostering / encouraging individual students to draw on their strengths, thereby minimizing their weaknesses.

The sample consisted of 143 undergraduate students enrolled in the Bachelor of Education Psychology level three course in the Faculty of Arts and Education, on the Mona campus of the University of the West Indies (U W I). Most students are in the matured age group of 30 to 50 years. Responses on the open-ended questionnaire were analysed by coding responses. Frequency distributions were calculated for the total sample. Responses were also analysed qualitatively by identifying recurring themes and issues from the written responses. There was evidence of moderate to high levels of support for the use of learning style inventories, especially, according to students, where the findings lead to greater awareness of students' preferred mode of learning and the desire of teachers to plan instructional activities using information from the inventory, thereby leading to improved student involvement and achievement. Recommendations are made regarding student development and better classroom interaction.

Introduction

Psychologists have argued, and researchers have shown, that what is learned is subject to the way different persons make sense of the same content. Certainly, all teachers operate on the assumption that the basic types of thinking and achievement outcomes can be improved by practice and application by those who are not mentally challenged. However, the evidence seems to suggest that many teachers are not concerned with meaningful learning, rather, they seem to be more concerned with the normal traditional way of regarding learning as an outcome in terms of, for example, "so many correct answers". Some teachers argue that the brighter students are born with this ability while others create considerable problems for the teacher. **"They just can't cut it"**, remarked one 3rd year frustrated Bachelor of Education (B. Ed.) student on teaching- practice (meaning these students cannot manage higher level thinking).

Cognitive or Learning Styles refer to the process we use in attacking problems, or a series of problems. Simply stated, a Learning Style involves the manner in which an individual perceives and organises information. There are several theories about Cognitive / Learning Styles: Franklin (1992) on "global and analytical approaches" used by Afro-American, Native American and Hispanic American children; Tharp (1989) using verbal / analytic to opposite style or orientation; Witkin **et al** (1977) on field dependent / field independent approaches, and Pask & Scott (1972) on holist / serialist learning strategies.

I assume that an awareness of the students' learning style / preferred mode of study is an asset to the teacher as well as to the student himself and that such knowledge can serve to increase student output and achievement goal. To do so, we must start early, and practice continuously, to increase student motivation and self awareness analysis. The tasks used however must be seen as helpful strategies and not just a fixation on stereotypic modes and styles.

If an awareness of individual learning styles is to be included in the teaching process, it must be integrated into day-to-day operations in the classroom. The knowledge cannot merely be appended to notes on a "lesson plan" but to the instructional activities, including formal and informal curriculum. Increasingly, educational leaders are recognising that the process of learning is critically important, and understanding the way individuals learn is the key to educational improvement.

Background

The approach learners use when they begin to concentrate on, process and conceptualise new and difficult information is called **"Learning Style"**, (Dunn, 1996). Students not only see the world in different ways, but also learn about the world in different ways and under different circumstances. It is not surprising therefore that different learners demonstrate different learning styles. Pask (1976) argued that:

> **"The general tendency to adopt a particular strategy is referred to as a Learning Style"** (in Entwistle (1986), p. 93).

At the Mona campus of the UWI, students, especially the more matured students in the Bachelor of Education (B. Ed.) Programme, entered their course of study with well established learning styles. The advent of the new millennium, with its focus on technology, makes it not only more imperative for faculty, in such circumstances, to be more sensitive to the diversity of learning styles of the student-intake but also to the potential impact of those styles on post UWI instructional delivery in schools. It is, for instance, often said as a regular criticism of graduate teachers: **"They don't bring back anything new."** This speaks to a situation where trained graduates after leaving the university are viewed, especially in high school situations, as not introducing any new or innovative ways of motivating students. Such criticisms are also derived when student achievement /output seem stagnant, or appear to have even deteriorated. It is possible our teachers need to know more about the process of learning and how students process information.

What is being advocated here is not an overemphasis on Learning Styles, since this may lead to inaccurate labelling and stereotyping. However, knowledge and an awareness of the different ways in which students learn and process information have implications for increased knowledge about students and improvement in the overall delivery of instruction and accountability, thereby giving each child a chance to develop to the maximum potential. Numerous researchers have seen the importance of varied approaches employed by students to learning and have developed instruments to elicit these. The Learning Style Inventory (LSI), the primary version of which was developed by Perrin (1981) for children in Kinder-garden through Grade 2 was a pictorial questionnaire. The Learning Style Inventory (Dunn, Dunn & Price, 1988) for youths in Grade 3 - 12 was a 104 item self-report questionnaire that identified 22 elements relating to the environment (Dunn, Dunn & Price, 1982) for adults was a 100 item self-report questionnaire that identified individual adult's preferences for conditions in a working and learning environment.

Instrumentation and Procedure

Although two (2) instruments were highlighted, only Instrument 2 was used as the focus of this chapter. Instrument 1. The first instrument administered to students was designed initially in 1968 by Entwistle **et al,** in Lancaster, Britain, but refined and modified considerably since then. This inventory included a number of different concepts proposed by Marton and Saljo (1976a, 1976b), Pask (1976) and Biggs, (1987, 1988), from their investigations with British university students geared at identifying their study strategies. The present form of the instrument consists of 30 Items divided into sub-scales labelled A, B, C, D, E, F, and G. The response mode was based on a 5-point design. An example of a sub scale is given below:

Sub-Scale D   - measures the meaning dimensions of deep approaches to learning, intrinsic and academic motivation. This instrument, though not the thrust of this chapter, is necessary here to give the reader an idea of its relationship to the present topic. As stated earlier, it was the administration of this inventory that motivated the focus of this research.

Instrument 2: This instrument was a question given to the students in order to elicit responses regarding their views as practitioners. It is a common cry of the policymakers that **"Teachers do not fulfil their roles in carrying out the mandates of the system."** However, very often teachers/ practitioners complain that they have been asked to carry out tasks with no initial input from themselves. This examination of the teachers/respondents' opinions was an effort to "give them a voice". Respondents were given the following question:

As a classroom teacher, what is your view on administering a Learning Style Inventory to students?

The respondents were encouraged to give their personal views, whether negative or positive. This second instrument was an open-ended question given to students of the Educational Psychology Level Three (3) course at the end the semester, requesting that they, from the teacher's perspective, state the significance of administering a Learning Style Inventory to students. This encouraged self evaluation and critical thinking. The inventory mentioned at Instrument 1, given to the respondents, prior to the open-ended question, was intended to allow them to analyse their personal styles to determine whether these styles reflected the true perceptions of themselves. The responses to the analysis were overwhelming, with most students expressing the view that the inventory should have been administered to them upon entry to the university. In the voice of one student: **"I would not have felt so lost if I had discovered my own style."**

Respondents (UWI Students)

The survey respondents were 143 students from three faculties of the university campus, from the Social Sciences (5), from Pure and Applied Sciences (3), and (135, being the majority) from the Faculties of Arts and Education and Social Sciences, with most of them being teachers in the educational system. The instrument showed up slight differences in the different disciplines in terms of preferred styles of learning, but another paper will focus on those results.

Table 1: Distribution of Respondents by Faculty (Number =143)

Age Range (Yrs)	Pure and Applied Sciences	Social Sciences	Arts and Education
20 - 30	2	1	10
30 - 50	1	4	117
Over 50	-	-	8
Total	3	5	135

N.B. The small number of students from Pure and Applied and Social Sciences did not warrant a focus on differences by Faculty at this time.

Most of the students fell within the matured age range of 30 to 50 years. Coordinating the data collection was quite a simple task since, firstly, students had to complete the inventory / surveys for an end of Semester paper and, secondly, the research question was derived from the inventory. The fact that students responded to the questions under controlled situations should not limit the importance of their expressions. The completion of the course brought together a group of students who demonstrated a level of motivation for understanding student diversity and the manner by which student output is increased. Most students requested copies of the inventory and the need to follow through upon resumption.

Methodology

The analysis of the data commenced with an open-coding of respondents' views (inductive study) and eighteen preliminary categories were grounded in the data (See Constant Comparative Method by Glaser and Strauss, 1967 and Strauss and Corbin, 1991). Peer review and random interviews with a smaller number of the respondents resulted in the reduction of the original eighteen (18) categories to the current seven (7). In a deductive process, the responses of the 143 respondents were analysed to confirm the results. **Auditing** was done by reporting back to a sample of respondents in the current study to verify interpretation and correct any misguided deductions I might have had. Data from a Learning Style inventory, as well as from an end of semester assignment, were analysed using simple statistical analyses such as frequency tables computed to provide descriptions of the data distribution, are reported elsewhere and are available from the author. Responses to the open-ended questions, based on the focus of this chapter, were analysed by coding responses. Frequency distributions were calculated for the entire sample. Responses were also analysed qualitatively by identifying recurrent themes derived from the written responses. [Further explanation of coding using the Constant Comparative Method, leading to a focus on recurring issues and themes, can be obtained from the author].

Results and Discussion

Seven categories were grounded in the data (see **Table 2**) describing situations relating to respondents'/ teachers' perspectives of administering the Learning Style.

INFORMATION REGARDING INSTRUCTIONAL PLANNING AND APPROACHES

This category consisted of 12 substantive codes describing situations within the areas of lesson planning (content), individual needs of students, student aptitudes, relationship of teaching method to subject matter and classroom arrangements (physical) and were reasons offered why the inventory administration was necessary. Ninety-four students regarded this category as important. One of the respondents stated:

> Learning Style is purposeful to the teacher in that it allows him / her to find out the different types of learners in the class and to design instruction to cater to all.

McCarthy (1987) suggested that there are distinct styles of learning and that, generally, individuals have a preferred learning style. The author believed that teachers could facilitate learning by implementing different instructional approaches that respond to the learning styles of each individual

Another respondent wrote:

> Teachers can vary their teaching to suit the subject...........science might be more formal, while Social Studies might be more informal.......less note taking and so on.

Table 2: Seven Categories and Examples of Substantive Codes Grounded in the Data from Educational Psychology Students

	Categories	Category No	%
1.	**Information regarding instructional planning and approaches**: - lesson planning, including strategies - individual needs - student aptitudes - relationship of teaching method to subject matter - classroom arrangements	115	80.4
2.	**Study Method Approaches (Information required on how students learn)** - variability of styles - personality characteristics - student evaluation - conditions under which students learn best - specific strategies employed by students	106	74.1
3.	**Motivation and Achievement Outcome**: - student motivation - teacher motivation - frustration reduction - student empowerment (through knowledge of particular style)	94	65.7
4.	**Organisation and Management of Time**:	5	3.5
5.	**Classroom Behavioural Management**: - discipline → teacher-imposed (understanding Ss help teacher expectations, groupings etc.) ↓ self-imposed	28	19.6
6.	**Teacher Development**: - critical/analytical thinking - increased knowledge content - de-emphasising teacher's own style - research focus	16	11.2
7.	**Teacher - Student Relationship**: - comfort level - classroom climate	88	61.5

Students felt that different subject matters warranted different instructional approaches and that some areas were more suited to particular styles of learners. They felt that teachers might even be able to use the knowledge of students' Learning Styles to encourage career choices. This request however was endorsed by only a few subjects. Individual needs of students were highlighted by almost all of the respondents who found that the knowledge of their own styles had helped them to become more self aware. The following are further verbatim expressions of respondents:

> **…planning lessons armed with this information guides the teacher to expect different responses from individual students.**
> **…understand that some students require a longer time to finish their work.**
> **…some students are global and some are more analytical.**
> **…the teacher will find ways in which to lay out the classroom to make it more conducive.**
> **…I will plan my lessons in future to accommodate these styles.**

It appeared that respondents were eager to discover their learning styles and even to measure the level of improvement anticipated. Griggs (1991) reiterated that:

> Everyone has a Learning Style. Our style of learning, if accommodated, can result in improved attitudes towards learning and an increase in productivity, academic achievement and creativity (p.3).

The seemingly committed group begged for copies of the Learning Style instrument to take home and enquired whether I would be mounting follow-up work in their particular schools.

Information Regarding How Students Learn

This category consisted of eight (8) substantive codes describing the need for focus and planning for instructional activities, variability of styles, personality characteristics, specific strategies employed by students, conditions which suited them better and the overall evaluation of each student style which were described as important factors for instructional planning. Andrews (1994) described a North Carolina elementary school principal's efforts to turn around two schools by adopting the Dunn & Dunn Learning Style Model. It was reported that the first school succeeded by recruiting all teachers, using small group techniques, redesigning classroom space and developing hands-on mathematics material for each grade level. Of note, was the commitment of both teachers and administrator which proved essential. Greater emphasis was placed on variability of instructional styles to ensure the treatment for the variability of styles especially in older High School students. Some comments follow:

> **…If we look at the characteristics of the learner we find that learners can be competitors or collaborators, avoiders or participants, dependents or independents.**
> **…The teaching strategies used should take into consideration all aspects of the learners characteristics.**
> **…I will be more aware of each student as an individual.**
> **…see what are the best possible ways they learn and use appropriate…**
> **…the teacher must be aware of each child's learning style because every child does not learn at the same rate and pace. Some children**

learn best in groups while others prefer to work independently.
Rita Dunn and her colleagues in an extensive research demonstrated that a variety of elements differentially affect individual's learning. A chart designed by Dunn and Dunn (1987) shows these elements (Figure 1). The focus here emphasises the benefits of allowing students to work in classroom settings in which physical, sociological and environmental factors were similar to those preferred by the students. This enhances student learning in a dramatic manner

Figure 1: Diagnosing Learning Styles

STIMULI	ELEMENTS					
ENVIRONMENTAL	Sound		Light	Temperature	space design	
EMOTIONAL	Motivation		Persistence	Responsibility	need for structure	
SOCIOLOGICAL	by self	In pairs	with peers	As a team	Adult	Varied
PHYSICAL	Perceptual		Intake	Time	Mobility	
PSYCHOLOGICAL	Global	Analytic	Hemisphericity		Impulsive	Reflective

Simultaneous and successive processing

(Source: Adapted from Rita Dunn and Kenneth Dunn. The Center for the Study of Learning and Teaching Styles. St. John's University.)

The fact that a student may have a preferred, or most comfortable mode, does not mean he / she cannot effectively function in others. In fact, the more flexible student who can move easily from one approach to another, based on the requirements of the situation, is definitely at an advantage over those limiting themselves to one style of thinking and learning. Such a learner is referred to as the **"versatile learner"** by Entwistle (**op cit**). Too often, teachers examine the failure of their students based on personal and social problems, without attending to the child's learning style (Jones & Jones, 1998). They argued that teachers who used the same instructional methods with every student, or who used a limited range of instructional activities, would create a situation in which some students would become frustrated, experience failure and respond by misbehaving (p.203). Although the increased attention perceived by such a strategy might initially appear to constitute additional work for the teacher, it is hoped that their enthusiasm was demonstrative of their true feelings and that perseverance would lead to success for both student and teacher.

MOTIVATION AND ACHIEVEMENT OUTCOME

This category comprised four (4) substantive codes - student motivation, teacher motivation, frustration and student empowerment. Respondents felt they were motivated to work "closer" or "better" with their students as a result of becoming more aware of the diversity of styles and what those diversities connoted. They agreed that when the teacher was motivated, he / she was more likely to encourage motivation in their students. Since some students are motivated by a particular type of reward, while those same rewards may not be too acceptable or desirable to others, a knowledge of Learning Styles is quite necessary in these circumstances. Witkin's field- independent learning is less reliant on teachers' praise than his field-dependent counterpart. Slavin (1997) on achievement motivation suggested that:

> Teachers can emphasise learning goals and positive or empowering attributions.......teachers' expectations can significantly affect students motivation and achievement. (p.380).

The respondents were of the view that the result of the inventory and interpretations of students' preferred mode were in keeping with this empowerment referred to. Teachers' understanding of students learning styles could serve to deter the traditional view that those students who **"always get the work right"** are perhaps benefiting from a particular style of teaching. The results of some views are highlighted below:

> **...this knowledge ......will minimise the chances of the teacher neglecting those students who will need special attention to make them more comfortable.**
> **...self-awareness and self- knowledge are empowering.**
> **...be encouraged to participate in class as well as be given a task to accomplish that will motivate and encourage his natural ability.**
> **...the knowledge of his style is good; the student's knowledge is empowering.**
> **...the student is more at ease in class because the teacher understands her...**

Guild (1994) stated that:

> Researchers and practitioners agree that Learning Styles stem from a nature / nurture combination; students of all styles can be successful learners; students are more successful when using their style strengths; and diverse teaching styles are essential. (p.13).

Students are more motivated to learn if the way they are instructed comes in varying modes and hence suits their styles if not all the time, at least sometimes. Sensitive and creative teachers can accommodate several learning styles. Students must however continue to be encouraged to be more self motivated and to use various approaches in their learning styles. Several researchers have found evidence to show that motivation bears some relationship to school performance (Ball, 1977; McClelland, 1985; Schunk, 1994). Awareness of their own learning styles can encourage self-efficacy in students. The feeling that he/she can succeed even with a different learning method from the other child should be comforting. Self-efficacy affects several aspects of learner behaviour and cognition such as task orientation, effort, persistence, beliefs, strategies used and performance (Bandura, 1993; Schunk, 1994. Locally, Leo-Rhynie (1978) found that successful "A" level students were usually highly motivated and had well organised study habits. The connection or relationship between the process of learning and learning itself should not be ignored by those who teach, The process or approaches used, when properly applied, tend to lead to greater success in students.

ORGANISATION AND MANAGEMENT

The category, Organisation and Management of time was included here for less emphasis since only two (2) individuals raised it as an issue. This was interpreted to mean that since a sub-scale of the inventory placed emphasis on the student who was organised and managed his time for studying, this factor or value should be encouraged in all students. Consequently, the encouragement of such behaviour in each student could serve to enhance and improve learning. Entwistle's point on organisation (**op.cit.**) in this regard linked this attribute to a well organised study method resulting in competitiveness and hope for success.

CLASSROOM BEHAVIOURAL MANAGEMENT

This category carried two (2) sub-codes. Classroom discipline was divided into teacher-imposed and self-imposed discipline. One respondent saw the need for the classroom teacher to **"control the discipline by insisting on student cooperation"**. It was not possible, without a further intervention, to clarify the point being made. However, the majority of respondents focused on encouraging self-discipline when **"understanding students and their styles help the teacher in terms of group work and such activities requiring students to perform certain tasks"**. This can be taken further, to another dimension, which sees the knowledgeable teacher not becoming too emotive when Johnny prefers to sit at the back of the classroom and near the window, nor when Sally Ann chooses to use her personal experience to make connection with the new information being learnt and discussed. Theorists like Gathercoal (1993) have demonstrated that the curriculum, as a basis for discipline in the classroom, serves to encourage students to achieve desirable behaviour. Since a level of comfort, as mentioned at category (7) leads to greater relationships, discipline as a whole, is likely to improve, and less emphasis needs to be placed on punishment. Examples of some responses follow:

...I believe that children give trouble in class when they don't understand.
...Sometimes teachers stick to one mode of teaching which does not work for other students.
...yes, many children would do better if they were understood or even like what was being taught.
...it is high time we, as teachers, explore ways of increasing better self discipline in the children; this might be a way.

Student behaviour in the classroom is greatly improved when learning is facilitated by varied approaches that respond to the student's learning style. McCarthy (1987) offered four (4) categories by which learning styles could be described. She encouraged teachers to develop lesson plans that included learning activities that responded systematically to the four categories in which students fall.

TEACHER DEVELOPMENT

This category resulted in the sub-scales (a) critical/analytical thinking, (b) increased knowledge content, (c) de-emphasising teacher's own style, and (d) research focus. It was heartening to see teachers being objective and emphasising a focus on the need for teacher development. They also asserted that an awareness of Learning Styles of the students would require further training and self evaluation on the practitioner's part. Educators and researchers also pointed to the need for teachers to keep abreast of developments in their field, as well as other related fields . It is however, also important for the teacher to become more broad-based and willing to increase his / her general knowledge whenever the opportunity presented itself.

Increased information in this case could be reflected in the teacher's understanding of the different styles of students and knowing that his / her style could not be imposed on the student but the teacher should become more versatile in an effort to cater to all students. Too often, students such as gifted learners, with preferred strategies like independent research, querying authenticity of information from teachers and finding creative and novel solutions to problems, soon **"fall out of grace"** with the teacher and find themselves ostracised and even alienated. An awareness of the student's style should serve to help the teacher not to personalise the issue, but to encourage more students to pursue similar approaches without feeling intimidated.

TEACHER / STUDENT RELATIONSHIPS

Over 61.5 percent of the students who responded in this category reported that they saw a better classroom climate emerging from the knowledge of student diversity, with each type being acknowledged and no greater importance being offered to the so-called "bright" student, or any negative attitude being demonstrated towards the more divergent student. They saw the development also of a greater comfort level of teachers and students alike when the latter are allowed to realise that **"nothing is wrong with them"** because they **"need more explanation from the teacher"** or **"work better on individual projects"**.

Other comments which illustrated respondents' views were:

...A digital learner who could be considered inquisitive, or even rude at times, as he/ she shows an eagerness to answer questions or voice his or her opinion.....the knowing teacher can help him to channel his energy into worthwhile.

...I see a relationship between socio-metric analysis and this where the student preference can help the teacher to place her in group-work.

...Once the child is aware of his style, he should become more comfortable in class.

This comfort level can be reached with the teacher's demonstration of sensitivity and awareness. In a study done by Shields & Shaver (1990), in the U.S.A., they found that when one teacher learned that Asian American students were often overwhelmed by the "hustle and bustle" of American schools, she tried to keep her classroom quiet and orderly. She also made a special effort to promote their participation by using open-ended questioning and by encouraging them to speak loudly and clearly. Anderson (1984), in her study, found that where the teacher had a good relationship with students, and had high expectations of them, the students were more academically achieved. The reverse was also true. The student who was in a situation of trust, where the teacher understood him/her, and assisted in increasing the student's strengths, was likely to achieve more, or at least would apply such effort to propel him/her to achieve, which is the goal of any institution.

Some approaches to teaching are likely to be find favour by students from one culture/situation than from another, according to Sleeter & Grant (1994). Accordingly, teachers should also pay attention to those students who might be attending that particular school from elsewhere. The teacher who is "alive" to the needs of the students is most definitely contributing to the comfort level of the his/her students, resulting in a better classroom climate for learning.

Summary and Major Findings

1. Most students agree that Learning Styles can be used for the enhancement of curricula and instruction.
2. Respondents in this study represented administrators and teachers within the local scene as well as some from other countries within the region. Consequently, dissemination of these results would serve very useful purposes.
3. Knowledge of students learning styles be used by teachers as a foundation for their instructional activities
4. Teachers should use students Learning Styles to cater to their individual needs. The commitment of both teacher and administrator is essential for successful use of this strategy.
5. Teachers, as classroom managers, demonstrated a willingness to foster increased learning-outcome by using the method of Learning Style Inventory.
6. Teachers in the region, and indeed those who study educational Psychology on the Mona campus, have argued that by addressing classroom environmental issues, as well as instructional methods, they could easily create a learning environment more relevant to the unique learning needs of many students.

Recommendations

1. Teachers should be encouraged to learn to use learning style since chances are good that most students will perform better after being introduced to instructional material through their correct styles.

2. Learning Styles can lead to more positive responses in children. How students learn, and the process by which they learn, are vital knowledge for teacher preparation and planning.
3. Although Learning Style is not a panacea, it is useful for student motivation.
4. Teachers' own style of learning can be made more versatile and students should be encouraged to be more flexible in their approach.

Bibliography

Anderson, S. R. (1984): *"The Effects of Certain Home Environmental Variables on Academic Motivation displayed by Primary School Students"* - unpublished Bachelor of Education (B. Ed.) study, UWI, Mona.

Andrews, R.H. (1994, January): *Three Perspectives of Learning Styles.* School Administrator, vol. 51, no.1, p.19, 22

Bandura, A. (1993): *Perceived Self-efficacy in Cognitive Development and Functioning.* Educational Psychology, 28(2), p.117-148.

Biggs, J. B. (1987): *Student Approaches to Learning and Studying* : Melbourne , Australia Council for Educational Research..

————(1988): *Approaches to Essay Writing.* In R. R. Scmek (Ed), Learning Strategies and Learning Styles, New York: Plenum.

Dunn, K. and Dunn, R. (1987). Displaying Out-moded beliefs about student learning. *Educational Leadership,* 44, 55- 62

Dunn, R., Dunn, K. & Price, J. (1982): *Manual: Productivity Environmental Preference Survey,* Lawrence , K. S. : Price Systems.

————(1985): *Manual: Learning Style Inventory,* Lawrence, K. S. : Price Systems.

Dunn, R. (1996): *How to Implement and Supervise a Learning Style Programme.* Association for Supervision and Curriculum, St. John University, New York.

Dunn, R., Beaudrey, J. AS. & Klavas, A. (1989): *Survey of Research on Learning Styles.* Educational Leadership 40(6), p. 50-58.

Entwistle, N.J. (1986): *Styles of Learning and Teaching,* New York, John Wiley and Sons, p.93.

Franklin, M. E. (1992): *Culturally Sensitive Instructional Practices for African-American Learners with Disabilities.* Exceptional Children 59, p. 115-122.

Gathercoal, F (1993): *Judicious Discipline* (3rd Ed.), San Francisco. Caddo Gap Press.

Glaser, B. A. & Strauss, A. L. (1967): *The Discovery of Grounded Theory: Strategies for Qualitative Research.* Chicago: Aldine.

Griggs, S. A. (1991, December): *Learning Styles,* ERIC Digest, ERIC Clearing House on Counseling and Personal Services, Ann Harbor, Michigan.

Guild, P. (1994): *The Culture/Learning Style Connection,* Educational Leadership, 51(8), p.16-21.

Jones, V.F. & Jones, L. S. (1998): *Comprehensive Classroom Management: Creating Communities of Support & Solving Problems,* Allyn & Bacon (p. 203).

Leo-Rhynie, E. A. (1983): *Study Habits and Practices of Jamaican 6th Formers preparing for the "A" Level Exams,* Current Psychological Research and Review, Spring 1985, Vol. 4, No.1, pp. 22-27.

Marton, F. & Saljo, R. (1976a): *On Qualitative Differences in Learning 1, Outcome and Process.* British Journal of Educational Psychology, Vol.46, No.1, pp.4-11.

————(1976b): *On Qualitative Differences in Learning 11, Outcome and Process,* British Journal of Educational Psychology, Vol.46, No.1, pp.115-127.

McCarthy, B (1987). *The 4-MAT System: Teaching to Learning Styles with right/left Mode Techniques,* Barrington, IL: Excel

McClelland, D. (1985): *Human Motivation.* Glenview, IL: Scott, Foresman

Pask, G.(1976): *Styles and Strategies for Learning.* British Journal of Educational Psychology, Vol. 46, pp.122-148.

Pask, G.& Scott, B.C.E.(1972): *Styles and Strategies and Individual Competence,* in Whitehead, J. M. (Ed.), Personality and Learning, Hodder and Stoughton, Open University.

Perrin, J. (1981): *Primary Version: Learning Style Inventory, Jamaica, NY:* Learning Styles Network, St. John's University

Schunk, D. (1994, April): *Goal and Self Evaluative Influences during Children's Mathematical Skill Acquisition.* Paper presented at the Annual Meeting of the Educational Research Association, New Orleans.

Shields, P. & Shaver, D. (1990, April): *The Mismatch between School and Home Cultures of Academically at-risk Students,* Paper presented at the Annual Meeting of the American Educational Research Association, Boston.

Slavin, R. E. (1997): *Educational Psychology: Theory and Practice,* Allyn and Bacon.

Sleeter, C. E. & Grant, C. A. (1994): *Making Choices for Multi-cultural Education* (2nd Ed.), New York, Merril.

Strauss, A. & Corbin, J. (1990): *Basics of Qualitative Research: Grounded Theory Procedures and Techniques.* Newbury Park, CA: Sage.

Tharp, R. G. (1989): *Psycho-cultural Variables and Constants: Effects on Teaching and Learning in Schools.* American Psychologists, 44, pp. 349-359.

Witkin, H.A., Moore, C. A., Goodenough, D. R. & Cox, P. W. (1977): *Field-dependent and Field-independent Cognitive Styles and their Educational Implications.* Review of Educational Research, Vol.47, pp. 1-64.

END

www.ingramcontent.com/pod-product-compliance
Lightning Source LLC
Chambersburg PA
CBHW080936300426
44115CB00017B/2837